# The AMERICAN HERITAGE®

# first
# dictionary

By the Editors of the AMERICAN HERITAGE® DICTIONARIES

HOUGHTON MIFFLIN HARCOURT

BOSTON • NEW YORK

Visit our websites: *hmhco.com* and *ahdictionary.com*

**Library of Congress Cataloging-in-Publication Data**
Names: Houghton Mifflin Harcourt Publishing Company.
Title: The American Heritage first dictionary / by the editors of the American Heritage Dictionaries.
Other titles: First dictionary
Description: New edition. | Boston : Houghton Mifflin Harcourt Publishing Company, [2019]
Identifiers: LCCN 2017026104 | ISBN 9781328753366 (softcover)
Subjects: LCSH: English language--Dictionaries, Juvenile. | BISAC: REFERENCE / Dictionaries. | JUVENILE NONFICTION / Reference / Dictionaries. | JUVENILE NONFICTION / Language Arts / Vocabulary & Spelling.
Classification: LCC PE1628.5 .A43 2019 | DDC 423--dc23
LC record available at https://lccn.loc.gov/2017026104

**Front cover photo credits: drum** Getty Images/C Squared Studios, Photodisc; **paint palette** Getty Images/Ryan McVay; **spinning top** Shutterstock/picturepartners; **linking blocks** © HMH/Sam Dudgeon; **paint cans** Getty Images/Fuse; **Bernese mountain dog** Shutterstock/Mikkel Bigandt

Manufactured in China

1 2 3 4 5 6 7 8 9 10-SCP-24 23 22 21 20 19 18

4500701766

## STAFF

**Senior Vice President, Publisher, General Interest Group**
Bruce Nichols

**Executive Editor**
Steven R. Kleinedler

**Project Editor**
Emily A. Snyder

**Senior Editor**
Peter Chipman

**Contributing Editor**
Katherine M. Isaacs

**Technology and Database Production Specialist**
Christopher Granniss

**Senior Art and Production Editor**
Margaret Anne Miles

**Print Production Director**
Donna Baxter McCarthy

**Lead Print Production Coordinator**
Diane Varone

**Text Design**
Margaret Anne Miles
Emily A. Snyder

*The staff wishes to acknowledge Joseph Pickett and Susan Spitz for their roles in the development of the previous edition of this title.*

# TABLE OF CONTENTS

## What Is a Dictionary?

A dictionary is a book about words. The dictionary tells you how to spell a word and what a word means. It also shows you how to use a word in a sentence.

## How to Find a Word

This dictionary has words in **ABC** order. You have to know the alphabet to find a word in the dictionary.

A B C D E F G H I J K L M N O P Q R S T U V W X Y Z
a b c d e f g h i j k l m n o p q r s t u v w x y z

All of the words that begin with **A** come before all the words that begin with **B** because **A** comes before **B** in the alphabet. And all the words that begin with **B** come before all the words that begin with **C** because **B** comes before **C** in the alphabet.

There are two **guidewords** at the top of most of the pages. They can help you find the word you are looking for. The guidewords are the first and last words you can look for on a page. The other words you can look for come after the first guideword and before the second guideword in **ABC** order. When the guidewords both begin with the same letter as the word you are looking for, look at the second letter of each guideword.

For example, on page 25, the guidewords are **bowl** and **branch**.

## bowl ◆ branch

If you wanted to find **boy**, you would know that it is on this page, because it comes between **bowl** and **branch** in **ABC** order.

You can also find the letter that words on a page begin with by looking at the alphabet border at the bottom of the pages. The letter that every word on the page starts with appears in a purple oval.

When a word is in this dictionary, it is called an **entry**. To read the **entries** in **ABC** order, start at the top of the left column and read to the bottom. Then, move to the top of the right column and read to the bottom.

branch

## Looking For a Word

Let's look at the letter **D.** All the words that begin with the letter **D** are in **ABC** order. Look at each letter of each word. When words begin with the same letter, you must look at the next letter.

**dam** comes before **damp** because **damp** has more letters

**d a m**
**d a m p**

**dark** comes before **date** because **r** comes before **t** in the alphabet

**d a r k**
**d a t e**

**dinner** comes before **dinosaur** because **n** comes before **o** in the alphabet

**d i n n e r**
**d i n o s a u r**

dinosaur

Now let's look up **paw.** Look for the pages that have words beginning with the letter **P.** Then find a guideword that begins with **pa** and has a third letter near the end of the alphabet. The guidewords at the top of page 165 are **paste** and **pea.** Now read the **P** words on the pages in **ABC** order. **Paw** comes in the ABC's after **path** but before **pay:**

**p a t c h**
**p a t h**
**p a w**
**p a y**
**p e a**

paw

### paw

A **paw** is the foot of some animals. Dogs, cats, bears, and rabbits all have four **paws.** The kitten raised his **paw.**

**Paw** and the other words you look up are in big purple letters. The page numbers are at the bottom corners of the pages.

## What You Can Learn About a Word in the Dictionary

What does the dictionary tell you about **paw**?

- The dictionary spells the word.
- The dictionary tells you what the word means.
- The dictionary gives you examples of the word in a sentence.
- The dictionary sometimes gives you a picture of the word.
- The dictionary sometimes has a note that tells you more about the word.

Sometimes a word will have more than one meaning. If you look up the word **orange**, you can see that it has two meanings. A number comes before each meaning when more than one meaning is given.

**orange**
>   **1.** An **orange** is a kind of fruit. It is about the size of a tennis ball. **Oranges** grow on orange trees. **2. Orange** is a color. Pumpkins and oranges are **orange**.

orange

## Different Forms of Words

Words can also have different forms. **Plurals** are words that name more than one thing. Most words add **-s** to name more than one.

books    hills    months

Words that end in **x, s, sh, ss,** or **ch** usually add **-es** to name more than one.

boxes    dishes    messes    watches

Words that end in **consonant-y** change the **y** to **i** and add **-es** to name more than one.

cherry    cherries        jelly    jellies

Some words have special spellings to name more than one. These special spellings are also shown after the meaning or meanings.

| child | children | tooth | teeth |
| mouse | mice | woman | women |

Words that tell what people do also have different forms. **Chase** and **chases** are forms of the word **chase** that you use to tell about something happening now.

- Maggie and Michael **chase** the soccer ball.

- Ben's dog **chases** him through the field.

**Chased** is the form you use to tell about something that happened in the past.

- Anna **chased** her kitten around the house yesterday.

It is usual to add **-ed** to words to show that something happened in the past.

**chase**

The last **e** in some words is dropped before adding **-ed.** These words usually end with **vowel-consonant-e.**

| care | cared | move | moved |

The last consonant in some words is doubled before adding **-ed.** These words usually have a short vowel sound followed by one consonant. These forms are shown after the word meaning or meanings in the dictionary.

| hop | hopped | nap | napped |
| hug | hugged | rub | rubbed |

Words that end in **consonant-y** change the **y** to **i** and add **-ed.** These forms are also shown after the word meaning or meanings. Some forms of short words like **tried** have their own place in the dictionary.

| hurry | hurried | try | tried |

**hug**

Some words have special forms that are not usual. **Go** is a word like this.

panda

- We like to **go** to the zoo and see the animals.
- Adam **goes** to the zoo often because he likes to see the animals.
- We **went** to the zoo last Saturday and saw a panda.
- We have **gone** to the zoo many times.

**Goes, went,** and **gone** are all special forms of the word **go.** In the dictionary, special forms like this are shown after the meaning or meanings and usually also have their own place in the dictionary. **Blow** is another word that has special forms.

**blow**

**1.** To **blow** means to push with air. The wind **blows** the leaves around on the ground. Daniela **blew** the seeds off a dandelion and made a wish. **2.** To **blow** means to make a sound by pushing air. We heard the whistle **blow.** It has **blown** five times. ▪ **blew, blown**

blow

If you look for **blew,** the dictionary will tell you that it is a form of **blow.**

**blew**

**Blew** is a form of **blow.** Yesterday the wind **blew** hard.

**Blown** is also a special form of **blow,** but it comes right after **blow** in the dictionary. It is given after the meanings of **blow** but does not have its own place in the dictionary's list of words.

Words that describe things also have different forms. These words usually end in -**er** or -**est** to show that one thing is being compared to another.

- My hair is **short**.
- His hair is **shorter** than mine.
- Your hair is the **shortest** of all.

If a word ends in **e**, then only -**r** or -**st** are added to it.

| free | freer, freest |
| gentle | gentler, gentlest |

The last consonant in some words is doubled before adding -**er** or -**est**. These words usually have a short vowel sound followed by one consonant. These forms are shown after the word's meaning or meanings.

| red | redder, reddest |
| thin | thinner, thinnest |

**thin**

Words that end in **consonant-y** change the **y** to **i** and add -**er** or -**est**. These forms are also shown after the word's meaning or meanings.

| angry | angrier, angriest |
| happy | happier, happiest |

Some of these words have special forms that are not usual. **Good** is a word like this.

- Our team had a **good** score.
- Mimi's team had a **better** score.
- My sister's team had the **best** score.
  They won the game.

**team**

Special forms like these are shown after the word's meaning or meanings. They also have their own place in the dictionary's list of words.

In this dictionary, some entries are followed by note boxes. These note boxes are shown in four different colors: **green**, **blue**, yellow, and **red**. Each color lets you know what kind of information the note will give you about the word.

**Green** note boxes are the most common. They tell you about other words that are related to the word you looked up.

> A person who **collects** things is called a **collector.** Some stamp **collectors** have stamps from around the world.

**Blue** note boxes sometimes tell you about a word that means the opposite of the word you looked up. Sometimes they tell you about a word that means the same as the word you looked up.

> The opposite of **under** is **over.** The ball flew **over** my head and went **under** the porch.

Yellow boxes tell you about the sounds of the word you looked up. They might tell you what words sound the same as the word you looked up. Or they might tell you about words that rhyme with the word you looked up.

> Can you think of a word that rhymes with **parrot?**

parrot

**Red** boxes tell you a fun fact about the word you looked up.

> People collect a sweet liquid from inside **maple** trees and make **maple syrup.** It tastes good on pancakes!

# A

## a

**A** means one. Red is **a** color. Our friends will stay with us for **a** day or two.

## able

Being **able** to do something means that you can do it. If you can run fast enough, you will be **able** to win a race.

## about

**1.** About means what something tells. The people in this story are Lisa and David. The story is **about** Lisa and David. **2. About** means nearly. That line is **about** four inches long.

## above

**Above** means higher. Emma sat on her father's shoulders and cleaned the fan that was on the ceiling **above** them.

◆ above

## absent

**Absent** means not here. Two students were **absent** because they were sick.

> The opposite of **absent** is **present**. The students who were **absent** from school yesterday are **present** today.

## accident

An **accident** is something you did not want or expect to happen. I broke my glasses by **accident**. Helmets protect the head during bicycle **accidents**.

## acorn

An **acorn** is a nut that grows on an oak tree. **Acorns** fall to the ground.

◆ acorn

1

## across

**Across** means from one side to the other. A bridge was built **across** the harbor.

## act

To **act** means to behave in some way. Alex **acts** like a clown.

> People who **act** in plays and movies by pretending to be someone else are called **actors.** The job they do is called **acting.**

## actually

**Actually** means really. Mila didn't think she would like the party, but when she got there, she **actually** had fun.

## add

**1.** To **add** means to put one thing together with another. Stevie drew a picture of his brother. Then he **added** a funny nose. **2.** To **add** also means to put numbers together. + is the symbol for **adding.** 3 + 1 = 4.

## address

An **address** is the name of a place. You put an **address** on a letter to tell the post office where to send it. Some people keep **addresses** in a book.

## adult

An **adult** is a person who is done growing and is no longer a child. Your parents and teachers are **adults.**

## adventure

An **adventure** is a new or unusual thing that people do. The first time that I went on a train was a big **adventure.** My friends and I like to read about **adventures** in the jungle.

## afraid

To be **afraid** means to think something bad will happen to you. The kittens were **afraid** of the dog.

## after

**After** means following. **After** the ball game, we went home. Vince ran fast when his brother came **after** him.

> The opposite of **after** is **before.** I always brush my teeth **after** breakfast and **before** going to bed.

## afternoon

**Afternoon** is the part of the day between noon and sunset. **Afternoons** are short in winter and long in summer.

## again

**Again** means one more time. Timmy went skiing on Friday. He went **again** on Sunday.

## against

**1. Against** means touching the side of something. Aiden leaned **against** the lockers. **2.** To be **against** someone means to try to beat them at a game. Two teams play **against** each other.

◆ against

## age

The **age** of something is how old it is. Debra is seven years old. She is tall for her **age.**

## ago

**Ago** means in the past. Dinosaurs lived a long time **ago.**

## agree

To **agree** means to share the same idea. Tamia, Christopher, and Katherine **agreed** to take turns.

## ahead

**1.** To be **ahead** of someone means to be in front of that person. I am in the middle of the line, Sophia is **ahead** of me, and Caleb is behind me. **2. Ahead** also means before. I ate quickly and finished breakfast **ahead** of my brother.

## air

**Air** is a gas that people breathe. **Air** is all around us. We cannot see **air**, but we can feel it when the wind blows.

## airplane

An **airplane** is a large machine. **Airplanes** have wings and fly in the air. **Airplanes** carry people from one place to another.

Airplanes can fly because they have wings with a special shape. When an **airplane** is moving very fast, the air pushes its wings up and lifts it off the ground. **Airplanes** have engines that make them move forward.

N O P Q R S T U V W X Y Z

## airport

An **airport** is a place where airplanes fly up into the air and land. **Airports** are usually near cities.

## alike

**Alike** means almost the same. Emery and Talia are wearing black coats and gray hats. They are dressed **alike**.

◆ alike

## alive

**Alive** means living and growing. Animals and plants are **alive** until they die.

## all

**All** means each one or each part. **All** horses have four legs. Beth ate **all** of her breakfast.

## alligator

An **alligator** is a very large reptile. It has short legs, a long tail, and strong jaws with sharp teeth. **Alligators** live in rivers and swamps where the weather is warm.

◆ alligator

## allow

To **allow** means to let someone do something. Our parents **allow** us to ride our bicycles on the sidewalk.

## almost

**Almost** means nearly. Marcel's birthday is next week. He is **almost** six years old.

## alone

**Alone** means by yourself. One of Mason's favorite things to do is to read stories **alone** in the library.

◆ alone

## along

**1. Along** means in a line with. The purple flowers grow **along** the fence. **2. Along** also means together. Charlotte went to the store and her younger brother went **along** with her.

(A) (B) (C) (D) (E) (F) (G) (H) (I) (J) (K) (L) (M)

## aloud

**Aloud** means so that other people can hear. Camille reads a story **aloud** to Brayden and Ariana.

## alphabet

An **alphabet** is the letters that people write with. Our **alphabet** is A, B, C, D, E, F, G, H, I, J, K, L, M, N, O, P, Q, R, S, T, U, V, W, X, Y, Z.

## already

**Already** means before this. Abdul missed the bus today. When he got to the bus stop, it had **already** gone.

## also

**Also** shows something added. Alexandra plays the piano. She can **also** play the trombone and the trumpet.

## always

**Always** means every time. Manuel is never late for soccer practice. He **always** comes on time.

## am

**Am** is a form of **be.** It is used with I. "Are you six years old?" "No, I **am** seven." My mother says that I **am** good at drawing pictures.

## amount

An **amount** is how much there is of something. An elephant needs a large **amount** of food. A mosquito makes a small **amount** of noise.

> The **amount** of money that we give when we buy something is called the **price.** The **price** of that hat is ten dollars.

## an

**An** is a form of **a.** It is used before words that begin with A, E, I, O, and before many words that begin with U and H. A new pair of shoes is nicer than **an** old pair.

## anchor

An **anchor** is a heavy object that helps a ship stay in one place. **Anchors** come in many different shapes.

◆ anchor

**and**

And joins two things together. Three **and** two are five. Elizabeth **and** Jane are best friends.

**angry**

To be **angry** means to feel very upset with someone. Alden's parents were **angry** because someone threw a ball through the window. ■ **angrier, angriest**

Another word for **angry** is **mad.** When people are **angry,** they sometimes show **anger** by shouting. If there is **anger** in their voices, they are speaking **angrily.**

**animal**

An **animal** is a living thing that is not a plant and can usually be seen without a microscope. **Animals** can move and eat plants or other **animals.** Dogs, cats, fish, birds, and insects are all **animals.**

**ankle**

An **ankle** is a part of the body. It joins the leg to the foot. Felipe hurt his **ankle** when he tripped over a step.

**another**

**Another** means one more. Lexi ate a carrot. She liked it so much she ate **another** one.

**answer**

An **answer** is what you give when someone asks a question. Ari knew the right **answers** to the teacher's questions.

**ant**

An **ant** is an insect. **Ants** live in large groups in trees or in tunnels in the ground.

◆ ant

**any**

**1. Any** means that it does not matter which one. Take **any** seat you like. **2. Any** also means some. Do you want **any** of my sandwich?

**anybody**

**Anybody** means any person. Steven didn't know **anybody** at the party.

**anyone**

**Anyone** means anybody. Invite **anyone** you like for dinner.

A B C D E F G H I J K L M

## anything

**Anything** means any thing. My brother will eat **anything.**

## anyway

**Anyway** means that something doesn't matter. Sol's foot hurt, but he tried to walk **anyway.**

## anywhere

**Anywhere** means in any place. Sit **anywhere** you like.

## apart

**1. Apart** means away from each other. The sun and the moon are far **apart. 2. Apart** also means in pieces. I like to take things **apart** to see how they work.

> The opposite of **apart** is **together.** My brother took the puzzle **apart,** but I put it back **together.**

## apartment

An **apartment** is a place to live that is part of a bigger building. **Apartments** have one or more rooms.

## ape

An **ape** is a kind of animal. **Apes** are like people in many ways. They have long arms and no tail and can stand up straight.

## appear

To **appear** means that something can be seen that was not seen before. The magician **appeared** suddenly when everyone in the audience sat down.

## appetite

**Appetite** means how hungry you are. My sister has a big **appetite** after she plays soccer. We lose our **appetites** if we eat snacks before meals.

## apple

An **apple** is a kind of fruit. **Apples** have red, yellow, or green skin.

## April

**April** is a month of the year. It has thirty days. **April** comes after March and before May.

## apron

An **apron** is something you wear to protect your clothes. **Aprons** are useful when you make food or paint.

◆ apron

## aquarium

**1.** An **aquarium** is a glass box or bowl that is filled with water. People who have fish at home keep them in **aquariums. 2.** An **aquarium** is also a place to look at fish and other animals that live in water. We saw some sharks at the **aquarium.**

## are

**Are** is a form of **be.** It is used with you, we, and they. "Where can my shoes be?" "They **are** in the closet."

## area

An **area** is a space. There are two **areas** of the library where we can talk.

## aren't

**Aren't** is a short way to say **are not.** Bananas **aren't** blue. They are yellow.

## arm

An **arm** is a part of the body. It is between the shoulder and the hand. Amy used both **arms** to carry her books.

## armor

**Armor** is a hard shell that protects someone's body in a fight. Knights often wore **armor.**

◆ armor

## army

An **army** is a large group of people who protect a country.
■ **armies**

## around

**Around** means on all sides. Benjamin's uncle built a white fence **around** his yard. Santiago looked **around** the entire house for his shoes, but didn't find them.

## arrive

To **arrive** is to come to a place. Emerson slept late, but he ran all the way to school so he would **arrive** on time. My cousin mailed me a letter over the summer, but it never **arrived.**

## arrow

**1.** An **arrow** is a stick with a point at one end. You can shoot **arrows** from a bow. **2.** An **arrow** is a symbol. It is used to point in one direction.

## art

**Art** is something made to be beautiful. Pictures, poems, and music are kinds of **art.** Jimena liked the **art** that we saw at the museum.

A B C D E F G H I J K L M

## artist

An **artist** is a person who makes art. You can see the work of many **artists** in a museum.

◆ artist

You can also find art outside. Some **artists** paint pictures on buildings in their neighborhoods. Other **artists** make statues for parks.

## as

**As** means in the same way. Maria and Hung are the same height. Maria is **as** tall **as** Hung.

## ash

**Ash** is what is left after something burns. It is a soft, gray powder. Malik watched his father clean the **ashes** out of the fireplace.

## ashamed

**Ashamed** means feeling bad because of something you did. I felt **ashamed** when my yelling woke up the baby.

## ask

**1.** To **ask** means to say a question. The teacher **asks,** "Who knows the answer?" **2.** To **ask** for something means to say that you want it. Oliver **asked** for more soup because he was hungry.

## asleep

**Asleep** means sleeping. Chris was **asleep** when his parents came home.

◆ asleep

The opposite of **asleep** is **awake.** I thought the baby was **asleep,** but he is **awake** now and wants to eat.

## astronaut

An **astronaut** is a person who goes into space. Some **astronauts** have walked on the moon.

◆ astronaut

## at

**1. At** tells where a person or thing is. Elena went to school this morning. She is **at** school now. **2. At** tells when something happens. School begins **at** nine o'clock. **3. At** also means toward. Jerry looked **at** the sky to watch for falling stars.

## ate

**Ate** is a form of **eat.** Darius eats three meals every day. Last night he **ate** pizza for supper.

## attention

**Attention** means looking and listening with care. The crowd watched the magician do tricks with cards. They were interested in what he did. The magician had the crowd's **attention.**

## attic

An **attic** is a room at the top of a house. People use their **attics** to store things they don't use every day. We have books and a chest in our **attic.**

◆ attic

## audience

An **audience** is a group of people who watch a show. I don't like noisy **audiences** when I go to the movies.

## August

**August** is a month of the year. It has 31 days. **August** comes after July and before September.

> **August** comes during the summer. Can you find **August** on a calendar?

## aunt

An **aunt** is the sister of a parent. An **aunt** is also the wife of a brother or sister of a parent.

## author

An **author** is a person who writes a story, a play, or a poem. Many **authors** write books for children.

## automobile

**Automobile** is another word for **car.** People drive **automobiles** on roads.

◆ automobile

(A) (B) (C) (D) (Ĕ) (F) (G) (H) (Ĭ) (J) (K) (L) (M)

## autumn

**Autumn** is a season. It comes after summer and before winter. School starts in **autumn**. Another word for **autumn** is **fall**.

> **Autumn** begins in September and ends in December. The leaves on some trees turn colors in **autumn.**

## avoid

**Avoid** means to stay away from someone or something. Charlotte is afraid of dogs. She **avoids** them.

## awake

**Awake** means not asleep. Sanjay tried to stay **awake** all night.

## award

An **award** is something you are given when you do something well. Dave won an **award** for writing the funniest story.

## away

**1. Away** shows distance. The ocean is three miles **away** from here. **2. Away** also shows direction. Bryan walked **away** from the house and toward the street.

> To **give away** something means to give it to someone else. Raven **gave away** her bicycle to her younger cousin.

## awful

**Awful** means very bad or terrible. When you have a cold, you feel **awful.**

## axe

An **axe** is a tool. It has a flat, sharp metal head and a long handle. **Axes** are used to cut wood.

◆ axe

# B

## baby

A **baby** is a very young child. **Babies** eat and sleep a lot.
■ **babies**

◆ **baby**

## back

**1.** The **back** is a part of the body. We like to lie on our **backs** and look up at the sky. **2. Back** is the opposite of **front.** I wrote my name on the **back** of my painting. **3.** To go **back** or come **back** means to return. Students go **back** to school every fall. We came **back** to our apartment after visiting our grandmother.

## backpack

A **backpack** is a cloth bag that you wear on your back so you can carry things. Most of the children in our class have **backpacks.**

## backward

**1. Backward** means in the opposite order. "Saw" spelled **backward** is "was." **2. Backward** also means toward the back. Kendra looked **backward** at Max in the wagon behind her.

## bad

**1. Bad** means not good. We couldn't eat the bananas because they were **bad. 2. Bad** also means not nice. Tammy is angry. She is shouting at everybody. Tammy is in a **bad** mood. **3. Bad** can mean able to hurt. Too much candy is **bad** for your teeth. **4. Bad** can also mean serious. Kaitlyn had a **bad** cold, so she stayed in bed all day. ■ **worse, worst**

## bag

A **bag** is used to hold things. It can be made of paper, plastic, cloth, or leather. We put our trash in a plastic **bag.**

◆ **backpack**

## bake

To **bake** is to cook in an oven. Jonathan **baked** his pie for an hour.

> A person whose job is **baking** is called a **baker.** Some foods that are **baked** are sold in a special store called a **bakery.**

## ball

A **ball** is an object that is used in sports and games. Most **balls** are round. They roll or bounce easily so players can throw, kick, or hit them. Terrence spins the **ball** on his finger.

◆ **ball**

## balloon

A **balloon** is a kind of bag filled with gas. They come in many different colors. People sometimes use **balloons** to decorate a room for a birthday party.

◆ **balloon**

## ballot

A **ballot** is a piece of paper used to vote for someone or something. Yesterday we had an election to pick our class play. Our teacher collected the **ballots** after we voted.

## banana

A **banana** is a kind of fruit. **Bananas** have a long, curved shape and yellow skin.

## band

A **band** is a group of people who play music together. Everyone at the parade watched the marching **bands.**

## bank

A **bank** is a safe place to keep money. A **bank** can be a small box or jar that you keep at home. **Banks** are also buildings where people can store or borrow money.

> A **piggy bank** is a little **bank** shaped like a **pig.** It is used to hold different kinds of coins.

## barber

A **barber** is a person who gives haircuts. **Barbers** also cut beards.

## bare

Bare means not covered with anything. I did not have any socks or shoes on. I touched the grass with my **bare** feet.

## bark

Bark is the skin of a tree. It is thick and rough. **Bark** covers the trunk and the branches.

## barn

A **barn** is a kind of building on a farm. Farm animals stay in **barns** at night.

◆ barn

## barrel

A **barrel** is used to hold things. It is made of wood or metal. The top and the bottom of **barrels** are flat circles. Some **barrels** have curved sides.

## base

**1.** A **base** is the bottom part of something. The statue in the park has a square **base**. The statue stands on its **base**. **2.** A **base** is a place where you are safe in a game. In baseball you try to run to all four **bases**.

## baseball

**1. Baseball** is a sport. It is played by two teams with a bat and a ball. **2.** A **baseball** is the hard, white ball used in a game of baseball. Our team hit two **baseballs** over the fence.

> **Baseball** is played on a special field that is shaped like a diamond. Each team has nine players.

## basement

A **basement** is the bottom room of a building. Many families store clothes, books, and other things in their **basements.**

## basket

A **basket** is used to hold things. It can be made of strips of wood or grass. **Baskets** are often shaped like bowls and have handles. We filled our **basket** with apples.

◆ basket

(A) (B) (C) (D) (E) (F) (G) (H) (I) (J) (K) (L) (M)

## basketball

**1. Basketball** is a sport. It is played by two teams with a ball and two goals that look like baskets. **2.** A **basketball** is the large rubber ball used in a game of basketball. We keep the **basketballs** in the shed.

◆ basketball

## bat

**1.** A **bat** is a long, thick piece of wood, metal, or plastic. **Bats** are used to hit a ball. **2.** A **bat** is a small animal. It has big wings and a body like a mouse. **Bats** sleep during the day and fly around at night.

In baseball, the player who tries to hit the ball with a **bat** is called the **batter.**

## bath

A **bath** is a time to sit and wash the body with water. Mariana gave the dog a **bath** in the back yard.

## bathroom

A **bathroom** is a room where you wash yourself. In Lee's house there are two **bathrooms.**

## bathtub

A **bathtub** is used to hold water for a bath. People sit in **bathtubs** to take baths.

## be

**1.** To **be** means to live or fill space. A person cannot **be** in two places at the same time. **2.** To **be** tells what something is like. Dogs can **be** big or small. Tomorrow will **be** sunny. ■ **am, are, is, was, were, been**

## beach

A **beach** is an area of sand at the edge of a lake or an ocean. **Beaches** are part of the shore.

**Beach grass** is a kind of grass that can grow in sand. It is tall and green and has deep roots. Sometimes **beach grass** is planted to protect the shore from the wind and ocean waves.

## beak

A **beak** is part of a bird's mouth. It is hard and ends in a point. **Beaks** can be large or small.

◆ beak

## bean

A **bean** is a kind of seed or seed cover. Some **beans** are vegetables. **Beans** taste good in soup.

A **string bean** is a kind of **bean. String beans** are long and green. They grow on bushes.

## bear

A **bear** is a large animal. It has thick fur and strong claws. Many **bears** sleep all winter.

◆ bear

## beard

A **beard** is the hair on a man's chin and cheeks. The elves in the story all had long, white **beards.**

## beat

**1.** To **beat** means to hit. Rich **beats** a drum when he marches in the parade. **2.** To **beat** eggs means to mix them up. You have to **beat** eggs to make a cake. Fred's father **beat** the eggs before he fried them in the pan. **3.** To **beat** also means to win a race or game against someone. Our team has lost all its games this year. We have not **beaten** anyone. ■ **beat, beaten**

## beautiful

**Beautiful** means very nice to look at or listen to. Rainbows and music are **beautiful.**

The opposite of **beautiful** is **ugly.** Those flowers are **beautiful,** but the dirty sidewalk around them is **ugly.**

## beaver

A **beaver** is a kind of animal. It has a flat tail and large, strong front teeth. **Beavers** build dams across streams. The dams are made of logs, sticks, and mud.

(A) (B) (C) (D) (E) (F) (G) (H) (I) (J) (K) (L) (M)

## became

**Became** is a form of **become.** Marcie wants to become a pilot one day. Her father **became** a pilot many years ago.

## because

**Because** tells why something happens. Mariah ate an apple **because** she was hungry. People read books **because** they want to learn.

## become

To **become** means to change into something. A caterpillar changes into a moth. It **becomes** a moth inside a cocoon. I mopped the floor because it had **become** dirty.
■ **became, become**

## bed

A **bed** is a kind of furniture. People sleep in **beds.**

## bee

A **bee** is a kind of insect. It can fly and likes flowers. Some **bees** make honey.

◆ bee

## beef

**Beef** is a kind of meat. It comes from cattle. Hamburger is made from **beef.**

## been

**Been** is a form of **be.** Van wants to be a farmer when he grows up. His parents have **been** farmers for many years.

## beetle

A **beetle** is a kind of insect. It has two pairs of wings. **Beetles** have hard wings on the outside that cover soft wings used for flying.

◆ beetle

## before

**1. Before** means that something comes first. Anita and Jonas wash their hands **before** they eat dinner. **2. Before** also means in the past. Alice rode in a plane for the first time last week. She had never been on a plane **before.**

N O P Q R S T U V W X Y Z

## begin

To **begin** means to start. Grass **begins** to grow in the spring. The birds **began** to sing when the rain stopped. We had **begun** to paint the house when it started to rain. ■ **began, begun**

When something **begins,** we say it is at the **beginning.** At the **beginning** of fall, the leaves **begin** to change color.

## behave

To **behave** means to do things in some way. Daniel **behaves** well when his family goes to a restaurant.

## behind

**Behind** means at the back. Michael and Malia's parents stood **behind** them.

◆ behind

## believe

To **believe** means to think something is true. I **believe** everything my sister says.

To **make believe** means to pretend. Faye likes to **make believe** she is a doctor.

## bell

A **bell** is a hollow piece of metal that rings when you hit or shake it. When the **bells** rang, the horses began the race.

A **doorbell** is a button on the door of a house or apartment. The button rings a **bell** when you push it.

## belong

**1.** To **belong** means to feel good in a place. Fish **belong** in the water. **2.** To **belong** also means to be owned by somebody. That toy **belongs** to me. It's my toy.

## below

**Below** means under. Roots grow **below** the ground.

The opposite of **below** is **above.** The sky is **above** me and the ground is **below** me.

A B C D E F G H I J K L M

## belt

A **belt** is a kind of clothing that you wear around the middle of your body. **Belts** are long and thin. They are usually made of leather, cloth, or plastic.

## beneath

**Beneath** means under or below. Aubrey put her shoes **beneath** her desk.

## bench

A **bench** is a long seat for two or more people. We sit on **benches** in the park.

## bend

To **bend** means to make a curve. Eliza **bends** over backward and touches the ground. I **bent** my knees and jumped. Sara's glasses were **bent** after she sat on them.
■ **bent**

◆ bend

## berry

A **berry** is a small fruit. **Berries** grow on bushes. Some kinds of **berries** are good to eat, but other kinds make you sick. ■ **berries**

◆ berry

## beside

**Beside** means at the side of. Madison and Charlotte are sitting on the couch. Madison sits **beside** Charlotte, and Charlotte sits **beside** Madison.

◆ beside

## best

**Best** means better than any other. Susie's **best** friend is the friend she likes most.

## better

**Better** means very good, but not the best. Jo is a **better** singer than Ava.

The opposite of **better** is **worse.** Do you feel any **better,** or is your cold **worse** today?

N O P Q R S T U V W X Y Z

19

## between

**Between** means in the middle. The letters **c a t** spell "cat." The **a** is **between** the **c** and the **t**. Mackenzie stands **between** her mother and grandmother.

◆ between

## beverage

A **beverage** is another word for a drink. Caden's favorite **beverages** are apple juice and milk.

## beyond

**Beyond** means on the other side of something. Luana climbed over a fence and into the field. She went **beyond** the fence. The planet Saturn is **beyond** the planet Jupiter.

## bib

A **bib** is a piece of cloth or plastic that is worn under the chin. Babies wear **bibs** to protect their clothes when they eat.

## bicycle

A **bicycle** is a kind of machine. **Bicycles** have two big wheels, two handles, and a seat. You make a **bicycle** go by moving your legs.

◆ bicycle

A person who rides a **bicycle** is called a **bicyclist**. Some **bicyclists** ride across the countryside in races that are hundreds of miles long.

## big

**Big** means not small. Whales and elephants are **big**. **Large** is another word for **big**. ■ **bigger, biggest**

## bill

**1.** A **bill** is a bird's beak. Ducks and some other birds have big **bills**. **2.** A **bill** is also a piece of paper money. A dollar **bill** is equal to one dollar. **3.** A **bill** is also a piece of paper that shows what you must pay for something. Kim's mother pays the electricity **bill** every month.

(A) (B) (C) (D) (E) (F) (G) (H) (I) (J) (K) (L) (M)

## bird

A **bird** is a kind of animal. It has two wings and is covered with feathers. Robins, chickens, eagles, and ostriches are all **birds.** Most **birds** can fly.

A **birdhouse** is a little box where birds can rest and build their nests. **Birdhouses** have small holes through which birds can enter and leave.

## birth

**Birth** is the moment when a person is born. Most **births** happen in hospitals.

## birthday

Your **birthday** is the day of your birth. Annabelle's **birthday** is on November 8. **Birthdays** are fun.

## bit

**1. Bit** is a form of **bite.** Eddie **bit** into an apple. **2. Bit** also means a small amount. Aaron put a **bit** of pepper into his soup. Kennedy and Nathaniel did a **bit** of homework after school before they went outside to play.

## bite

**1.** To **bite** means to cut with your teeth. Christopher **bites** into his apple. Then he chews and swallows. I had **bitten** into the apple when I lost my tooth.
**2.** A **bite** is a small amount you can cut off with your teeth. Aliyah has taken some **bites** of her sandwich. She will eat the rest later.
■ **bit, bitten**

◆ bite

## bitter

**Bitter** means having a sharp taste. Debbie tasted the medicine and made a face. It was very **bitter.**

## black

**Black** is a color. It is very dark. This sentence is printed in **black** ink.

A **blacktop** is a smooth, black surface that covers part of the ground. We play basketball on the **blacktop** after school.

## blacksmith

A **blacksmith** is a person who makes things out of iron. **Blacksmiths** make horseshoes.

## blanket

A **blanket** is a large, soft cloth. People cover themselves with **blankets** to keep warm.

◆ blanket

## blend

To **blend** means to mix together. Kwami **blended** the milk and eggs when he made the birthday cake.

A **blender** is a small machine used to **blend** different foods. Some people make drinks by mixing fruit and juice in a **blender**.

## blew

**Blew** is a form of **blow**. Yesterday the wind **blew** hard.

## blind

**Blind** means not able to see. A person who cannot see is **blind**.

## block

**1.** A **block** is a piece of wood, plastic, or stone. It has straight sides and is usually shaped like a square or a rectangle. Children play with **blocks**. **2.** A **block** is an area of a city. It has four streets for sides. Evan and Rosie walked around the **block**.

## blood

**Blood** is a red liquid inside our bodies. Nobody can live without **blood.**

## blossom

A **blossom** is a flower. The **blossoms** on Samaira's favorite tree are white.

## blow

**1.** To **blow** means to push with air. The wind **blows** the leaves around on the ground. Daniela **blew** the seeds off a dandelion and made a wish. **2.** To **blow** means to make a sound by pushing air. We heard the whistle **blow**. It has **blown** five times. ■ **blew, blown**

◆ blow

(A) (B) (C) (D) (E) (F) (G) (H) (I) (J) (K) (L) (M)

## blue

**Blue** is a color. The sky is **blue** during the day.

Blueberries, bluebirds, bluefish, and **blue sharks** all got their names because they are the color **blue.**

## board

**1.** A **board** is a long, flat piece of wood. **Boards** are used to build houses. **2.** A **board** is also a flat surface that you play a game on. Checkers are placed on a **board.**

## boat

A **boat** carries people and things on the water. **Boats** can be made of wood, metal, or plastic. Most **boats** have engines to make them move. Some **boats** have sails.

## body

A **body** is all the parts of a person or animal. Human **bodies** have a brain, a heart, and two lungs. ■ **bodies**

## boil

To **boil** is to change from a liquid into a gas. When water **boils** it makes bubbles, and steam rises into the air.

## bone

A **bone** is a hard part of the body. People and many animals have **bones** under their skin and muscles.

## book

A **book** is a group of pages. The pages have words and sometimes pictures on them. The pages are held together with thread or glue. Dictionaries are **books.** Emma likes to read a **book** before she goes to sleep.

## boot

A **boot** is a large shoe. **Boots** are made of rubber or leather. Most people wear **boots** in the rain or snow to keep their feet dry and warm.

◆ boot

## border

A **border** is an edge. It is a line where one area ends and another area begins. Two **borders** of stones separated the lawn from the path. The **border** between two states is sometimes a river.

## born

**Born** means brought into life. Terry is one day old. She was **born** yesterday.

## borrow

To **borrow** means to use something that belongs to somebody else. You can use it for a small amount of time. Wally **borrowed** a book from the library. He has to return it in two weeks.

The opposite of **borrow** is **lend.** Pedro **borrowed** five dollars from Carmen. This means that Carmen **lent** five dollars to Pedro.

## both

**Both** means two together. Sarah uses **both** hands to eat lunch.

◆ both

## bother

To **bother** means to give trouble. The bugs in the yard **bothered** us.

## bottle

A **bottle** is used to hold liquids. Many **bottles** are made of plastic. I drank a **bottle** of juice.

## bottom

The **bottom** is the lowest part of something. A tree has roots at the **bottom.**

## bought

**Bought** is a form of **buy.** Most people buy food at a store. Fran **bought** some milk this morning.

## boulder

A **boulder** is a very big rock. **Boulders** are found on the ground or in the soil.

## bounce

To **bounce** means to move back after hitting something. The ball **bounced** when it hit the street.

## bow

**1.** A **bow** is a curved piece of wood. A piece of string is tied to the ends of it. **Bows** are used to shoot arrows. **2.** A **bow** is also a knot made with ribbon or string. It has two circles and two ends. I tie my shoes with a **bow. 3.** A **bow** can also be a thin, long stick used to play some instruments. A violin is played with a **bow. 4.** To **bow** means to bend the body forward. In the story the knight **bows** to the king.

A **bow** that you use rhymes with **go** and **blow.** When you **bow** down, **bow** rhymes with **cow.**

## bowl

A **bowl** is a kind of dish that is round and hollow. People can eat soup, cereal, and fruit out of **bowls.**

◆ bowl

## bowling

**Bowling** is a sport. **Bowling** is played with a heavy ball and pieces of wood shaped like bottles. You roll the ball toward the pieces of wood and try to knock them down.

## box

A **box** is used to hold things. It has four sides and a flat bottom. Some **boxes** have tops, too. We have a lot of large **boxes** in the attic.

## boy

A **boy** is a male child. My brothers Isaac and Aaron are **boys.**

## braces

**Braces** are thin metal wires that a dentist puts on your teeth. **Braces** are worn to make your teeth straight.

## braid

A **braid** is a strip of hair. It is made by dividing the hair into three parts and placing each part of loose hair over one of the other parts. My sister wears her hair in **braids** every day.

◆ braid

## brain

The **brain** is a part of the body. It is inside your head. The **brain** makes our arms, legs, hands, feet, eyes, and ears work. People think with their **brains.**

## branch

A **branch** is a part of a tree. **Branches** grow out from the trunk of a tree or from other **branches.** Leaves grow from the **branches.**

◆ branch

N O P Q R S T U V W X Y Z

## brave

**Brave** means without fear. The knight in the story was very **brave.** He did not run away from the dragon.

## bread

**Bread** is a kind of food. It is made with flour and water and other things mixed together. **Bread** is baked in an oven.

## break

**1.** To **break** means to divide into pieces. If a window **breaks,** it becomes pieces of glass. A window **breaks** when a ball goes through it. **2.** To **break** also means not to work. If a machine **breaks,** someone has to fix it. Then it will work again. **3.** To **break** the law means to do something against the law. Someone who robs a bank is **breaking** the law.
■ **broke, broken**

## breakfast

**Breakfast** is a meal. It is the first meal of the day. At **breakfast** Meghan usually eats cereal with milk.

Some people have a big **breakfast** of eggs and fruit. Other people have pancakes. What is your favorite **breakfast** food?

## breath

A **breath** is an amount of air. The air comes through our mouths and noses and into our bodies. The doctor asked Aisha to take deep **breaths.**

## breathe

To **breathe** is to take in breaths of air. Jeff **breathes** fast when he runs.

## breeze

A **breeze** is a gentle wind. Savannah enjoyed the **breezes** when her parents took her on a boat ride.

## brick

A **brick** is a very hard piece of clay shaped like a rectangle. Many houses and other buildings are made of **bricks.**

## bridge

A **bridge** is used to cross from one side of something to the other side. **Bridges** are often built over water.

◆ **bridge**

(A) (B) (C) (D) (E) (F) (G) (H) (I) (J) (K) (L) (M)

## bright

**Bright** means giving a lot of light. The sunrise over the field was very **bright.**

◆ bright

## bring

To **bring** means to take something with you. When Chantal goes to a birthday party, she **brings** a present.
■ **brought**

## broke

**Broke** is a form of **break.** It is easy for glass to break. Yesterday I dropped a glass. It **broke** into pieces.

## broken

**Broken** is a form of **break.** The glass dish was **broken** into many pieces. The cat knocked it off the table.

## broom

A **broom** is a kind of tool. It is a long stick with straw or thin pieces of plastic on one end. Most people use **brooms** to clean dirt off floors.

## brother

A **brother** is a boy who has the same parent or parents as somebody else. My **brothers** and I walk home together.

## brought

**Brought** is a form of **bring.** Christine **brought** her dog when she came to visit.

## brown

**Brown** is a color. Toast and chocolate are **brown.** Some people have **brown** hair.

## brush

**1.** A **brush** is a kind of tool. It looks like a small broom. Some **brushes** are used to paint with. Other **brushes** are used to clean things. **2.** To **brush** means to clean with a brush. Alan **brushes** his teeth every morning and night.

## bubble

A **bubble** is a round shape with air in it. **Bubbles** can be made in soap and water. **Bubbles** are also made when water boils.

◆ bubble

## bucket

A **bucket** is used to carry things. It can be made of wood, metal, or plastic. It has a flat, round bottom and a handle. **Buckets** are often used to carry water.

◆ **bucket**

## bug

**1.** A **bug** is an insect. When we go on picnics, **bugs** crawl on our blanket. **2.** To **bug** means to bother. The noise from the television **bugs** me sometimes when I am trying to read.

## build

To **build** means to put together. Everyone joined together to **build** a new house. ■ **built**

## building

A **building** is a place that has been built. Houses, hotels, schools, and barns are all **buildings.**

## built

**Built** is a form of **build.** Mom and Dad **built** our tree house.

## bull

A **bull** is a large animal. **Bulls** have horns and eat grass. They are male cattle.

## bulldozer

A **bulldozer** is a very strong tractor. **Bulldozers** push dirt and rocks from one place to another.

## bump

**1.** To **bump** means to hit against something. Duncan **bumped** his head on the table by accident. **2.** A **bump** is a round place that sticks out. The road has a lot of **bumps** in it.

## bunch

A **bunch** is a group of things of the same kind that are next to each other. Grapes grow in **bunches** on vines. My father brought my mother a **bunch** of pink and yellow flowers on her birthday.

◆ **bunch**

## buried

**Buried** is a form of **bury.** The squirrels **buried** acorns in the yard.

## burn

To **burn** is to be changed by fire. We like to watch the logs **burn** in the fireplace. Gasoline and other things are **burned** to make energy and give off heat.

## bury

To **bury** means to put something in a hole in the ground and then cover it with dirt or sand. The pirate filled the chest with gold and **buried** it in the sand. ▪ **buried**

## bus

A **bus** is a machine. It has four wheels, an engine, and many seats and windows. **Buses** carry many people from one place to another.

◆ bus

A **school bus** takes children to and from school.

## bush

A **bush** is a plant. It has many branches and leaves. **Bushes** are not as big as trees. Flowers grow on **bushes.**

## busy

**Busy** means doing many things. Abby has a lot of work to do. She is very **busy** today. ▪ **busier, busiest**

## but

**1. But** is used to put two opposite ideas together. The weather was cold yesterday, **but** today it is warm. **2. But** means except. Tina, Jed, and Liam liked the new car. Albert did not like it. Everybody **but** Albert liked the new car.

## butter

**Butter** is a kind of food. It is made from cow's milk. **Butter** is soft and yellow. Some people eat it on bread.

**Buttercups** are yellow flowers that have the same color as **butter.** They grow in marshes and meadows.

## butterfly

A **butterfly** is a kind of insect. It has four thin wings. These wings can have many colors. Some caterpillars change into **butterflies.** ▪ **butterflies**

◆ butterfly

## button

**1.** A **button** is a small piece of plastic, wood, or metal. **Buttons** are often round. They are sewn on clothes to help keep parts of clothes together. **2.** A **button** is also something that you push to make something happen. Joaquin pushed a **button** on the TV to turn it off.

◆ **button**

## buy

To **buy** means to give money for something. You can **buy** many kinds of food at a supermarket.
■ **bought**

## buzz

To **buzz** is to make the sound of a bee. The bees **buzzed** around the flowers.

## by

**1.** **By** shows who or what does something. The question was asked **by** Dana. **2.** **By** also shows how something is done. We made a garden **by** planting some flowers. **3.** **By** can mean before some time. Nicki is usually hungry **by** the time she gets home from school.

(A) (B) (C) (D) (E) (F) (G) (H) (I) (J) (K) (L) (M)

# C

## cabin

A **cabin** is a small house. When we go to summer camp, we stay in **cabins.**

## cabinet

A **cabinet** is a box that is used to store things. **Cabinets** have drawers and shelves inside them.

## cactus

A **cactus** is a kind of plant. **Cactuses** grow in hot, dry places. They have thick stems and very thin leaves.
■ **cactuses, cacti**

◆ **cactus**

## cage

A **cage** is a kind of box. The sides are made of metal or wood poles. Birds and other animals are sometimes kept in **cages.**

## cake

A **cake** is a kind of food. It is made of flour, sugar, eggs, and milk. It is baked in an oven. **Cakes** are sweet.

## calendar

A **calendar** is a group of pages that show the days, weeks, and months in a year. Cua and her friends make **calendars** at school when the new year begins.

## calf

**1.** A **calf** is a young cow or bull. The cow and her **calf** are eating grass in the field. **2.** A **calf** is also the back part of your leg that is below your knee. My **calf** hurts sometimes after a long walk. ■ **calves**

## call

**1.** To **call** means to say in a loud voicc. Gabriella heard the teacher **call** her name. **2.** To **call** means to use the telephone. James **calls** his friends on the telephone when he wants to play. **3.** To **call** means to give a name to. Alexandra **calls** her doll Emily. **4.** A **call** is a loud sound made by a person. The police heard someone's **call** for help.

## calm

**1. Calm** means quiet and not moving. The wind is **calm** today. **2. Calm** means quiet and not bothered. Tim is very **calm** about his first day at school.

## calves

**Calves** means more than one **calf.** They let us feed the **calves** at the farm we visited last week.

## came

**Came** is a form of **come.** Malcolm **came** into the kitchen to eat supper. We **came** outside to see the rainbow.

## camel

A **camel** is a large animal. It has a long neck. It also has one hump or two humps on its back. **Camels** can carry people and things across the desert.

◆ camel

## camera

A **camera** is a small machine that makes pictures. Many phones include **cameras.**

## camp

**1.** A **camp** is a place where people live outside for a short time. They sleep in tents or huts. Our family goes to a **camp** in the woods every summer. **2.** A **camp** is also a place where children play in the summer. Sheryl goes to **camp** during the day. Her older brother goes away to soccer **camp** for two weeks. **3.** To **camp** means to live in a camp. My family **camped** near the lake.

◆ camp

A **campground** is a place for **camping.** Some **campgrounds** have tables for picnics and trails for walking.

## can

**1.** A **can** is used to hold things. It is usually made of metal and comes all in one piece. You can buy paint in **cans.** **2. Can** means to be able to. Kelly **can** run fast. Sal **can** speak two languages. ■ **could**

(A) (B) (C) (D) (E) (F) (G) (H) (I) (J) (K) (L) (M)

## candle

A **candle** is a stick of wax with a piece of string in it. **Candles** make light when they burn. Some **candles** smell nice.

## candy

**Candy** is a kind of food. It is made of sugar and is very sweet. **Candies** can be made with chocolate, nuts, or fruit.
■ **candies**

> **Candy apples** are **apples** covered with melted **candy**.

## cannot

**Cannot** means to be not able to. A dog can run, but it **cannot** fly.

## canoe

A **canoe** is a kind of small boat. It is long, narrow, and light. **Canoes** go through the water very quietly.

◆ canoe

## can't

**Can't** is a short way to say **cannot**. Fish can swim, but they **can't** talk.

## cap

A **cap** is a kind of soft hat. People who play baseball wear **caps**. **Caps** made of wool keep your head warm.

## cape

A **cape** is a kind of clothing that you wear over your shoulders. **Capes** have no sleeves. Kirsten is wearing a pink **cape**.

◆ cape

## capital

**1.** A **capital** is a city where a state or country has its government. Dominic knows the **capitals** of all of the states.
**2. Capital** is also a way that you write letters of the alphabet. The letters **A, B**, and **C** are **capital** letters. The letters **a, b,** and **c** are small letters.

## captain

A **captain** is a person who leads other people. Firefighters, sailors, and sports teams all have **captains**.

## car

**1.** A **car** is a machine. It has four wheels, an engine, seats, and windows. People travel over roads in **cars**. **2.** A **car** is also one part of a train. It is like a big room on wheels. Most trains have many **cars.**

Babies and young children sit in **car seats** when they ride in **cars.**

## card

**1.** A **card** is a small piece of thick paper. It is shaped like a rectangle. **Cards** have numbers and pictures on them. People play games with **cards. 2.** A **card** is also a small, folded piece of paper with a message on it. You send **cards** to people in the mail. Jada got a **card** on her birthday.

## care

**1. Care** means a slow, steady way of doing things so that nothing bad will happen. You have to handle tools with **care. 2.** To take **care** of means to keep someone or something safe. Parents take **care** of their children. **3.** To **care** means to have a special interest in something. Nancy **cares** about her pets.

◆ carrot

## careful

To be **careful** means to use care. Juanita is very **careful** when she crosses the street.

## carnival

A **carnival** is a place where people go to have fun. You can win prizes at **carnivals.** Many **carnivals** have rides and games.

## carousel

A **carousel** is a kind of ride you see at a park or fair. It is sometimes called a **merry-go-round. Carousels** have seats shaped like horses or other animals that move in a circle.

## carpenter

A **carpenter** is a person who builds things with wood. **Carpenters** also fix the wood parts of houses and ships.

◆ carpenter

## carriage

A **carriage** is a box on wheels that is used to move people from one place to another. Some **carriages** are pulled by horses.

## carrot

A **carrot** is a kind of vegetable. It is long and orange. **Carrots** grow under the ground.

(A) (B) (C) (D) (E) (F) (G) (H) (I) (J) (K) (L) (M)

◆ carry

## carry

To **carry** means to hold something and take it somewhere. Isabella **carries** a basket of laundry.

■ **carries, carried**

## cartoon

A **cartoon** is a kind of picture. It is drawn by an artist in a simple way. **Cartoons** are usually funny.

## cash

**Cash** is another word for **money.** Christopher's mother gets **cash** from the bank every week.

## castle

A **castle** is a large building with high, thick walls. **Castles** were built a long time ago. Kings, queens, and knights lived in **castles.**

◆ castle

## cat

A **cat** is a small animal. It has four legs, soft fur, and a long tail. Many people have **cats** as pets.

◆ cat

## catch

**1.** To **catch** means to take and hold something that is moving. Greg throws the ball for Mindy to **catch.** He threw the ball, and she **caught** it. **2.** To **catch** also means to arrive in time for something. Dylan ran to **catch** the bus. He did not want to miss it. **3. Catch** is also a game that people can play by throwing a ball back and forth. Zoey and Avery like to play **catch** in the park. ■ **caught**

The **catcher** of a baseball team stays behind the batter. The pitcher throws the ball. If the batter misses it, the **catcher** tries to **catch** it.

N O P Q R S T U V W X Y Z

## caterpillar

A **caterpillar** is a kind of insect. It looks like a worm. **Caterpillars** change into butterflies or moths.

◆ caterpillar

## cattle

**Cattle** are large animals that are raised for milk and meat. They have four legs and two horns. Cows and bulls are **cattle.**

## caught

**Caught** is a form of **catch.** Axel kicked the ball, and Luca **caught** it.

◆ caught

## cause

**1.** To **cause** is to make something happen. When Will dropped the plate, he **caused** it to break. **2.** A **cause** is the person or thing that makes something happen. The storm was the **cause** of the flood.

## cave

A **cave** is a hollow place that goes deep under the ground. **Caves** are very dark inside.

## ceiling

A **ceiling** is the top side of a room. You walk on the floor. You look up at the **ceiling.**

## celebrate

To **celebrate** means to have a good time when something special happens. The city **celebrated** the holiday with fireworks.

## cellar

A **cellar** is a room under a house. **Cellars** are a good place to store things.

## cent

A **cent** is an amount of money equal to a penny. A nickel is five **cents,** and a dollar is one hundred **cents.**

The word **cent** sounds the same as **sent.**

## center

The **center** is the middle of something. Tiffany stood in the **center** of the room.

## century

A **century** means one hundred years. Our country fought a war for independence more than two **centuries** ago. ■ **centuries**

## cereal

**Cereal** is a kind of food. Many **cereals** are made from corn, wheat, or rice. Most people eat **cereal** with milk.

## chair

A **chair** is a kind of furniture. It has four legs and a seat. People sit on **chairs.**

◆ chair

A **chair** that a baby sits in is called a **highchair.**

## chalk

**Chalk** is something you write or draw with. I use **chalk** to draw pictures on the sidewalk. Rain washes the **chalk** away.

## chance

**1. Chance** means luck. I found three dollars by **chance.**
**2. Chance** means that something may happen. There is a **chance** it will rain today. **Chances** are it will be sunny tomorrow.

## change

**1.** To **change** means to become different. In the fall, the leaves on many trees **change** color from green to red, orange, and yellow. **2.** To **change** means to put on other clothes. After school, Sebastian and Pablo **change** before they go outside to play with their friends. **3. Change** means coins. Samantha has a dollar bill and some **change.**

## chapter

A **chapter** is a part of a book. The mystery book that Katherine is reading has eight **chapters.**

## chase

**1.** To **chase** means to run after something to try to catch it. Ben's dog **chased** him through the field. **2.** A **chase** is when someone follows something quickly. Many car **chases** end in crashes.

◆ chase

## cheap

**Cheap** means not costing a lot. Cole didn't have a lot of money, so he was glad the book he needed was **cheap.**

> **Cheap** is the opposite of **expensive.**

## check

**1.** A **check** is a mark. You make a **check** next to something to show that it is right. A **check** looks like this: ✔ . **2.** To **check** also means to look for something. I can't find my shoe. My mom tells me to **check** under her bed. **3.** A **check** is also a piece of paper that says what a meal costs. **Checks** are given to people in restaurants.

## checkers

**Checkers** is a game for two people. It is played with a board and round, flat pieces. One set of pieces is white or red, and the other is black. Antoinette is very good at **checkers.**

◆ checkers

## cheek

A **cheek** is a part of the body. Your face has two **cheeks.** They are the wide, soft areas below your eyes.

## cheerful

To be **cheerful** means to act happy. Our new neighbor smiles a lot. He says nice things to everybody. He is always **cheerful.**

## cheese

**Cheese** is a kind of food. It is made from milk. Many **cheeses** are yellow or white.

> A hamburger with **cheese** on top is called a **cheeseburger.**

## cherry

A **cherry** is a small fruit. It is round and red. **Cherries** grow on **cherry** trees.

◆ cherry

## chest

**1.** The **chest** is a part of the body. It is between your neck and your stomach. Your heart and lungs are in your **chest.** **2.** A **chest** is a strong box. Many **chests** have locks.

(A) (B) (C) (D) (E) (F) (G) (H) (I) (J) (K) (L) (M)

## chew

To **chew** means to break something into small pieces with the teeth. Our puppy **chewed** an old shoe.

## chicken

1. A **chicken** is a large bird. **Chickens** are raised for eggs and meat.
2. **Chicken** is a kind of meat. It comes from a chicken.

◆ chicken

## chief

A **chief** is a person who leads other people. **Chiefs** decide how a group of people will do their jobs. Firefighters and police have **chiefs.**

## child

A **child** is a very young person. Boys and girls are **children.**
■ **children**

## chimney

A **chimney** is a long, hollow part above a fireplace. Smoke and gas from the fireplace go up the **chimney** to the outside.

## chin

A **chin** is a part of the body. It is at the bottom of your face, below your mouth.

**Chin** rhymes with **pin, thin, tin, twin,** and **win.**

## chocolate

**Chocolate** is a kind of food. It is usually brown and very sweet. **Chocolate** candies are called **chocolates.**

## choice

A **choice** is something you can choose. The dinner **choices** were chicken, soup, or pizza. My father's **choice** for dessert was a bowl of fruit.

## choose

To **choose** means to take one thing from a lot of things. There are many books to **choose** from at the library. Abe **chose** a book about horses. ■ **chose, chosen**

## chop

To **chop** means to cut into smaller pieces with a sharp tool. Chase's uncle **chopped** potatoes, carrots, and onions for dinner with a knife. Axes are used to **chop** wood into pieces that will fit in a fireplace.
■ **chopped**

## chose

**Chose** is a form of **choose.** Marie and Etta **chose** to play soccer last spring.

## chosen

**Chosen** is a form of **choose.** Ann must choose a kind of sandwich for lunch. She has **chosen** a cheese sandwich.

## circle

A **circle** is a round shape. It is made by a line that turns until the two ends touch. **Circles** do not have any corners or straight parts.

◆ circle

A triangle, a rectangle, and a square are shapes too. They are different from a **circle** because they have straight sides and corners.

## circus

A **circus** is a kind of show. **Circuses** usually happen in a big tent. You can see clowns and magicians at the **circus.**

## citizen

A **citizen** is a person who belongs to a country. Some people are born in the country that they are part of. Other people become **citizens** after they move to a new country and live there for a long time.

## city

A **city** is a place where many people live and work. It has many streets and tall buildings. There are a lot of **cities** in our country. ■ **cities**

## claim

**1.** To **claim** means to say something that you believe is true. Grayson **claimed** that he could swim faster than me. **2.** A **claim** is something that you say is true. I believed Paige's **claim** that she finished first.

## clap

To **clap** means to hit the palms of your hands together. People **clap** after something that they like happens. The audience **clapped** after we finshed the play. ■ **clapped**

## class

**1.** A **class** is a group of students who learn together. Our **class** went on a trip to the science museum. **2.** A **class** is also what a group of people come together to learn. My mother goes to a tennis **class** every Saturday and Sunday.

A **classroom** is a **room** in a school where students learn.

(A) (B) (C) (D) (E) (F) (G) (H) (I) (J) (K) (L) (M)

## claw

A **claw** is a part of the foot of an animal or a bird. It is sharp and curved. Birds hold on to branches with their **claws.**

◆ claw

## clay

**Clay** is a kind of earth. Pots and cups can be made from **clay.**

## clean

**1. Clean** means without any dirt. Blake keeps his dog **clean.** He gives her a bath every Saturday. **2.** To **clean** is to take away dirt. Dorie **cleaned** her face with soap and water.

## clear

**1. Clear** means easy to see through. The water in the ocean was so **clear** that Leo could see the fish. **2. Clear** also means easy to understand. The directions to school were very **clear.**

## clever

**Clever** means able to think quickly. Jaime always invents good stories. She is very **clever** with words.

## climate

**Climate** means what kind of weather a place has. Palm trees grow in warm, wet **climates.**

## climb

To **climb** means to move up or down. I **climbed** the wall at the gym.

## clock

A **clock** is a kind of machine. **Clocks** tell what time it is. This **clock** says it is 10:10.

◆ clock

## close

**1. Close** means near. Some flowers grew **close** to that wall. **2.** To **close** something means to move something so that nothing can come in or go out. Amber **closed** the door and the windows. **3.** To **close** means to not allow people inside. The store **closes** at 9:00 every night.

## closet

A **closet** is a very small room. People keep clothes, shoes, and other things in **closets.**

## cloth

**Cloth** is used to make clothes. It comes from cotton, wool, and other things.

## clothes

**Clothes** cover a person's body. Coats, shirts, pants, and socks are all kinds of **clothes.**

## clothing

A piece of **clothing** is anything that you wear. My parents gave me new **clothing** to wear on the first day of school.

## cloud

A **cloud** is made up of many drops of water. **Clouds** in the sky have many shapes. Rain comes from **clouds.**

## clown

A **clown** is a person who makes other people laugh. **Clowns** wear funny costumes. Many **clowns** work in a circus.

## coach

**1.** A **coach** is a person who gives directions to a sports team. Our soccer **coach** talks to us before every game. **2.** A **coach** is also a large carriage with four wheels, a top, and a seat outside for the driver. In stories, kings and queens ride in **coaches** pulled by horses.

◆ coach

## coat

A **coat** is something that covers your body. **Coats** are usually made from thick cloth. Madelyn's pink **coat** keeps her warm when the weather is cold.

◆ coat

## cocoon

A **cocoon** is a ball of threads made by some caterpillars. These caterpillars live in **cocoons** before they change into moths.

## coin

A **coin** is a kind of money. **Coins** are usually round. They are made of metal. Pennies, nickels, dimes, and quarters are all **coins.**

◆ coin

## cold

**1. Cold** means having no heat. **Cold** is the opposite of **hot.** Snow and ice are very **cold.** **2.** A **cold** is also something that makes you sick. Your head may hurt. You may sneeze a lot and want to rest in bed. Riley stayed home from school because he had a **cold.**

(A) (B) (C) (D) (E) (F) (G) (H) (I) (J) (K) (L) (M)

## collect

To **collect** means to put things together in a group. We **collected** our toys and books into a pile.

A person who **collects** things is called a **collector.** Some stamp **collectors** have stamps from around the world.

## color

**1. Color** is the kind of light that comes from a thing. Most things have a **color.** Red, yellow, green, orange, purple, and blue are **colors. 2.** To **color** means to add color to something. Indira **colors** with crayons.

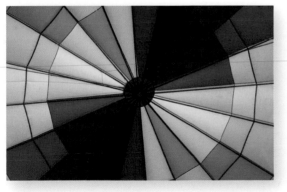

◆ color

## comb

A **comb** is a small tool used to make hair smooth and neat. Jesse carries a red **comb** to school every day.

## come

**1.** To **come** is to move toward. My mother asked me to **come** to the table to eat supper. I **came** quickly because I was hungry. **2.** To **come** also means to happen or be. Spring **comes** before summer. ■ **came, come**

## comfortable

**Comfortable** means that something feels good. Our new couch is **comfortable** to sit on.

The opposite of **comfortable** is **uncomfortable.**

## community

A **community** is a group of people who live together. A neighborhood is a small **community.** Cities are large **communities.** ■ **communities**

## compare

To **compare** means to see how things are alike or different. At camp we **compared** different kinds of leaves.

## complete

**1. Complete** means with all the parts together. We worked on the puzzle until it was **complete. 2.** To **complete** means to finish something. After we **complete** our homework, we can watch TV.

## computer

A **computer** is a machine. It helps you find information about things. **Computers** can work very quickly.

## concert

A **concert** is a show where people sing or play music on instruments. Our city orchestra plays in a **concert** every year.

## cone

**1.** A **cone** is a shape that has a circle at one end and a point at the other. Some party hats are shaped like **cones**. **2.** A **cone** is a part of some kinds of trees. A pine **cone** has the seeds for new pine trees inside it.

◆ cone

## confuse

**1.** To **confuse** means to cause someone to not understand something. I don't understand your plan. It **confuses** me. **2.** To **confuse** also means to think one thing is another. My teacher sometimes **confuses** me with my twin.

When something **confuses** you, it is **confusing**. Is your homework **confusing** sometimes?

## consonant

A **consonant** is a kind of letter. B, C, D, F, G, H, J, K, L, M, N, P, Q, R, S, T, V, W, X, Y, and Z are **consonants**. All of the letters of the alphabet are **consonants** or vowels.

## container

A **container** is something that is used to store things. Boxes, cans, jars, and barrels are **containers**.

◆ container

## contest

A **contest** is a kind of game to see who can win. Two or more people can be in a **contest**.

## continent

A **continent** is a very large area of land. There are seven **continents** on the earth.

## continue

**1.** To **continue** means to happen without stopping. The rain began in the morning and **continued** all day. I **continued** reading the book until I finished it. **2.** To **continue** also means to start again. We played baseball in the morning but stopped for lunch. Then we **continued** the game in the afternoon.

## control

To **control** something means to make it do what you want it to do. Amir **controls** his kite with a long string. ■ **controlled**

## cook

**1.** To **cook** is to heat food to make it ready to eat. We **cooked** the turkey in the oven for four hours. **2.** A **cook** is a person who makes meals. **Cooks** work in kitchens.

> A **cookbook** is a **book** that explains how to make different kinds of food. **Cookbooks** have many recipes.

## cookie

A **cookie** is a kind of food. It is like a small, flat cake. **Cookies** are sweet.

## cool

**Cool** means not very cold. The weather was **cool** this morning, but it got warm this afternoon.

> A **cooler** is a box that keeps food **cool**. Some people put sandwiches and drinks in a **cooler** to take to the beach.

## cooperate

To **cooperate** means to work well with someone else. Our whole class **cooperated** in writing a story for the school newspaper.

## copper

**Copper** is a kind of metal. Many wires are made from **copper**. **Copper** gives pennies their brown color.

## copy

**1.** A **copy** is something made to look like something else. Laura drew a picture. Then she made **copies** to give to her friends. **2.** To **copy** something is to make another one like it. Abel writes a poem on a piece of paper. He **copied** the poem out of a book. ■ **copies, copied**

## corn

**Corn** is a kind of vegetable. It grows on a tall, green plant. **Corn** can be yellow or white.

> A **cornfield** is a **field** where **corn** grows.

◆ corn

## corner

A **corner** is the place where two sides come together. Squares and rectangles have four **corners**.

## correct

**1. Correct** means without mistakes. Jack's answer was **correct**. **2.** To **correct** means to check for mistakes in something. The teacher **corrects** all our tests.

## cost

**1.** To **cost** means to have a price of some amount of money. The book Jo wants **costs** ten dollars. **2.** The **cost** of something is how much money you pay to buy it. The **cost** of the toy I wanted was too much. I didn't have enough money to buy it.
■ **cost**

## costume

A **costume** is a set of special clothes. People wore **costumes** in the school play. Sophia's **costume** was a nurse's uniform.

## cottage

A **cottage** is a small house that is usually in the country. Some families have **cottages** where they go on vacation.

◆ costume

## cotton

**Cotton** is soft, light, and white. It grows on a **cotton** plant. It is made into cloth. People wear clothes made from **cotton** in the summer.

◆ cotton

## couch

A **couch** is a kind of furniture that two or three people can sit on at one time. **Couches** are comfortable for reading and watching television.

◆ couch

## cough

**1.** A **cough** is a noise that happens when you suddenly push air out of your lungs. My mother's **coughs** kept me awake at night. **2.** A **cough** is also a sickness that causes you to make this noise often. Jackson stayed home from school when he had a **cough**. **3.** To **cough** is to make a cough. The smoke in the air caused Mia to **cough**.

A B C D E F G H I J K L M

## could

**Could** is a form of **can**. Jonathan can whistle. He **could** whistle when he was five years old.

## couldn't

**Couldn't** is a short way to say **could not**. Last year I **couldn't** read as well as Tyrone, but now I can.

## count

To **count** means to add. Katie **counted** the pencils on her desk. There were five pencils.

## country

**1.** A **country** is a large place where a group of people live. All the people in one **country** share the same laws. There are many cities in each **country** and many **countries** in the world. **2.** A **country** is also the group of people who live in a country. Our **country** votes for a president every four years. **3.** The **country** is the area away from a city. There are forests, fields, and farms in the **country**.
■ **countries**

> Land that is in the **country** is sometimes called the **countryside.**

## courage

**Courage** is what you have when you are brave. The firefighters showed **courage** when they went into the burning building to save people.

## cousin

Your **cousin** is the child of your aunt or uncle. Angelina has lots of **cousins.**

## cover

**1.** To **cover** means to put something on top of something else. Wendy **covered** herself with thick blankets to keep warm. **2.** A **cover** goes on the top or outside of something. Books and magazines have **covers.** Pots and pans also have **covers.**

◆ cover

## cow

A **cow** is a large, female animal that lives on a farm. **Cows** are raised for milk and meat.

## cowboy

A **cowboy** is a man who takes care of cattle. **Cowboys** work on big farms. They often ride horses.

## cowgirl

A **cowgirl** is a woman who takes care of cattle. **Cowgirls** work on big farms. They often ride horses.

## crab

A **crab** is a small animal. It has a hard shell and five pairs of legs. **Crabs** usually live in or near the ocean.

There are many types of **crabs.** The **spider crab** has long legs like a spider. The **blue crab** has blue claws. The **king crab** is one of the largest **crabs.** It weighs more than ten pounds.

## crack

**1.** A **crack** is a small place that looks like a crooked line. The ground had **cracks** in it. **2.** To **crack** is to break so that cracks are seen. Toby's mirror **cracked** after she dropped it on the floor.

◆ crack

## crane

**1.** A **crane** is a large bird with a long neck, long legs, and a long beak. **Cranes** often live in marshes. **2.** A **crane** is also a large machine with a long metal arm. **Cranes** lift and move heavy objects.

◆ crane

## crash

**1.** To **crash** means to hit something and break with a lot of noise. During the storm, a boat **crashed** into the dock. **2.** A **crash** is a loud noise. We heard a **crash** in the next room.

## crawl

To **crawl** is to move on your hands and knees. Babies **crawl** until they learn to walk.

## crayon

A **crayon** is a piece of colored wax. It is used to draw and write with. **Crayons** come in many colors.

## cream

**Cream** is a kind of food. It is part of the milk that comes from a cow. Butter is made from **cream.**

## creature

A **creature** is something that is living. Camden likes to see the sea **creatures** at the aquarium.

## crib

A **crib** is a special kind of bed with high sides. Babies sleep in **cribs** so that they are safe.

## cricket

A **cricket** is a kind of insect. Some male **crickets** make noises by rubbing their front wings together.

## cried

**Cried** is a form of **cry.** My brother **cried** when he fell on the ice.

## crocodile

A **crocodile** is a very large reptile. It looks like an alligator with a long, narrow jaw. **Crocodiles** live in rivers and swamps.

◆ crocodile

## crooked

**Crooked** means not straight. Lightning looks like a **crooked** line in the sky.

◆ crooked

## cross

**1.** A **cross** is a shape. It is made by two lines that touch in the middle. It looks like this: + .
**2.** To **cross** means to go to the other side. The bridge **crosses** the river. We **crossed** the street.
**3.** To **cross** also means to draw a line through something. Our teacher tells us to **cross** our t's.

## crow

A **crow** is a large bird with black feathers. **Crows** can make a loud noise.

## crowd

A **crowd** is a large group of people. **Crowds** come to watch football games.

## crown

A **crown** is a special hat worn by kings and queens. Many **crowns** are made of metal and have jewels on them.

## cruel

**Cruel** means not kind. In the story I am reading, the people in the village don't like their **cruel** king.

**Cruel** is another word for **mean.**

## crumb

A **crumb** is a very small piece of foods that are baked. Bread, cake, and cookies make **crumbs** when we eat them.

## crush

To **crush** is to push or squeeze something until it breaks or changes its shape. Jayden **crushed** the can when he stepped on it.

◆ crush

## crutch

A **crutch** is a kind of pole that helps people walk when they are hurt. After Jeremiah fell, he needed **crutches** to help him walk.

## cry

To **cry** is to have tears fall from your eyes. People sometimes **cry** when they are sad or when they get hurt.
■ **cries, cried**

## cub

A **cub** is a young bear, wolf, or lion. Some bear **cubs** stay with their mother for two or three years.

◆ cub

## cup

A **cup** is a small, open container with a flat bottom used for drinking. You can drink milk, juice, or water from **cups.**

A **teacup** is a little **cup** with a handle.

## cure

A **cure** is something that makes a sick person get better. After the doctor gave Amy the **cure** for her fever, she felt better.

## curious

To be **curious** is to want to learn. Hailey and her brother ask a lot of questions. They are very **curious.**

(A) (B) (C) (D) (E) (F) (G) (H) (I) (J) (K) (L) (M)

## curly

**Curly** means twisting around in small circles. Leigh's hair is **curly.** ■ **curlier, curliest**

◆ curly

## curtain

A **curtain** is a piece of cloth used to cover a window. We have blue cotton **curtains** on our kitchen windows.

## curve

**1.** A **curve** is a round line. The bottom of a **U** is a **curve. 2.** To **curve** means to follow a round line. The road **curves** back and forth.

## cushion

A **cushion** is a kind of soft, cloth pillow. You can sit, lie, or rest on it. Our couch has two large, round **cushions.**

## customer

A **customer** is someone who buys something. Sebastian helps the **customers** find what they need at his parents' store.

## cut

To **cut** is to divide something into pieces with a sharp tool. Dan used scissors to **cut** pictures out of the newspaper. Diana **cut** her fried chicken before she ate it. ■ **cut**

◆ cut

# D

## dad

A **dad** is someone's father. My **dad** reads stories to me before I go to bed.

## daisy

A **daisy** is a kind of flower. Most **daisies** are white with yellow centers. ▪ **daisies**

## dam

A **dam** is a wall across a river. It causes a lake to form behind it. **Dams** control how fast water goes from the lake to the other side of the **dam.**

> Some animals build **dams.** Beavers build **dams** out of sticks and branches.

## damp

**Damp** means only a little wet. Erika used a **damp** cloth to wash the table.

## dance

To **dance** means to move your body to music. Marta **danced** with her friends at the party.

## dandelion

A **dandelion** is a kind of flower. **Dandelions** are round and yellow. When they become white, their seeds are blown away by the wind.

## dangerous

**Dangerous** means not safe. Tornadoes can be very **dangerous.**

◆ dandelion

> **Danger** is something that is **dangerous.** We are careful to stay out of **danger** when we swim in the ocean.

◆ dam

(A) (B) (C) (D) (E) (F) (G) (H) (I) (J) (K) (L) (M)

## dark

**Dark** means without light. At night it is **dark** outside.

> Where there is no light, there is **darkness**. When the electricity didn't work, we were in **darkness**.

## date

A **date** is any one day. July 7 is a **date**. November 20 is also a **date**. Every day has a **date**.

## daughter

A **daughter** is a person's female child. Liza and Kit are my teacher's **daughters**.

## day

**1.** A **day** is the time from one morning to the next morning. There are 24 hours in one **day**. There are seven **days** in one week. **2. Day** is the time when it is light outside. Rolf played outside all **day**. He only went in the house when it got dark.

## dead

**Dead** means not alive. Plants and flowers die without water. They become **dead**.

## deaf

**Deaf** means not able to hear. A person who cannot hear is **deaf**.

## dear

Something **dear** is something you love. People also use **dear** to begin a letter. Susan's letter to her aunt began with "**Dear Aunt Sonia**."

## December

**December** is the last month of the year. It has 31 days. **December** comes after November and before January.

## decide

To **decide** means to choose. Ramona **decided** to wear a red shirt and blue pants to the school picnic.

## decorate

To **decorate** means to add colors, designs, or objects to something to make it look prettier. Madelyn and Logan **decorated** the kitchen with balloons for Zoe's birthday party.

## deep

**Deep** means that there is a lot of space between the top and the bottom of something. The ocean is **deep**.

> The opposite of **deep** is **shallow**. This end of the pool is **shallow**, but the other end is **deep**.

## deer

A **deer** is a kind of animal. It has four legs and soft, brown fur. **Deer** live in forests and fields. ▪ **deer**

◆ deer

## delicious

**Delicious** means very good to taste. For dinner we ate turkey, rice, and broccoli. It was **delicious!**

## delighted

**Delighted** means very happy. Shoshanna and her brother were **delighted** when their cousins moved into the house across the street.

## dentist

A **dentist** is a kind of doctor. A **dentist** takes care of people's teeth. **Dentists** teach you how to keep your teeth healthy.

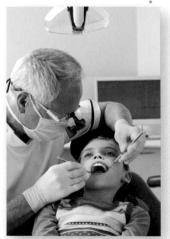

◆ dentist

## describe

To **describe** means to tell or write all about something. I **described** my summer vacation to my friends.

The way something is **described** is a **description.** My book has a good **description** of how bees make honey.

## desert

A **desert** is a large, dry area of land. Not much rain falls there. **Deserts** are covered by sand.

## design

A **design** is a group of different lines or shapes. **Designs** are usually drawn or painted. The blanket has pretty **designs** on it.

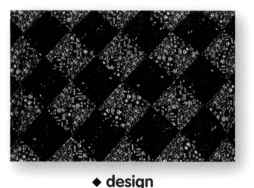

◆ design

## desk

A **desk** is a kind of furniture. It has a large, flat top and legs. People sit at **desks** to read and write.

(A) (B) (C) (D) (E) (F) (G) (H) (I) (J) (K) (L) (M)

## dessert

A **dessert** is a kind of food. It is the last part of a meal. **Dessert** is usually sweet. Ice cream, pie, cake, and fruit are **desserts.**

## diamond

**1.** A **diamond** is a jewel. **Diamonds** are clear and very hard. **2.** A **diamond** is also a shape. It has four sides and four corners. One corner is at the top, and another is at the bottom.

◆ **diamond**

## diary

A **diary** is a book that you can write your thoughts in. Jamie and Sam both have **diaries.**

## dictionary

A **dictionary** is a kind of book. **Dictionaries** show how words are spelled. They also explain what words mean. This book is a **dictionary.** ■ **dictionaries**

## did

**Did** is a form of **do.** Alexa and Joey **did** something together. They went to the movies.

## didn't

**Didn't** is a short way to say **did not.** Zac was sick. He **didn't** feel well. He **didn't** go to school.

## die

To **die** means to become dead. The cold weather made all the flowers **die.** The leaves on the trecs **died** too.

## different

**Different** means not alike. Dogs and cats are very **different** kinds of animals. A monkey's tail is **different** from a fish's tail.

◆ **different**

The opposite of **different** is **same.** My brother and I live in the **same** house. My cousin lives in a **different** house.

## dig

To **dig** means to make a hole in the earth. Aiden likes to **dig** in the sand. ■ **dug**

## dime

A **dime** is a coin. One **dime** is the same as ten pennies or two nickels. A dollar is ten **dimes.**

## dinner

**Dinner** is a meal. It is usually the biggest meal of the day. Most people eat **dinner** at night.

## dinosaur

A **dinosaur** is a reptile that lived a long time ago. Some **dinosaurs** were huge, and some were very small. Some **dinosaurs** ate plants, and some ate meat.

◆ dinosaur

## dip

**1.** To **dip** means to put something in liquid and then take it out quickly. Dawn **dips** her brush in the bucket of paint. **2. Dip** is also a kind of soft food. Sam likes to eat carrots with **dip**.
■ **dipped**

## direction

**1.** A **direction** is somewhere you can look or point or go. North, south, east, and west are **directions**. **2. Directions** tell you how to get somewhere. Matthew and Adrianne gave us the **directions** to their house. **3. Directions** can also tell you how to do something. Games usually come with **directions** that tell you how to play.

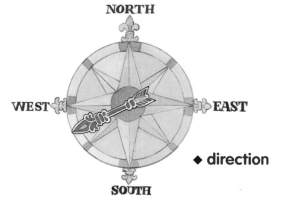

NORTH

WEST  EAST

SOUTH

◆ direction

## dirt

**Dirt** means earth. The ground is made of **dirt** and rocks. Harper gets **dirt** on her gloves when she works in the garden.

◆ dirt

**Dirty** means covered with dirt. Our dog gets **dirty** when he swims in the swamp.

## disappear

To **disappear** means to stop being seen. The sun **disappeared** behind a cloud.

(A) (B) (C) (D) (E) (F) (G) (H) (I) (J) (K) (L) (M)

## discover

To **discover** means to find out something. I looked down and **discovered** that I was wearing two different socks.

## dish

A **dish** is something to put food in. **Dishes** are usually round. Miguel washed all the **dishes** after supper.

◆ dish

## distance

**Distance** is the space between two things. Airplanes can travel long **distances** in a few hours.

## distant

**Distant** means far away. Letters from **distant** countries can take a long time to arrive.

## dive

To **dive** means to jump in the water with your hands and head first. Elsa learned how to swim and **dive** at the pool.

A **diver** is a person who **dives**.

## divide

To **divide** means to change one big thing into two or more smaller things. Louisa **divided** the apple into two halves. Benjamin **divides** his toys into three piles.

## do

To **do** means to make something happen. Hannah always **does** a good job cleaning her room. She has always **done** it without being asked. Bridget and Kimberly **did** some work together. ■ **does, did, done**

## dock

A **dock** is a place to tie up a boat. **Docks** are built where land and water meet. Tyler tied his boat to the **dock** so it wouldn't float away.

## doctor

A **doctor** is a person who helps sick people get well. Many **doctors** work in hospitals.

## does

**Does** is a form of **do**. Ben **does** his homework every night. Fatima **does** hers too.

## doesn't

**Doesn't** is a short way to say **does not**. Larry **doesn't** like to eat carrots, but he does like to eat corn.

## dog

A **dog** is a kind of animal. It has four legs, fur, and a tail. Many people have **dogs** as pets. There are many kinds of **dogs.**

## doll

A **doll** is a kind of toy. **Dolls** usually look like babies or small children.

## dollar

A **dollar** is an amount of money. A **dollar** is usually made of a piece of green paper shaped like a rectangle. One **dollar** is equal to one hundred pennies. My lunch cost five **dollars.**

## dolphin

A **dolphin** is a kind of animal that lives in the sea. **Dolphins** are mammals that are smaller than whales. Sometimes, **dolphins** jump above the water.

◆ dolphin

## done

**Done** is a form of **do.** Jo and Taryn have fed their pets. They have **done** their job for the day.

## donkey

A **donkey** is a kind of animal. It looks like a small horse with long ears. **Donkeys** can carry heavy loads.

◆ donkey

## don't

**Don't** is a short way to say **do not.** Fish live in water. They **don't** live in trees. I like to eat apples, but I **don't** like to eat bananas.

## door

A **door** is a place in a wall where you can move through along the floor. **Doors** usually open and close.

◆ door

## dot

A **dot** is a small, round spot. Miranda's skirt has black and green **dots** on it.

## doughnut

A **doughnut** is a small cake. Many **doughnuts** are round and have a hole in the center. Some have jelly inside.

## down

**1. Down** means going from a high place to a low place. A big balloon came **down** in our garden. **2. Down** means in a low place. There is water **down** in the well.

The opposite of **down** is **up**. The balloon was **up** in the sky, but it fell **down** to the ground.

## dozen

A **dozen** is a group of 12 things. I bought a **dozen** eggs. There are two **dozen** students in Padma's class. ▪ **dozen**

## Dr.

**Dr.** is a short way to write **doctor**. People use **Dr.** with a doctor's name. Our family doctor is **Dr.** Chan.

## dragon

A **dragon** is a monster in stories. It is not real. **Dragons** look like huge reptiles with wings and claws. They breathe fire.

## drank

**Drank** is a form of **drink**. Sam **drank** water before she played outside.

◆ dragon

## draw

To **draw** is to make a picture. You can **draw** with pencils, pens, or crayons. Abbie has **drawn** many cartoons. ▪ **drew, drawn**

A picture that you **draw** is called a **drawing**. Myra made a **drawing** of her house.

## drawer

A **drawer** is a container that slides in and out of a piece of furniture. Lucas keeps his shirts in a **drawer**.

◆ drawer

## dream

**1.** A **dream** is a story or a picture that happens in your mind when you sleep. **2.** To **dream** means to imagine stories while you sleep. One night Fiona **dreamed** she could fly. **3.** A **dream** is also something you wish for. Nick's **dream** is to fly to the moon in a rocket.

# dress

**1.** To **dress** means to put clothes on. Jae's father helped him **dress** for the party.
**2.** A **dress** is a kind of clothing. It is one piece that covers the top and the bottom of the body. Riya has many **dresses**, but her favorite **dress** is yellow with pink flowers on it.

◆ **dress**

# drew

**Drew** is a form of **draw.** Andy used a red crayon to draw a circle on the paper. Then he **drew** some squares with a blue crayon.

# dried

**Dried** is a form of **dry.** After we washed the car, we **dried** it with old towels.

# drink

**1.** A **drink** is a liquid you can swallow. Orange juice is Ella's favorite **drink. 2.** To **drink** means to take liquid into your mouth and swallow it. Mateo always **drinks** milk with supper.
■ **drank, drunk**

◆ **drink**

# drive

To **drive** is to make a car, a truck, or a bus go. Yesterday, my mom **drove** our car to the park. She has **driven** to the park a lot. ■ **drove, driven**

A **driveway** is a small road that leads from a street to a house. We park our car in the **driveway.**

# drop

**1.** A **drop** is a very small amount of liquid. I felt **drops** of rain on my nose. **2.** To **drop** something means to let it fall. Tomas **dropped** most of the clothes he was carrying upstairs.
■ **dropped**

◆ **drop**

# drove

**Drove** is a form of **drive.** When Carla missed the bus, her father **drove** her to school.

# drugstore

A **drugstore** is a store where people can buy medicine. **Drugstores** also sell snacks and other things.

## drum

A **drum** is an instrument. To play **drums,** you beat on them with your hands or with sticks.

◆ drum

## drunk

**Drunk** is a form of **drink.** I drink a lot of water. I have **drunk** a whole bottle today.

## dry

**1. Dry** means not wet. During the storm my brother and I stayed warm and **dry** inside. **2.** To **dry** means to take all the water from something. The towel hangs outside to **dry.** The sun **dries** it in a few hours.
■ **dries, dried**

## duck

A **duck** is a kind of bird. It has a wide, flat bill and short legs. **Ducks** swim in water.

◆ duck

A young **duck** is called a **duckling.** Five **ducklings** swim behind their mother.

## dug

**Dug** is a form of **dig.** Taylor digs in the sand at the beach. She **dug** a big hole with her pail and shovel.

## dull

**1. Dull** means not sharp. It is hard to cut anything with **dull** scissors. **2. Dull** also means not interesting. Anthony didn't like the story. He thought it was **dull.**

## dump

To **dump** is to drop something. Rachel **dumped** her books on the table.

## during

**During** means for the whole time. It is light outside **during** the day. We stayed inside **during** the storm.

## dust

**1. Dust** is tiny pieces of dirt. **Dust** can make you sneeze. The cowboy's horse left a lot of **dust** behind it. **2.** To **dust** means to take dust off with a cloth or brush. My brother and I **dusted** the furniture yesterday.

**Dusty** means covered with **dust.** We had to clean the table because it was **dusty.**

# E

## each

Each means with none left out. Nan ate **each** berry in the bowl.

> **Each other** means one and the other. Karen and Joy gave **each other** presents.

## eagle

An **eagle** is a large bird. **Eagles** have curved beaks and strong wings.

## ear

An **ear** is a part of the body. There is one **ear** on each side of your head. People hear with their **ears**.

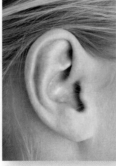

◆ ear

## early

**1. Early** means happening near the beginning. Ian wakes up **early** in the morning. **2. Early** also means before the usual time. Last night I went to bed **early.** ■ earlier, earliest

> The opposite of **early** is late.

## earn

To **earn** is to get something for what you do. Carly **earns** money sometimes by working in her neighbors' yards.

## earth

**1. Earth** means soil. There is good **earth** in the garden for the plants to grow in. **2.** The **earth** is our world. The **earth** is covered by land and oceans.

## earthquake

An **earthquake** happens when a part of the earth moves suddenly. During **earthquakes,** the ground shakes.

## east

**East** is a direction. The sun rises in the **east**. **East** is the opposite of **west.**

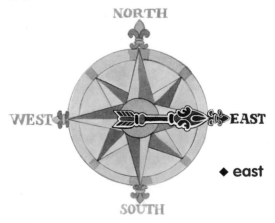

◆ east

## easy

**Easy** means not hard to do. Katherine likes doing math. She thinks it is **easy.** ■ **easier, easiest**

> The word **easily** means in an **easy** way. Liz is very good at swimming. She swam across the pool **easily.**

## eat

To **eat** means to take food into the body through the mouth. People **eat** when they feel hungry. Agustín **ate** chicken and peas for dinner. My grandparents have **eaten** their pizza. ■ **ate, eaten**

◆ eat

## echo

**1.** An **echo** is a sound that comes back again. If you shout at a mountain, you may hear **echoes** of your voice. **2.** To **echo** means to make an echo. The coach's voice **echoed** in the gym during our basketball game. ■ **echoes, echoed**

## edge

An **edge** is the line or place where something ends. Tanya hung on the **edge** of the pool. Knives have very sharp **edges.**

◆ edge

## education

**Education** means what you learn in school. A good **education** helps you when you look for a job.

## egg

An **egg** is a smooth, round shell with a baby animal inside of it. Birds grow inside **eggs** until they are ready to hatch. Sometimes you can find bird **eggs** in a bird's nest. Many people eat **eggs** from chickens.

◆ egg

## eight

**Eight** is a number. **Eight** is one more than seven. **Eight** is written **8.** $7 + 1 = 8$.

## either

**1. Either** means one or the other. Adrianna wants **either** a puppy or a kitten for her birthday. She would be happy to get **either** of them. **2. Either** also means that you also do not have something or do not want to do something. Warren did not want to play soccer. He did not want to play basketball **either.**

## elbow

An **elbow** is a part of the body. Your arm bends at the **elbow.** Mei sat with her **elbows** on the table.

## election

An **election** is when people vote for someone or something. We have **elections** at school every year for our team captains.

When we have an **election,** we **elect** someone. My cousin Alexis was **elected** president of her class.

## electricity

**Electricity** is a kind of energy. Lamps make light when **electricity** goes through them. **Electricity** also makes refrigerators, computers, and many other things work.

Things that use **electricity** are called **electric.** The singer in my favorite band also plays the **electric** guitar.

## elephant

An **elephant** is a very large animal. It has thick, gray skin, big ears, and a long trunk. **Elephants** are the biggest animals that live on land.

◆ elephant

## elevator

An **elevator** is a machine that takes people up and down in a building. People sometimes use **elevators** when they don't want to use the stairs.

(A) (B) (C) (D) (E) (F) (G) (H) (I) (J) (K) (L) (M)

## elf

An **elf** is a creature in stories that is often small. **Elves** can usually use magic. ■ **elves**

## else

**Else** means other or different. Mackenzie did not want a turkey and cheese sandwich for lunch. She wanted something **else.**

## emerald

An **emerald** is a kind of jewel. **Emeralds** are green.

## empty

**Empty** means with nothing inside. Cameron ate all of the peanut butter. He left the **empty** jar on the table.
■ **emptier, emptiest**

> The opposite of **empty** is **full**. **Empty** boxes are easier to carry than **full** boxes.

## end

**1.** An **end** is the last part of something. Jamie went to the **end** of the line to buy an ice cream cone. **2.** An **end** is also either side of something long. My brother sat at one **end** of the table, and I sat at the other. **3.** To **end** means to come to the last part. The story **ends** with a surprise.

## energy

**Energy** is something that you need to do work. People, animals, and plants make **energy** from food. Heat, steam, light, and electricity are forms of **energy** that machines make or use.

## engine

An **engine** is a kind of machine. It burns oil, gas, or wood to do work. Cars, ships, and planes have **engines** to make them move.

◆ engine

## engineer

**1.** An **engineer** is a person who drives a train. **Engineers** control the engines at the front of trains. **2.** An **engineer** is also someone who tells people how to build engines, machines, roads, bridges, and other things.

## enjoy

To **enjoy** something means to like it. The first grade class **enjoyed** having a picnic at the end of the year.

## enough

**Enough** means as much or as many as you need. We have **enough** food for everybody.

## enter

To **enter** means to go into a place. Tara and P.J. **entered** the building together.

## entrance

An **entrance** is where you enter a place. We keep a plant beside the **entrance** to our house. There were two **entrances** to the fair.

◆ entrance

> The opposite of an **entrance** is an **exit.** Our class walked in through the **entrance** of the museum and left through the **exit.**

## environment

The **environment** is what is all around a living thing. Air, water, land, and buildings are all part of the **environment.** Cactuses grow best in desert **environments.**

## equal

**Equal** means the same in amount or size. One dime is **equal** to ten pennies. I wanted a slice of cake that was **equal** to my sister's slice.

◆ equal

## erase

To **erase** means to make something disappear by rubbing it. Christopher **erased** his math homework after he made a mistake.

> An **eraser** is something that you can use to erase. Pencils often have **erasers** on one end.

## escape

To **escape** means to become free. Emma's hamster **escaped** from his cage.

## especially

**Especially** means more than anything else. Joellen likes to do a lot of things for fun. She **especially** likes to act in the school plays.

(A) (B) (C) (D) (E) (F) (G) (H) (I) (J) (K) (L) (M)

## even

**1. Even** means having the same size or amount. Please cut the cake into **even** slices. **2.** An **even** number is a number that you can get to when you start at zero and count by twos. Two, four, six, eight, and ten are **even** numbers.

## evening

**Evening** is the part of the day between the afternoon and the night. The sun sets during the **evening**. We stay at home most **evenings**.

## event

An **event** is something that happens. My cousin's wedding was a fancy **event**.

## ever

**Ever** means at any time. Have you **ever** seen a peacock? Going to the fair is the most fun I have **ever** had.

## every

**Every** means each one. Nobody could read **every** book in the library.

**Everybody** and **everyone** mean the same as **every** person.

## everything

**Everything** means each thing. Before we left the beach, we checked that we had picked up **everything** we had brought with us. After the storm, the snow covered **everything**.

◆ everything

## everywhere

**Everywhere** means in every place. Deanna cannot find the book she borrowed from the library. She looks in her house, at school, and at the park. She looks **everywhere**!

## evil

To be **evil** is to be very mean. In the story, the **evil** giant would not let the people cross the bridge.

The opposite of **evil** is **good**. In the movie, the **good** king sends the **evil** prince away from the palace.

## example

An **example** is something that is chosen because it is like other things of the same kind. Water is an **example** of a liquid.

We say **for example** when we want to show an **example**. The zoo has animals from other countries, **for example,** monkeys and elephants.

## excellent

**Excellent** means very, very good. T.J. tells **excellent** stories.

## except

**Except** means leaving out. Everyone **except** Ivy was in school today. She was the only one who wasn't there.

## exciting

To be **exciting** is to make people feel a lot of energy. Ava and Tom thought the ride was **exciting.**

◆ exciting

## excuse

An **excuse** explains the reason for something. Students must bring a written **excuse** from their parents if they are late for school.

## exercise

**1. Exercise** is running and jumping and moving your body around. We get a lot of **exercise** when we play soccer.
**2.** An **exercise** lets you practice how to do something. We are learning to add by doing the **exercises** in our book.

◆ exercise

## exit

**1.** An **exit** is the way out of a room or a building. The gym in our school has two **exits** that lead outside. **2.** To **exit** means to leave a room or a building. Emmett and Sadie got hungry during the movie, so they **exited** the theater to get snacks.

(A) (B) (C) (D) (E) (F) (G) (H) (I) (J) (K) (L) (M)

## expand

To **expand** is to get bigger. A balloon **expands** when you blow air into it.

◆ expand

## expect

To **expect** is to think something will happen. Laila **expects** her father to be home in a few minutes.

## expensive

**Expensive** means costing a lot of money. Robert's parents wanted to buy a new car, but it was too **expensive.**

## experiment

An **experiment** is a test to find out something. Our class did **experiments** with magnets to find out what they do. We saw how they stick to some metals.

## explain

To **explain** means to tell about something so that other people can understand it. Aria **explained** the rules of the game so we could all play it.

## explore

To **explore** means to go into a place you have never been before to see what is there. Matt **explored** the field until he found a spider's web.

◆ explore

A person who **explores** is called an **explorer.**

## extra

**Extra** means more than what you need or expect. Mr. Chen gave Isabella twelve dollars to clean his car. She got an **extra** three dollars for washing the tires.

## eye

An **eye** is a part of the body. People and animals see with their **eyes.** Your **eyes** are in the middle of your face, one on each side of your nose.

# F

## face

**1.** The **face** is the front of the head. The eyes, the nose, and the mouth are all part of the **face**. **2.** The **face** of a clock shows what time it is. Clock **faces** have numbers on them. **3.** To **face** means to look in some direction. Eric **faced** the front of the room.

## fact

A **fact** is something that is true. Scientists try to find out **facts**.

## factory

A **factory** is a building where people use machines to make things. Many people work at different jobs in large **factories**. ■ **factories**

◆ **factory**

## fair

**1.** To be **fair** means to treat everyone the same. Breaking the rules is not **fair**. **2.** A **fair** is a place where people go to have fun. Some people show animals, vegetables, and other things that they have raised or made. At most **fairs** there are rides and games.

## fairy

A **fairy** is a small person in a story. **Fairies** can often perform magic. ■ **fairies**

## fall

**1.** To **fall** is to go down. Shira still **falls** sometimes when she skates. All the leaves had **fallen** off the trees in our yard by winter. **2.** To **fall** asleep means to go to sleep. Pascale **falls** asleep easily at night. **3.** **Fall** is a season. It comes after summer and before winter. **Fall** is another word for **autumn**. ■ **fell, fallen**

## false

**False** means not true. It is **false** to say that frogs can fly.

## family

Your **family** has in it your parents, sisters, brothers, aunts, uncles, and cousins. There are many different kinds of **families**.
■ families

## fan

**1.** A **fan** is an object that can make air move to make a breeze. Some **fans** are machines. Others are made of paper that you wave with your hand. **2.** A **fan** is also a person who likes something a lot. Kennedy is a **fan** of adventure stories.

◆ fan

## fancy

**Fancy** means prettier or better than usual. Samantha wore a **fancy** dress and new shoes to her aunt's wedding. ■ **fancier, fanciest**

## far

**Far** means at a great distance. The moon is **far** away from here. It takes a long time to get there.

The opposite of **far** is **near**. I live **near** my school but **far** from the train station.

## farm

A **farm** is an area of land. People grow food and raise animals on **farms.**

◆ farm

A **farmer** is a person who works on a **farm. Farmers** start to work early in the morning.

## farther

**Farther** means at a greater distance. The sun is **farther** from us than the moon is.

## fast

**Fast** means quickly. A rocket goes very **fast**.

## fat

**Fat** means big and round. Pigs and hippopotamuses are **fat**.

The opposite of **fat** is **thin.** My **fat** puppy became **thin** when he ate less food.

## father

A **father** is a man who has a child. **Fathers** and mothers take care of their children.

## favorite

**Favorite** means what you like the most. Holly's **favorite** color is purple.

## fear

**1. Fear** is what you feel when you are afraid. Sy's **fears** about school disappeared when he met his new teacher. **2.** To **fear** is to be afraid. Charlie **fears** the water because he doesn't know how to swim yet.

## feast

A **feast** is a very large meal. Many families have **feasts** on Thanksgiving and other holidays.

## feather

A **feather** is part of a bird. Most birds are covered with them. **Feathers** are light and soft.

◆ feather

## February

**February** is the second month of the year. It has 28 or 29 days. **February** comes after January and before March.

## feed

To **feed** means to give food to. Yesterday my mom **fed** a carrot to the rabbit. ■ **fed**

◆ feed

## feel

**1.** To **feel** is to touch. Sofia **feels** the dolphin's smooth skin.
**2.** To **feel** is also to be some way. When you are happy, you may **feel** like singing. When our friends are sick, we **feel** sorry for them. ■ **felt**

A **feeling** is the way you **feel** about something. Joy and love are **feelings**.

## feet

**Feet** means more than one **foot**. People have two **feet**. Dogs and cats have four **feet**. Luis is more than four **feet** tall.

## fell

**Fell** is a form of **fall**. Allie **fell** off her bicycle. Evelyn **fell** asleep.

(A) (B) (C) (D) (E) (F) (G) (H) (I) (J) (K) (L) (M)

## felt

**Felt** is a form of **feel.** Yesterday Angelo **felt** too sick to go out. The cat's fur **felt** soft when I touched it.

## female

**Female** is a kind of person or animal. It is the opposite of **male.** Girls and women are **female** people.

## fence

A **fence** is something that is built outside to keep two places apart. **Fences** can be made of wood, metal, or stone.

◆ fence

## festival

A **festival** is a special party where people celebrate something that is important to them. **Festivals** often have food, music, and dancing.

## few

**Few** means not many. Glenn ate a **few** bites of his supper because he wasn't very hungry.

## field

**1.** A **field** is a large, flat area of land. No trees grow there. Farmers grow corn and other plants in **fields. 2.** A **field** is also where some sports are played. Baseball and football are played on different kinds of **fields.**

◆ field

When you go on a **field trip,** you leave school to visit another place with your teacher and your class. Ms. Carr's class took a **field trip** to the zoo.

## fight

**1.** To **fight** is to get mad at someone when you cannot agree. People often shout when they **fight. 2.** A **fight** is what happens sometimes when people do not agree. Ethan and I had a **fight** yesterday. ■ **fought**

## fill

To **fill** means to make something full. Marcus **filled** two glasses with milk.

◆ fill

## find

**1.** To **find** is to see where something is. Matt looks around his room for his shoes. He **finds** them under the bed. Yesterday he **found** three socks there. **2.** To **find** out something is to get information about it. In school we **found** out that glass is made from sand. ■ **found**

## fine

**Fine** means very good. Today is a **fine** day for a walk. Jenny was sick last week, but she feels **fine** now.

## finger

A **finger** is a long, thin part of the hand. People have five **fingers** on each hand.

The **nails** on your **fingers** are called **fingernails.** We must cut our **fingernails** when they grow too long.

## finish

To **finish** is to come to the end of something. Tino had so much homework that he couldn't **finish** it.

## fire

**Fire** is flame, heat, and light. It is what happens when something burns. We cut wood for the **fires** at our camp.

A **fire engine** is a kind of truck. **Fire engines** carry hoses and ladders to a fire. Firefighters use them to put out the fire.

## firefighter

A **firefighter** is a person who puts out fires. **Firefighters** can work in buildings, in forests, or on boats.

## fireplace

A **fireplace** is a safe place to have a small fire inside a house. It is made of stone, bricks, or metal. **Fireplaces** must have a chimney for the smoke to go up.

◆ fireplace

(A) (B) (C) (D) (E) (F) (G) (H) (I) (J) (K) (L) (M)

## fireworks

**Fireworks** make light, smoke, and a lot of noise in the sky. **Fireworks** shoot off into the sky on small rockets.

## first

**1. First** means before all the others. The letter **A** is the **first** letter in the alphabet. **2.** At **first** means in the beginning. At **first** our team was not very good, but we got better as we practiced.

## fish

**1.** A **fish** is an animal that lives in water. **Fish** have tails and can swim very well. **2.** To **fish** means to try to catch fish. When people do this, they are **fishing. 3. Fish** is a kind of food that comes from a **fish.** I ate **fish** for lunch.

◆ fish

## fisherman

A **fisherman** is a person who fishes. Some **fishermen** work on very large boats. Others use a pole and a hook. ■ **fishermen**

◆ fireworks

## fist

A **fist** is a hand that is closed tight. Theo and Jasmine knocked on the door with their **fists.**

## fit

**1.** To **fit** means to be the right size. Leah's favorite shirt **fit** her last year, but now she is too big for it. The children were **fitted** with costumes for the play. **2.** To **fit** is to put something into a small space. Jared **fit** all of his toys into one large box. ■ **fit, fitted**

## five

**Five** is one more than four. **Five** is written **5.** $4 + 1 = 5$.

## fix

To **fix** is to make something work again when it is broken. Libby's zipper was broken, but her mother **fixed** it.

## flag

A **flag** is a piece of cloth with colored shapes on it. Every country has a **flag.** Some **flags** are simple, and others are fancy. Sometimes people hang **flags** on poles.

◆ flag

The **flag** of our country is red, white, and blue. There are 50 stars, one for each state. There are 13 stripes.

## flame

A **flame** is the bright, moving part of a fire. **Flames** are very hot. Finn blew out the **flame** of the candle.

## flash

To **flash** is to show a bright light for a short moment. The light from the camera **flashed** when my mother took our picture.

## flashlight

A **flashlight** is a small lamp that you can carry in your hand. People carry **flashlights** when they go out at night. Dave uses a **flashlight** to read in bed at night.

◆ flashlight

## flat

**Flat** means smooth and without any bumps. Floors and tables are **flat.**

## flavor

**Flavor** is what something tastes like. My favorite **flavors** are orange and cherry.

## flew

**Flew** is a form of **fly.** The pilot **flew** his airplane over our house.

## flip

To **flip** is to turn something over so that its other side is up. When one side of the pancake was cooked, Imogen **flipped** it over to cook the other side.
■ **flipped**

A B C D E F G H I J K L M

## float

**1.** To **float** is to sit on top of the water. James **floats** on a green toy while his older sister swims behind him. **2.** To **float** is also to stay in place in the air. At my birthday party, balloons **floated** above the presents.

◆ float

## flock

A **flock** is a large group of animals that live, move, and feed together. Birds and sheep live in **flocks**. Some dogs know how to keep **flocks** of sheep together.

## flood

A **flood** is what happens when water comes up over the edges of a river. **Floods** usually come after there is a lot of rain. Sometimes they happen when snow melts.

## floor

A **floor** is the bottom part of a room. People put rugs on **floors** to cover them.

## flour

**Flour** is a white or brown powder. It is made from wheat, rice, or potatoes. **Flour** is used to make bread and cake.

◆ flour

The word **flour** sounds the same as the word **flower.**

## flow

To **flow** means to move without stopping. Water **flows** in a stream or a river. When I cry, tears **flow** down my cheeks.

## flower

A **flower** is part of a plant. Some **flowers** become fruits. **Flowers** come in many colors, shapes, and sizes. People like to smell them and to look at them.

◆ flow

### flown

**Flown** is a form of **fly**. Neela goes to visit someone in an airplane every year. She has **flown** to many different cities.

### flute

A **flute** is an instrument that you blow air into to make music. **Flutes** are tubes made of metal or wood that have holes in them. You put your fingers over the holes to make different sounds.

### fly

**1.** A **fly** is a kind of insect. It is small and has thin, clear wings. There are many kinds of **flies**. **2.** To **fly** is to travel through the air. Most birds can **fly**. **3.** To **fly** also means to make something **fly**. A pilot **flies** an airplane. ▪ **flies, flew, flown**

◆ fly

### fog

**Fog** is a cloud that is near the ground. You cannot see very far in the **fog**.

**Fog** rhymes with **dog, frog, jog,** and **log**.

### fold

To **fold** is to bend together. Emmeline can **fold** paper to make the shape of a hat or a bird. Silas helps his father **fold** the laundry before they put it away.

### follow

**1.** To **follow** is to go behind. Christina likes to **follow** her older brother around the house. She **follows** him everywhere he goes. **2.** To **follow** also means to come later. December **follows** November every year. Mom said that dessert will **follow** dinner.

### food

**Food** is what people or animals eat. Elena's favorite **foods** to eat for lunch are hamburgers and peanut butter and jelly sandwiches. Many animals, such as cows and sheep, eat grass for **food**.

◆ fog

(A) (B) (C) (D) (E) (F) (G) (H) (I) (J) (K) (L) (M)

## foot

**1.** The **foot** is a part of the body. It is at the end of your leg. The toes and the heel are parts of the **foot.** People and birds have two **feet.** Cats and dogs have four **feet. 2.** A **foot** is an amount of length. One **foot** equals 12 inches. Darryl is four **feet** tall. ■ **feet**

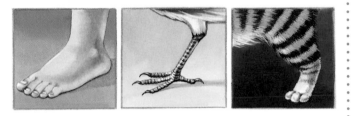

◆ foot

## football

**1. Football** is a sport. It is played by two teams on a field. One team tries to throw, carry, or kick a ball down the field. The other team tries to stop them. **2.** A **football** is the ball used in a football game. **Footballs** have a point at each end.

◆ football

## for

**1. For** tells why something is there. That carpenter has a box **for** his tools. I bought this book **for** you. **2. For** also means toward. People can reach **for** the sky, but they can't touch it. **3. For** tells how long something continues. We played baseball **for** two hours.

> The word **for** sounds the same as the number **four.**

## force

A **force** is something that pushes or pulls an object. The **force** of gravity keeps things on the ground.

## forest

A **forest** is a place with many trees. Many kinds of animals live in **forests,** but few people live in them.

## forget

To **forget** means not to remember. Joseph often **forgets** where he put his shoes. Rebecca **forgot** to put her bicycle in the garage, so it got wet in the rain. Rona has **forgotten** to bring her lunch to school twice this week. ■ **forgot, forgotten**

## fork

A **fork** is a kind of tool to eat with. **Forks** are made of metal or plastic and have sharp points.

## form

**1.** The **form** of something is its shape or what it is like. Clouds have many different **forms**.
**2.** To **form** something is to give it a shape. David **forms** a piece of clay into a pot. He **formed** another piece of clay into a plate.
**3.** A **form** is also a kind of something. Ice is another **form** of water. A word can have more than one **form**. "Children" is a **form** of "child."

◆ form

## fort

A **fort** is a building or place with strong walls. **Forts** protect people who are inside them.

## forward

**1. Forward** means in the usual order. Aria counted **forward** from one to ten. **2. Forward** also means toward the front. Joaquin stepped **forward** when his name was called.

The opposite of **forward** is **backward.**

## fossil

A **fossil** is an animal that died a very long time ago and turned into stone. There are many **fossils** in the museum.

◆ fossil

## fought

**Fought** is a form of **fight.** Yesterday Don and Kenneth had a big fight, but today they have forgotten what they **fought** about.

## found

**Found** is a form of **find.** Noah always finds something under his bed. Last night he **found** his baseball bat there.

## fountain

A **fountain** is something that is built to give off a stream of water. Some **fountains** you can drink from. Other **fountains** are used just to decorate a park or a building.

## four

**Four** is one more than three. **Four** is written **4. 3 + 1 = 4.**

A B C D E F G H I J K L M

## fox

A **fox** is a kind of animal. It looks like a small dog. **Foxes** have thick fur, especially on their tails.

◆ fox

## free

**1.** To be **free** means that you can do what you like. Benita doesn't have to go to school today. She is **free** for the whole day.
**2.** **Free** also means that you do not have to pay for something. Air and sunlight are **free.**

## freeze

To **freeze** is to change from a liquid into a solid. When water **freezes,** it becomes ice. ■ **froze, frozen**

## fresh

**1.** **Fresh** means not too old to use. Bread, fruit, and vegetables are best to eat when they are **fresh. 2.** **Fresh** air is air that is clean and good to breathe. **3.** **Fresh** water is water that has no salt in it. There is **fresh** water in rivers, ponds, and lakes.

## Friday

**Friday** is a day of the week. **Friday** comes after Thursday and before Saturday.

## fried

**Fried** is a form of **fry.** Many people like to eat **fried** chicken.

## friend

A **friend** is someone that likes you and that you like too. Molly and Madison play together and share many secrets. They are best **friends.**

When people are **friends,** they have a **friendship.**

## friendly

To be **friendly** means to like to meet people. Some animals are **friendly,** but others are not.
■ **friendly, friendliest**

## frog

A **frog** is a small animal. It has smooth skin, large eyes, and strong back legs. **Frogs** live near water and eat flies.

◆ frog

(N) (O) (P) (Q) (R) (S) (T) (U) (V) (W) (X) (Y) (Z)

## from

**1. From** means away. Mackenzie was at school. Then she went to the library. She went **from** school to the library. **2. From** also means apart. The moon is a long way **from** the earth. **3. From** also tells where something is found in nature. Apples come **from** trees. **4. From** also tells what is used to make something. Paper is made **from** wood.

## front

**Front** is the part of something that you see first. Many shirts have buttons in the **front.**

## frost

**Frost** is water that freezes outside into small pieces of ice. You can see **frost** on the leaves on cold days.

◆ frost

## frosting

**Frosting** is a type of sweet food that you spread on top of a cake. We put chocolate **frosting** on the cake.

## frown

**1.** A **frown** is an unhappy look on a person's face. A **frown** is the opposite of a **smile.** Many **frowns** appeared when it began to rain during the picnic. **2.** To **frown** means to make a frown. Carl **frowned** because he could not go to the playground.

◆ frown

## froze

**Froze** is a form of **freeze.** Last night it was so cold that the lake **froze.**

## frozen

**Frozen** is a form of **freeze.** Ice is water that has **frozen.**

## fruit

A **fruit** is a part of a plant. It has the seeds of the plant in it. Apples, oranges, and tomatoes are all **fruits.** Many **fruits** are good to eat.

◆ fruit

(A) (B) (C) (D) (E) (F) (G) (H) (I) (J) (K) (L) (M)

## fry

To **fry** is to cook in very hot oil. On Thursdays Jake's father **fries** chicken for the family's supper. ▪ **fries, fried**

## full

Full means that something cannot hold any more. Bernardo poured juice into his glass until it was **full,** and then he stopped.

◆ full

> The opposite of **full** is **empty.**

## fun

**Fun** is a happy feeling you get when you do something you like. Landon and his three brothers wore costumes at Halloween. Everybody had a lot of **fun.**

## funny

**1.** To be **funny** means to make people laugh. Deon's uncle tells **funny** jokes to Deon and his cousins. **2. Funny** also means strange. Gabriella's flute made a **funny** sound. ▪ **funnier, funniest**

## fur

**Fur** is soft, thick hair. Cats, dogs, bears, and other animals are covered with **fur.** It keeps them warm in cold weather.

◆ fur

> If something has **fur,** we say that it is **furry.** There are a lot of **furry** animals at the zoo.

## furniture

**Furniture** is objects that people sit on, work on, eat on, and sleep on. Chairs, desks, tables, and beds are all **furniture.**

## future

The **future** is the part of time that has not happened yet. Tomorrow is in the **future.** Maybe one day in the **future,** people will live in space.

# G

## gallon

A **gallon** is an amount of a liquid. It is the same as four quarts. There are **gallons** of milk and juice sold at the supermarket.

## game

A **game** is a way to play or have fun. Some **games** are played with cards. Others are played with a ball. Every **game** has rules or directions.

◆ gallon

A **board game** is a **game** that is played on a board. Checkers is a **board game.**

## garage

A **garage** is a building where cars and trucks are kept. Many houses have **garages.** A big **garage** in the city can hold hundreds of cars.

## garden

A **garden** is a place where plants are grown. People grow flowers and vegetables in **gardens.**

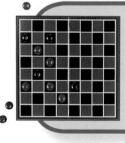

◆ garden

## gas

**1.** A **gas** is something that is so light that it fills up whatever space it is in. Air and steam are **gases. 2. Gas** also means a group of gases that are mixed together and burned to make energy and heat. Our house is heated by **gas. 3. Gas** is also a short way to say **gasoline.**

## gasoline

**Gasoline** is a kind of liquid that can burn. It is burned in cars and trucks to make them go.

## gate

A **gate** is a door in a fence. Some **gates** swing in, and others swing out.

## gather

To **gather** means to come together or put together. People often **gather** to listen to music. Lincoln **gathered** up all his toys and games and put them in one box.

## gave

**Gave** is a form of **give.** Eva gives her brother some of the books she has read. Last year she **gave** him a book about the stars and planets.

## geese

**Geese** means more than one **goose.** In the fall you can watch **geese** flying south for the winter.

## gentle

**Gentle** means in a soft way that doesn't hurt someone or something. Valentina was very **gentle** when she held the puppy.

## germ

A **germ** is a tiny living thing that can make you sick. **Germs** are too small to see without a microscope.

## get

**1.** To **get** means to have something come to you. Lara **gets** a new sweater from her grandmother every year. **2.** To **get** also means to go and take. Helena was hungry, so she **got** an apple from the refrigerator. **3.** To **get** can mean to become. Doug **gets** tired from running all the way home. **4.** To **get** also means to be able to or be allowed to. My older brother **gets** to stay up later than I do. **5.** To **get** means to arrive. The day the bus broke down, everyone **got** to school late. **6.** To **get** up means to stand up. Burt **got** up to leave after the movie. ▪ **got, gotten**

## giant

**1. Giant** means much bigger than usual. We picked out a **giant** pumpkin. **2.** A **giant** is a very tall person. Many children's stories have **giants** in them.

◆ **giant**

## gift

A **gift** is something that is given. On her birthday, Caroline got **gifts** from six of her friends.

> Another word for **gift** is **present**.

## gigantic

**Gigantic** means as big as a giant. We saw **gigantic** rocks when we got to the top of the mountain.

## giggle

**1.** To **giggle** is to laugh in a silly way. Nathaniel **giggled** when his father told him a joke.
**2.** A **giggle** is the noise you make when you giggle. When Savannah heard **giggles** in the closet, she knew her brother Jacob was hiding in there.

## ginger

**Ginger** is the root of a plant. It is made into a powder and used in some foods.

## gingerbread

**Gingerbread** is a kind of cake made with ginger. Mona ate a piece of **gingerbread** for dessert.

◆ gingerbread

## giraffe

A **giraffe** is a very tall animal. It has long legs and a very long neck. **Giraffes** are covered with brown spots. Their necks are long so that they can eat leaves from the tops of trees.

◆ giraffe

## girl

A **girl** is a female child. My sisters Emma and Julie are **girls.**

## give

To **give** is to let someone else have something. Hiro **gives** his cousins tickets to the school play every year. Brian has **given** away some of his toys. ■ **gave, given**

## glad

**Glad** means happy. We went to a ball game yesterday. We were **glad** because the weather was sunny and warm. ■ **gladder, gladdest**

A B C D E F G H I J K L M

## glass

**1. Glass** is what windows are made from. You can see through **glass.** It feels hard, but it is easy to break. Did you know that **glass** is made from sand? **2.** A **glass** is used to hold liquid that you drink. Dylan can pour his juice into a **glass**. **3. Glasses** are made to help people see better. **Glasses** are made of glass or plastic. They fit over your nose and in front of your eyes.

> **Sunglasses** are a special kind of **glasses.** You wear them to protect your eyes when the sun is very bright.

## glide

To **glide** is to move easily and quickly. Lucy and Chester **glided** over the ice in their ice skates. When I throw my paper airplane, it **glides** across the room.

## globe

A **globe** is a model of the earth. **Globes** are round and show all of the continents and oceans.

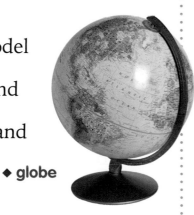

◆ globe

## glove

**1.** A **glove** fits over your hand to protect it. It is made of cloth, wool, leather, or plastic. People usually wear **gloves** to keep their hands warm in cold weather. **2.** Baseball players wear a special kind of **glove** to help them catch the ball. There are several kinds of baseball **gloves.**

◆ glove

## glue

**Glue** is a thick liquid. After it dries, **glue** holds things so they do not come apart.

## go

**1.** To **go** is to move from one place to another. Pam **goes** to school in the morning. She **went** to school late yesterday because the weather was bad. **2.** To **go** also means to leave a place. It is very late, so we have to **go**. **3.** To **go** can mean to lead somewhere. The road **goes** through the forest. It **goes** all the way to the city. **4.** To **go** to sleep means to begin sleeping. Harry closed his eyes, but he could not **go** to sleep. ■ **goes, went, gone**

## goal

**1.** A **goal** is something you want to do in the future. My **goal** is to become a doctor. People work hard to reach their **goals**. **2.** A **goal** is also a space or net where players in some sports try to put a ball. Caden stopped the ball from entering the **goal**. **3.** A **goal** happens when someone puts the ball in the goal. How many **goals** were there in the game?

◆ goal

## goat

A **goat** is an animal. Many goats have hair on their chins and curved horns. **Goats** are raised for their milk and wool.

## gold

**Gold** is a yellow metal. It comes from streams or from underground. **Gold** is used to make rings, coins, and many other things.

◆ goat

## goldfish

A **goldfish** is a kind of fish. **Goldfish** are usually small and orange. We keep two pet **goldfish** in a bowl at home.

## gone

**Gone** is a form of **go**. Daniela has **gone** to school. I came to meet her, but she was already **gone**.

## good

**1.** A thing is **good** when people like it. Chuck's bicycle is easy to ride. It is a **good** bicycle. **2. Good** also means doing things well. Kay's mother is a **good** cook. **3. Good** can also mean that something helps you be healthy. Cold weather is **good** for penguins. ■ **better, best**

> The opposite of **good** is **bad**. I had a **good** time at the picnic, but the weather was **bad**. It rained all day.

## goodbye

**Goodbye** is the last thing a person says to another person when they finish talking. When the party was over, Jill said "**Goodbye**" to Caitlin and then went home.

## gooey

To be **gooey** means to stick to everything. Honey sticks to the spoon you use to get it out of the jar. It sticks to your fingers. Honey sticks to the bread that you put it on. Honey is very **gooey.** ■ **gooier, gooiest**

## goose

A **goose** is a bird. It is like a large duck and has a long neck. Some **geese** fly long distances every spring and fall. ■ **geese**

## gorilla

A **gorilla** is a kind of ape. **Gorillas** are large and have dark hair all over their bodies. They live on the ground and like to eat plants.

◆ gorilla

## got

**Got** is a form of **get.** Wesley **got** several birthday cards in the mail last week. Mackenzie wanted something to read, so she **got** a book from the library. Jordan almost **got** sick from eating too much. Eddie **got** home late after baseball practice. The next morning he **got** up early to go fishing.

## gotten

**Gotten** is a form of **get.** Lindsey has **gotten** more gloves than she knows what to do with. I offered to get a banana for my sister, but she had already **gotten** one. Kelsey has never **gotten** too tired to play. Adam had already **gotten** up by seven o'clock.

## government

A **government** is a group of people who lead a country, city, or town. In our country we vote for our **government. Governments** make laws and decide many other things.

Every state has its own **government.** The person who leads a state's **government** is a **governor.**

## grab

To **grab** means to take something suddenly. Noah's brother **grabbed** the toy from Noah's hand. ■ **grabbed**

## grade

A **grade** is where you are in school. In her first year Penny was in the first **grade.** This year she is in the second **grade.** There are six **grades** in Penny's school.

## grain

**1. Grain** means the seeds of wheat, rice, corn, and some other plants. Flour and cereal are made from **grain**. **2.** A **grain** also means a very tiny piece. **Grains** of sand are very, very small.

◆ grain

## gram

A **gram** is a small amount of weight. A penny weighs almost three **grams.**

## grandfather

A **grandfather** is the father of your mother or father. Alex has two **grandfathers.**

> **Grandfathers** and **grandmothers** are called **grandparents.**

## grandmother

A **grandmother** is the mother of your mother or father. Jamie has two **grandmothers.**

## grape

A **grape** is a kind of fruit. It is small and round. **Grapes** can be either purple or green. They grow on vines in big bunches.

◆ grape

## grapefruit

A **grapefruit** is a round, yellow fruit. **Grapefruits** are larger than oranges, and they are not as sweet. Some people eat **grapefruits** at breakfast.

## grass

**Grass** is a kind of plant. It grows in yards, fields, meadows, and parks. There are many different kinds of **grass.**

■ grass

## grasshopper

A **grasshopper** is a large insect. It has long, strong back legs. **Grasshoppers** can jump many feet in one hop.

◆ grasshopper

(A) (B) (C) (D) (E) (F) (G) (H) (I) (J) (K) (L) (M)

## gravity

**Gravity** is a force in nature that pulls objects toward the center of the earth. **Gravity** makes things fall to the ground when we drop them.

## gravy

**Gravy** is a sauce. It is made from the juice that comes out of meat during cooking. ■ **gravies**

## gray

**Gray** is a color. Elephants, rhinoceroses, and rain clouds are **gray.**

When you mix together the colors black and white, they become **gray.**

## great

**1. Great** means very important. Alex has pictures of many **great** people. **2. Great** can mean very good. We had a **great** time on our vacation. **3. Great** also means very large. We stayed inside during the **great** storm last week.

## greedy

To be **greedy** is to wish for more things than you need. The king had a lot of gold, but he was **greedy** and wanted more. ■ **greedier, greediest**

## green

**Green** is a color. Leaves and grass are **green** in the summer. Many vegetables, such as lettuce and zucchini, are also **green.**

## greenhouse

A **greenhouse** is a special building to grow plants in. **Greenhouses** usually have glass roofs. The air inside is always warm.

◆ greenhouse

## grew

**Grew** is a form of **grow.** Tomatoes and berries **grew** in our garden last summer. When Alexandra was young, she wanted to be a scientist. When she **grew** up, that is what she became.

## grin

A **grin** is a big smile. Carita cut her pumpkin so it had a big **grin** for Halloween. She thinks pumpkins with **grins** look funny.

◆ grin

## grocery

A **grocery** is a store that sells food and other things you need at home. These things are called **groceries**. ■ **groceries**

> A person who sells **groceries** is called a **grocer.**

## ground

The **ground** is the earth. Jonathan was playing in the yard, but he fell on the **ground** and hurt his knee. Plants grow out of the **ground.**

## group

A **group** is a number of people or things together. Two **groups** of students took a trip to the country. Each **group** had a good time.

◆ group

## grow

**1.** To **grow** is to get bigger. Animals and plants **grow** as they get older. This bush has **grown** bigger than me! **2.** To **grow** up means to become an adult. When you **grow** up, you may be taller than your father. ■ **grew, grown**

## grownup

A **grownup** is someone who is an adult. Our parents are **grownups.**

## grumble

To **grumble** means to talk about something in an unhappy way. I **grumbled** about having to do homework on my birthday.

## grumpy

To be **grumpy** means to be in a bad mood. I was **grumpy** today because I went to bed too late last night. ■ **grumpier, grumpiest**

## guard

**1.** To **guard** is to watch something so that nothing bad happens to it. I **guarded** the picnic basket so that ants would not get inside of it. **2.** A **guard** is a person who watches over something. There are always **guards** in front of the queen's palace.

(A) (B) (C) (D) (E) (F) **(G)** (H) (I) (J) (K) (L) (M)

## guess

To **guess** is to try to think of the answer. Shelley does not know where her cat is. She **guesses** that the cat is up in a tree. If she finds the cat in the garage, she will know she **guessed** wrong.

## guide

A **guide** is someone or something that shows you what to do. At the museum, the **guides** took us to see the photographs. My mother bought a **guide** and read about the best things to see in the city.

A **guide dog** is a **dog** that helps blind people know where to go.

## guitar

A **guitar** is an instrument that you hold in your arms. **Guitars** are made of wood and have six strings. You hit or pull on the strings with your fingers to make music.

◆ guitar

## gum

**Gum** is a kind of sweet, flavored candy that you chew but do not swallow.

## gym

A **gym** is a place inside a building where people play games and exercise. Most schools have large **gyms**.

## habit

A **habit** is something you do often. Ryder has a **habit** of drinking a glass of water every night before he goes to bed. People can have good **habits** or bad **habits.**

## had

**Had** is a form of **have.** Ryan and Lucy have four dollars in their bank. Last month they only **had** two dollars.

## hadn't

**Hadn't** is a short way to say **had not.** Justin wanted to watch television, but he **hadn't** done his homework yet.

## hair

**Hair** is what grows on your head. People and some animals have **hair. Hair** can be straight or curly.

When someone cuts your **hair,** you get a **haircut.** Jackie gets several **haircuts** every year.

## half

A **half** is one of two pieces that are the same size. Jeremy gave **half** of his sandwich to me when I forgot my lunch yesterday. ■ **halves**

◆ **half**

## hall

A **hall** is a place inside a building. It leads from one room to another room or rooms. Some **halls** are short, and some are long and narrow.

## Halloween

**Halloween** is a holiday that comes on October 31. People wear costumes on **Halloween.** Sometimes they go out to collect candy in their neighborhoods.

## halves

**Halves** means more than one **half.** Andrew cut his apple into two **halves.**

## ham

**Ham** is a kind of meat. It comes from pigs. You can buy **ham** at the supermarket.

## hamburger

**1. Hamburger** is a kind of beef. It has been cut up in very small pieces so you can make it into different shapes. **2.** A **hamburger** is a kind of sandwich. It is made of two pieces of bread with cooked hamburger in between. Penelope likes to eat **hamburgers** on a roll with lettuce and tomatoes.

## hammer

A **hammer** is a tool. It has a handle and a heavy, metal head. It is shaped like a **T.** Most **hammers** are used to hit nails into wood.

◆ **hammer**

## hamster

A **hamster** is a small animal that has short fur and a short tail. **Hamsters** make good pets.

## hand

A **hand** is a part of the body. Your **hands** are at the ends of your arms. People use their **hands** to hold things. The fingers, the thumb, and the palm are parts of the **hand.**

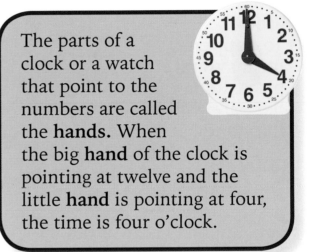

The parts of a clock or a watch that point to the numbers are called the **hands.** When the big **hand** of the clock is pointing at twelve and the little **hand** is pointing at four, the time is four o'clock.

## handkerchief

A **handkerchief** is a piece of cloth. You put it over your nose when you sneeze. Many **handkerchiefs** are white.

## handle

**1.** A **handle** is a part of something that you can hold with your hand. Cups and tools have **handles. 2.** To **handle** something is to hold or touch it with your hands. Sharp tools must be **handled** with care.

## hang

**1.** To **hang** is to be held above the ground or floor by something. Vivian likes to **hang** by her arms on the playground.
**2.** To **hang** is also to put something up so it **hangs**. I **hung** my coat in the closet.
■ **hung**

◆ hang

## happen

To **happen** means to take place. Rana told her parents what **happened** at camp.

## happy

To be **happy** means to feel good. At the fair, Ronnie smiled and laughed because she was **happy**. ■ **happier, happiest**

## harbor

A **harbor** is a safe area in the water where ships can stay. Ships in **harbors** are protected in storms.

◆ harbor

## hard

**1.** When something is **hard**, it cannot be shaped with your fingers. Most rocks are **hard**. **2. Hard** also means that you have to work a lot to do something. **Hard** is the opposite of **easy**. Sometimes homework is **hard**.

To **harden** means to become **hard**. We heat the clay until it **hardens**.

## hardly

**Hardly** means almost not at all. There were so many clouds that we **hardly** saw the sun all day.

## harp

A **harp** is a tall instrument with many strings. You pull on the strings with your fingers to make melodies. **Harps** are sometimes part of an orchestra.

## harvest

To **harvest** means to gather fruits, vegetables, and other foods from a field when they are ready to eat. Pumpkins and corn are **harvested** in the fall.

## has

**Has** is a form of **have**. Juan **has** two dollars. Aaron **has** two dollars too. Together they have four dollars.

## hat

A **hat** is something you wear on your head. **Hats** come in many different shapes and sizes.

◆ hat

## hatch

To **hatch** is to break out of an egg. Birds and reptiles **hatch** when they are born. Baby turtles are very small when they **hatch.**

◆ hatch

## hate

To **hate** means to not like something in a very strong way. **Hate** is the opposite of **love.** I **hate** tomatoes, but I **love** strawberries.

## have

**1.** To **have** something means that it is with you. Jamal **has** a book in his hand. This morning he **had** two books. Cats **have** soft fur. **2.** To **have** to do something means that there is no choice about it. We **have** to brush our teeth every morning.
■ **has, had**

## haven't

**Haven't** is a short way to say **have not.** Selena and Serena **haven't** seen their new baby brother yet.

## hawk

A **hawk** is a large bird. It has a short, curved beak and strong claws. **Hawks** fly high in the sky and catch small animals on the ground.

## hay

**Hay** is a kind of tall grass that has been cut and dried. Horses and cows eat **hay.**

## he

**He** means a male person. Edward is a boy. **He** and his brother Freddie are twins.

## head

**1.** The **head** is a part of the body. Your face and your ears are parts of your **head. 2.** A **head** also means a part of a tool. It is the heavy part that does the work. Hammers and axes have **heads.**

A **headstand** is when you put your **head** on the floor and your legs in the air. Clowns in the circus sometimes do **headstands.**

N O P Q R S T U V W X Y Z

## heal

To **heal** is to get better when you are hurt. When you cut your finger, it will **heal** in a few days if you keep it clean.

## healthy

**Healthy** means not sick. Tamiko eats good food and gets exercise so that she will stay **healthy**. ■ **healthier, healthiest**

## hear

To **hear** is to know what something is like by using your ears. Mick **heard** a loud noise in the other room. ■ **heard**

## heart

The **heart** is a part of the body. It is near the center of your chest. Our **hearts** make the blood move through our bodies.

## heat

**1.** **Heat** is a kind of energy that makes things warm or hot. The **heat** from the sun helps plants grow. The **heat** in the oven cooks food. **2.** To **heat** is to make warm. The fire in the fireplace **heated** the room.

> A **heater** is a machine that can make something warm or hot. A **water heater** makes water warm for washing.

## heavy

**Heavy** means hard to lift. Rocks and bowling balls are **heavy,** but pillows are light. My older brothers helped carry the **heavy** couch up the stairs. ■ **heavier, heaviest**

◆ heavy

## heel

**1.** The **heel** is a part of the body. It is the back part of the foot. When you put your feet into shoes, your toes go in first, and your **heels** go in last. **2.** The **heel** is a part of a shoe. It is the part under the heel of your foot. Some shoes have high **heels**.

◆ heel

## height

The **height** of something is how high it is. Sandy is five feet tall. Her **height** is five feet. The balloon rose to a **height** of one thousand feet.

## held

**Held** is a form of **hold.** Lana lifted the baby and **held** it in her arms. Colleen tried to put all her toys in one box, but it only **held** half of them.

## helicopter

A **helicopter** is a machine. It carries people through the air. **Helicopters** do not have wings like airplanes. They have propellers on the top. The propeller turns around and lifts the **helicopter** off the ground.

◆ helicopter

## hello

**Hello** is the first word people say to each other when they talk. When people answer the phone, they usually say "Hello."

## helmet

A **helmet** is a special kind of hat. It is hard and protects your head. Jason wore a red and yellow **helmet.**

◆ helmet

## help

**1.** To **help** is to give what someone or something needs. Brooklyn **helped** her mother rake the leaves. The rain **helps** the grass to grow.

◆ help

**2. Help** is also what you give when someone needs something. I asked my sister for **help** with my homework.

## hen

A **hen** is a female chicken. **Hens** sit on eggs before they hatch.

## her

**1. Her** means a female person or animal. Jackson borrowed a book from Annabelle. He gave it back to **her** after he finished reading it. **2. Her** also means belonging to a female person or animal. Carrie has a room in the house where she keeps **her** things. It is **her** room. She keeps **her** toys and **her** clothes inside it.

## herd

A **herd** is a group of one kind of animal. Cows, sheep, elephants, and other animals live in **herds.**

◆ herd

## here

**Here** means in this place. We are waiting for the bus, but it is not **here** yet.

The opposite of **here** is **there.** We are standing **here** in front of the school, and we want to go to the post office. Do you know how to get **there**?

## hero

**1.** A **hero** is a person who is very brave and does great things to help other people. The firefighters who run into burning buildings are **heroes.** **2.** A **hero** is also the most important person in a story or poem. The **hero** of my book is a girl who loves horses. ▪ **heroes**

## hers

**Hers** means belonging to her. Sebastian has his own room, and his sister Catherine has **hers.** Everything in her room is **hers.**

## herself

**Herself** means her and nobody else. Willa set the table by **herself.**

## hi

**Hi** is another way to say hello. People say "**Hi**" to their friends when they see them. People also say "**Hi**" when they meet someone for the first time.

## hide

**1.** To **hide** something is to put it where nobody will see it. Gabriel **hid** his mother's present behind the sofa. **2.** To **hide** also means to go where no one can see you. Vic's sister has **hidden** behind the house. ▪ **hid, hidden**

## high

**1. High** means far above the ground or bottom. Brandi stood **high** above the pool before she dived into the water. **2. High** also means greater than usual. On hot days the temperature is **high.**

(A) (B) (C) (D) (E) (F) (G) **(H)** (I) (J) (K) (L) (M)

## hill

A **hill** is a big bump in the ground. You can climb up one side of a **hill** and down the other side. **Hills** are like small mountains.

◆ hill

A **hilltop** is the highest part of a **hill**. It took us a long time to climb to the **hilltop**.

## him

**Him** means a male person or animal. On Dean's birthday, his grandfather took **him** to a baseball game.

## himself

**Himself** means him and nobody else. Samar folded the laundry by **himself**.

## hippopotamus

A **hippopotamus** is a very large animal. It is as big as a small car. **Hippopotamuses** have short legs and large mouths. They swim in lakes and rivers and eat grass.

◆ hippopotamus

## his

**His** means belonging to him. This watch belongs to Alberto. It is **his** watch.

## history

**History** is what has happened in the past. In school we study the **history** of our state and our country.

## hit

To **hit** is to move very hard against something. Baseball players try to **hit** the ball with a bat. An apple fell from the tree and **hit** the ground. ■ **hit**

## hive

A **hive** is a home for bees. Bees make honey inside of **hives**.

## hobby

A **hobby** is something you like to do when you have time. Some **hobbies** are collecting things, drawing, and playing music. ■ **hobbies**

## hockey

**Hockey** is the name of two sports. In field **hockey,** a player runs on the ground and hits a ball with a stick into a goal. In ice **hockey,** a player skates on ice and hits a piece of rubber with a stick into a goal. Ice **hockey** players wear ice skates.

## hold

**1.** To **hold** is to have something in your hands or arms. People can **hold** very large things in their arms. They can **hold** small things in their hands. You **hold** a pencil or pen when you write something down on paper. Paige **held** the puppy in her arms.
**2.** To **hold** also means to have room for. A small car will only **hold** five people, but a larger car can **hold** seven people.
■ **held**

◆ hold

## hole

A **hole** is an empty place in something. Some birds and animals live in **holes** in trees or in the ground.

## holiday

A **holiday** is a special day. Some people do not go to school or work on **holidays.** Sometimes there are parades and fireworks on **holidays.**

Different countries have their own special **holidays.** In our country, Thanksgiving is a **holiday** that comes in November.

## hollow

**Hollow** means with an empty space inside. Basketballs are **hollow.** Some animals live in **hollow** trees.

◆ hollow

## home

A **home** is a place where people or animals live. Most people have **homes** in houses or apartments.

## homework

**Homework** is something that you bring from school to do at home. You bring it back to school for the teacher to correct.

(A) (B) (C) (D) (E) (F) (G) (H) (I) (J) (K) (L) (M)

## honest

To be **honest** means to tell the truth. Bennett tries to be **honest** so that people will trust him.

## honey

**Honey** is a thick, sweet liquid. It is made by bees. **Honey** is good to eat on toast, in cereal, and with many other foods.

## hood

A **hood** is a kind of clothing that covers your head and neck. Most **hoods** are parts of shirts and coats.

◆ hood

## hook

A **hook** is a curved piece of metal. It is shaped like a **J**. Some **hooks** have points on the end and are used to catch fish. Other **hooks** are used to keep clothes off the floor.

◆ hook

## hoot

To **hoot** is make the sound of an owl. Owls **hoot** at night.

## hop

**1.** To **hop** is to jump up in the air. Rabbits, frogs, grasshoppers, and kangaroos **hop** from place to place. **2.** A **hop** is a jump. Colette jumped over the stream in one **hop**.
■ **hopped**

## hope

To **hope** is to believe something good may happen. We want to swim in the lake tomorrow. We **hope** tomorrow will be sunny. Jaylen **hopes** his father will cook something good for dinner.

## hopped

**Hopped** is a form of **hop**. The kangaroos **hopped** across the plain.

## horn

**1.** A **horn** is part of an animal's body. Bulls, goats, and some other animals have two **horns** on their heads. **2.** A **horn** is also an instrument. Kaylee blows into her **horn** to make music. **3.** A **horn** is also something that makes a loud noise in the air. We heard the truck's **horn** blow two times.

## horse

A **horse** is a large animal with long legs. **Horses** can run fast. They live on farms. People like to ride **horses.**

◆ horse

A **horseshoe** is a piece of iron that is shaped like a **U. Horses** wear **horseshoes** to protect their feet.

## hose

A **hose** is a tube made of rubber or cloth. Firefighters put out fires with water from **hoses.** People use **hoses** to give water to the plants on their lawns.

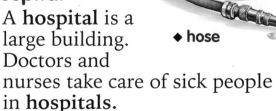

◆ hose

## hospital

A **hospital** is a large building. Doctors and nurses take care of sick people in **hospitals.**

## hot

**Hot** means something that has a lot of heat. **Hot** is the opposite of **cold.** The sun is **hot** on bright summer days. The inside of an oven is **hot.**

## hot dog

A **hot dog** is a kind of food. It is made from meat and other things. People often eat **hot dogs** in long rolls with mustard on them.

## hotel

A **hotel** is a big building with many rooms. People who are away from home stay in them. Big cities have many **hotels** because many people come to visit the city.

## hour

An **hour** is an amount of time. There are 24 **hours** in one day. One **hour** has 60 minutes in it.

When you are telling the time, the small hand of the clock points to the **hour.** The big hand points to the minute.

## house

A **house** is a building where people live. There are two yellow **houses** in Pilar's neighborhood.

(A) (B) (C) (D) (E) (F) (G) (H) (I) (J) (K) (L) (M)

## how

**1. How** tells the way something is done. Mercedes wanted to know the way to make a rabbit come out of her hat. "**How** did you make that rabbit come out of your hat?" she asked the magician. He did not tell her **how** he did it. **2. How** much tells the amount of something. **How** much rain did we get yesterday? **How** much money does that book cost? **How** much time do we have before the movie starts?

## howl

To **howl** means to make a loud cry. The wolf **howled** in the forest. I **howled** when my friend stepped on my foot by accident.

## hug

To **hug** is to put your arms around someone and hold that person tight. Some people **hug** each other to show that they are glad to see each other.
■ **hugged**

◆ hug

## huge

**Huge** means very big. Joel made himself a sandwich with turkey, ham, cheese, lettuce, tomato, and three pieces of bread. That was a **huge** sandwich.

◆ huge

## hugged

**Hugged** is a form of **hug**. I **hugged** my grandparents when they arrived at the airport.

## human

**Human** means about people. A **human** body is the body of a person. Babies, children, and adults are **human.**

## hump

A **hump** is a bump on an animal's back. Some camels have two **humps.** Other camels have one **hump.**

## hundred

A **hundred** is a number. It is written **100.** It takes ten tens to make one **hundred.** There were **hundreds** of people in the audience.

N O P Q R S T U V W X Y Z

## hung

**Hung** is a form of **hang.** Mateo's mother asked him to hang his shirt in the closet. He said he had **hung** it up already.

## hungry

To be **hungry** is to want to eat. Betsy has not eaten her breakfast yet. She is very **hungry.** ■ **hungrier, hungriest**

## hunt

**1.** To **hunt** means to look around for something. Avery **hunted** through the art closet looking for the crayons. **2.** To **hunt** also means to search for an animal to eat. Wolves **hunt** deer.

## hurry

To **hurry** is to try to go quickly. When you are late, you have to **hurry.** ■ **hurries, hurried**

Another word for **hurry** is **rush.** When people **hurry** or **rush,** they sometimes forget things.

## hurt

**1.** To **hurt** is to break something or make someone feel bad. If you fall on the sidewalk, you may **hurt** yourself. **2.** To **hurt** also means to feel bad. Luciana's back was burned in the sun and **hurt** for several days. ■ **hurt**

## husband

A **husband** is a married man. My teacher's **husband** works at the post office. Both **husbands** and wives came to the picnic.

## hut

A **hut** is a very simple, small house. **Huts** are usually built in places where the weather is warm.

◆ hut

(A)(B)(C)(D)(E)(F)(G)(H)(I)(J)(K)(L)(M)

# I

## I

I is a word you use when you speak about yourself. This coat belongs to me. **I** wear it during the winter to keep me warm.

## ice

Ice is water that has frozen. It is hard and cold. Annabel skates on the **ice** that covers the pond. Brandon put **ice** in his drink to keep it cold.

> An **ice skate** is a skate with a sharp edge for skating on **ice.**

## ice cream

Ice cream is a kind of food. It is a frozen dessert. **Ice cream** is made from cream or milk, eggs, and sugar. There are many flavors of **ice cream.**

## idea

An **idea** is something that you think of. You can have an **idea** about anything. Mitch and Muhammad often get **ideas** for new inventions.

## if

If tells what might happen. Mack may decide to go to the store, or he may not. **If** he goes, he will buy some bread. **If** it rains today, we will need to use our umbrellas.

## igloo

An **igloo** is a kind of house. It is made of blocks of snow. People who live in cold places where there are no trees sometimes build **igloos.**

◆ igloo

## ill

Ill means sick. Richard is too **ill** to go outside today.

## I'll

I'll is a short way to say **I will.** After I finish this book, **I'll** be glad to let you borrow it.

## I'm

**I'm** is a short way to say **I am**. **I'm** almost as tall as my brother.

## imagine

To **imagine** is to see a picture in your mind. When the snow is falling outside her window, Leora likes to **imagine** that it is summer. She **imagines** herself at the beach in the warm sun.

## important

**Important** things are things you care about or need. Tracy will feel sad if she does not learn to ski. It is **important** to her to learn to ski. Teachers and scientists do work that helps other people. They do **important** work.

## impossible

**Impossible** means that something cannot be. It is **impossible** for the sun to come up in the west.

## in

**1. In** tells where something is. Fish swim **in** the water. **2. In** tells when something happens. Connor's birthday is **in** May. We will have dinner **in** one hour.

## inch

An **inch** is an amount of length. There are 12 **inches** in one foot.

## independent

**Independent** means not controlled by anyone else. An **independent** country makes its own laws.

## information

**Information** is facts that you know. You can get **information** from teachers in school, reading books, and listening to other people. My mother gets **information** from reading the newspaper every day.

> When you give **information** to people, you **inform** them. The principal **informed** us that our teacher was sick.

## injure

To **injure** means to hurt. Two people were **injured** in the accident.

## ink

**Ink** is a liquid that people write with. You can use either a brush or a pen to write with **ink.** Many pens have blue or black **ink.**

◆ ink

(A) (B) (C) (D) (E) (F) (G) (H) (I) (J) (K) (L) (M)

## insect

An **insect** is a small animal. All **insects** have six legs. Some **insects** can fly. Flies, ants, butterflies, grasshoppers, and bees are all **insects,** but spiders are not.

◆ insect

## inside

**1.** To be **inside** means to be in something. The sisters stayed **inside** the tent until the weather got cold. Then they went **inside** the house to get warm. **2.** The **inside** of something is the stuff that is inside that thing. The **inside** of a banana is soft. Make sure the **inside** of the hamburger is cooked!

## instant

An **instant** is a very short amount of time. **Instants** are almost too short to notice. Lightning only flashes for an **instant.**

## instead

**Instead** means in the place of. Melissa wanted to eat an orange. But she only found pears in the refrigerator. So she ate a pear **instead.**

## instrument

**1.** An **instrument** is something that makes music. Pianos, flutes, trumpets, drums, violins, trombones, and guitars are all **instruments.** There are many **instruments** in an orchestra. **2.** An **instrument** is also a small tool that some people use when they work. Doctors and dentists use special **instruments** when they take care of people.

◆ instrument

## interest

An **interest** is something you like to learn more about. Elisa has a great **interest** in drawing. She has many other **interests,** too.

When you are **interested** in something, you want to learn or hear more about it. You think it is **interesting.** My uncle told me many **interesting** stories about his vacation.

## into

**1. Into** tells where something goes. My father drives the car **into** the garage. Then he comes **into** the house. **2. Into** also tells what something becomes when it changes. Caterpillars change **into** moths and butterflies.

## invent

To **invent** means to make something that nobody has ever made before. My uncle has **invented** many useful machines.

> An **invention** is a thing that someone **invents.** Cars, radios, and computers are important **inventions.**

## invite

To **invite** is to ask someone to come and visit you. Jillian **invited** three of her friends for dinner.

> An **invitation** is a note you write to **invite** someone. Alexander gave everyone in the class **invitations** to his party.

## iron

**1. Iron** is a kind of metal. It is gray or black. **Iron** is very hard and strong. **2.** An **iron** is used to take wrinkles out of clothes. The bottom of the **iron** is flat and gets very hot. Some **irons** make steam.

◆ iron

## is

**Is** is a form of **be.** Last year Ian was six years old. This year he **is** seven. Next year he will be eight.

## island

An **island** is an area of land that has water all around it. Rivers, ponds, lakes, and oceans can all have **islands** in them.

◆ island

## isn't

**Isn't** is a short way to say **is not.** "Is Karina home?" "No, she **isn't.**"

(A) (B) (C) (D) (E) (F) (G) (H) (I) (J) (K) (L) (M)

## it

**1. It** means a thing. Jon took his bicycle out of the garage. Then he rode **it** to the store. **2. It** also means the way things are. **It** is raining today. If **it** is cold enough tomorrow, **it** may snow.

## itch

To **itch** is to make you want to scratch. Mel's head **itches** under his helmet.

> Something that makes you **itch** is **itchy**. Sometimes sweaters are **itchy**.

## its

**Its** means belonging to it. Sometimes a dog or cat will chase **its** own tail.

## it's

**It's** is a short way to say **it is.** What a beautiful day it is. **It's** too nice to stay inside.

## itself

**Itself** means it and nothing else. There is a tree standing by **itself** in the middle of the meadow.

## I've

**I've** is a short way to say **I have.** I would like to go to the circus. **I've** never been to one before.

## ivy

**Ivy** is a kind of plant. **Ivies** are vines that can climb up the trunks of trees or the walls of buildings. They have green leaves. ■ **ivies**

> **Poison ivy** is a plant that has three leaves. If you touch it, it can make your skin itch a lot.

# J

## jacket

A **jacket** is a short, light coat. **Jackets** are good to wear when the weather is cold or cool, or when it is raining.

## jail

A **jail** is a kind of building. Sometimes it has metal poles on the windows and doors. People who break the law have to stay in **jail.**

## jam

**Jam** is a kind of food. It is made from fruit and sugar boiled together. **Jams** are thick and sweet.

## January

**January** is the first month of the year. It has 31 days. **January** comes after December and before February.

## jar

A **jar** is used to hold things. It looks like a fat bottle with a wide top. Jam, peanut butter, mustard, and other foods come in **jars.**

## jaw

A **jaw** is a part of the body. It is a bone at the bottom of your face. When you speak, your **jaw** moves. Sharks have large **jaws.**

## jelly

**Jelly** is a kind of food made from fruit juice and sugar boiled together. **Jellies** are smooth and sweet. ■ **jellies**

**Jellybeans** are a kind of candy made like **jelly.** They are made by boiling sugar. **Jellybeans** are hard on the outside and soft on the inside.

## jellyfish

A **jellyfish** is a kind of animal. It has a soft body and floats in the ocean. **Jellyfish** can hurt you if they touch you. ■ **jellyfish**

◆ **jellyfish**

## jet

A **jet** is a kind of airplane. Its engines do not use propellers. **Jets** fly faster than other planes.

## jewel

A **jewel** is a kind of stone that has been made smooth or cut into a shape. **Jewels** are used to decorate things like rings and crowns.

**Jewelry** is things we wear that are made of **jewels**.

## job

A **job** is the work someone has to do. It is Wade's **job** to help wash the dishes after supper. When people become grownups, they get **jobs** to earn money. Barbara is a carpenter. That is her **job**.

## jog

To **jog** is to run. People who **jog** do not try to run fast. They **jog** to exercise and to keep themselves healthy. Jenny **jogged** with her mother yesterday.
■ **jogged**

◆ **jog**

## join

**1.** To **join** is to put together. Nicholas and Kaylee **joined** the pieces of the puzzle. **2.** To **join** also means become a part of. Both boys and girls can **join** our singing group. **3.** To **join** also means to come together. Our families **joined** for the holiday.

## joke

A **joke** is a short, funny story. Mackenzie likes to make her friends laugh by telling them **jokes**.

## jolly

To be **jolly** means to laugh and smile a lot. Gabrielle's father was very **jolly** at the school carnival. ■ **jollier, jolliest**

## journal

A **journal** is a book that you write your thoughts in. Some people use **journals** to write about what happened to them that day.

## journey

**1.** A **journey** is a long trip. The movie we saw is about some friends and their **journeys** through space. **2.** To **journey** is to go on a long trip. In the story, the boys **journeyed** down the river on a raft.

## joy

**Joy** is the feeling you have when you are very happy. Danny felt great **joy** when the dentist took off his braces.

> When you feel great **joy,** you are **joyful.**

## judge

**1.** A **judge** is a person who decides things. **Judges** help to decide who is right when people cannot agree. Sometimes **judges** decide the winner of a contest. **2.** To **judge** is to decide. Kristen and Trevor asked their teacher to **judge** who drew the better picture.

## juggle

To **juggle** means to keep two or more things up in the air at one time by throwing and catching them one after the other. At the party, Grayson **juggled** three balls for five minutes!

◆ juggle

## juice

**Juice** is the liquid inside foods. People drink the **juice** of apples, oranges, grapes, tomatoes, and many other fruits.

◆ juice

> When something has a lot of **juice,** we say it is **juicy.** Grapes are **juicy.**

## July

**July** is a month of the year. It has 31 days. **July** comes after June and before August.

## jump

To **jump** is to push yourself into the air with your legs. Katya **jumped** up to catch the ball and won the game. If our dog **jumps** when we ask him to, we give him a treat.

> A **jump rope** is a **rope** that a person **jumps** over for fun or exercise. It is held by one or two people.

## June

**June** is a month of the year. It has 30 days. **June** comes after May and before July.

## jungle

A **jungle** is a place where many trees and plants grow and where many animals live. **Jungles** are found where it is warm and there is a lot of rain.

## junk

**Junk** is things that people do not want to keep. Old cars and broken furniture are **junk.**

◆ junk

## just

**1. Just** means only. Catherine thought she heard a monster outside the window, but it was **just** a squirrel. **2. Just** also means a little before. Sebastian's birthday was yesterday. He has **just** turned seven. **3. Just** can also mean the right amount and no more. The ice cream cone Alexandra wanted cost four dollars. She had four dollars in her pocket. Alexandra had **just** enough money to buy the ice cream cone.

## jut

To **jut** is to stick out from something. The dock **juts** out into the lake. ■ **jutted**

◆ jut

# K

## kangaroo

A **kangaroo** is a large animal. **Kangaroos** have strong back legs for jumping. **Kangaroo** mothers carry their babies in a pocket in front of their stomachs.

◆ **kangaroo**

## keep

**1.** To **keep** means to have and not give away. Ava gave me a book. She said I could **keep** it as long as I wanted. I **kept** the book for one week. **2.** To **keep** also means to put in a special place. Mark **kept** his jackets in the closet until the winter. **3.** To **keep** can also mean to continue to be. I have to **keep** quiet while my baby sister is sleeping. **4.** To **keep** a promise means to do what you say you will do. Abe said he would come to the party, and he **kept** his promise. **5.** To **keep** a secret means to not tell it to anyone. My best friend **keeps** my secrets. ▪ **kept**

## ketchup

**Ketchup** is a kind of food. It is a thick, red liquid made from tomatoes. **Ketchup** is good to eat on hot dogs and hamburgers.

## kettle

A **kettle** is a big pot. Water is boiled in **kettles**.

◆ **kettle**

## key

**1.** A **key** is a piece of metal. It opens a lock. People use **keys** to open the doors of their homes and cars. **2.** A **key** is also a part of a piano. The **keys** are where you put your fingers to play. There are black **keys** and white **keys** on a piano.

On a piano, the white and black **keys** together are called a **keyboard**.

## keyhole

A **keyhole** is the hole in a lock. To open a lock, put the key into the **keyhole** and turn it.

## kick

To **kick** is to hit something with your foot. Nolan **kicked** the soccer ball all the way across the field.

◆ kick

## kid

**1. Kid** is another word for **child**. The **kids** in my family like to go skating. **2.** A **kid** is also a young goat. There are lambs, **kids,** and calves at the little zoo down the road.

## kill

To **kill** is to cause something to die. Bad things in the water **killed** the fish.

## kilometer

A **kilometer** is an amount of length. One **kilometer** is a thousand meters. A **kilometer** is a little more than one half of one mile.

## kind

**1. Kind** means a form of something. Lettuce is one **kind** of vegetable. Carrots and potatoes are other **kinds. 2.** To be **kind** is to try to help others. Sari tries to be **kind** to people who have no home.

## kindergarten

**Kindergarten** is a class in school. It is the year before first grade. My favorite part of **kindergarten** was learning how to read.

## king

A **king** is a man who rules a country. **Kings** are usually the sons of **kings** or queens.

A **kingdom** is a place where a **king** or a queen rules. People do not vote for kings and queens in **kingdoms.**

## kiss

**1.** To **kiss** is to touch with the lips. Seth **kissed** his mother before he went to bed. **2.** A **kiss** is a touch with the lips. Christina and Cameron give their father **kisses** when he comes home.

## kit

**1.** A **kit** is a set of things that you have to put together. **Kits** usually come with directions. You can buy **kits** to make model cars and airplanes. **2.** A **kit** is also a set of tools or other things that are used to do something. We always pack a sewing **kit** when we go on vacation.

## kitchen

A **kitchen** is a room in a house where people cook food. Most **kitchens** have a stove, an oven, and a refrigerator. Sometimes people eat meals at a table in the **kitchen**.

## kite

A **kite** is a kind of toy. It is made of sticks covered with paper or cloth. The wind holds a **kite** up in the sky. You hold on to it with a string. **Kites** are often decorated with bright colors or other designs.

◆ kite

## kitten

A **kitten** is a young cat. Most **kittens** like to drink milk. Hailey wanted to get a pet for her birthday. Her parents gave her a gray **kitten**.

◆ kitten

## knee

The **knee** is a part of the leg. It bends like an elbow. People bend their **knees** when they sit down.

When you sit with one or both of your **knees** on the ground, you are **kneeling**. Nicolas **kneeled** when they took his photograph.

## knew

**Knew** is a form of **know**. Savannah **knew** how to write her name when she was four years old.

## knife

A **knife** is a kind of tool. It has a handle and a piece of metal with a sharp edge. Pete used a **knife** to cut an apple. ■ **knives**

## knight

A **knight** is a person who rode a horse in the army of a king or queen. **Knights** lived long ago. Sometimes they wore armor.

## knives

**Knives** means more than one **knife**. We cut our meat with **knives**.

(A) (B) (C) (D) (E) (F) (G) (H) (I) (J) (K) (L) (M)

## knob

A **knob** is a round handle that you can turn or pull to open something. Drawers and doors have **knobs**.

The knob on a **door** is called a **doorknob**. You turn a **doorknob** to open the door.

## knock

To **knock** means to hit. Ellen **knocked** on the door three times before her friend Renee opened it.

◆ knock

## knot

A **knot** is a place where two things are tied together. People make **knots** in string, rope, and ribbon. When you tie your shoelaces, you make a kind of **knot**.

## know

**1.** To **know** something means to have something that is true in your mind. Our teacher **knows** the names of all the students in the class. We **know** where the train station is. **2.** To **know** someone is to be able to say who he or she is. My brother **knew** all the teachers in his school. Al and Mandy have **known** each other for two years. **3.** To **know** how means to be able to do something. Celine **knows** how to spell "rhinoceros." Marty has **known** how to write for a long time.
■ **knew, known**

The **k** in words that begin with **kn-** is silent. **Knot** sounds like **not**. **Know** sounds like **no**.

◆ koala

## koala

A **koala** is a furry animal that lives in trees. It eats leaves and bark. **Koala** mothers carry their babies in a pocket in front of their stomachs.

# L

## laboratory

A **laboratory** is a room or building used for science experiments or research. In the school science **laboratories,** students look at pond water under microscopes.
■ **laboratories**

◆ laboratory

## lace

**Lace** is a fancy kind of cloth. It is made of very thin threads with spaces between them. Maura only wears her **lace** shirt on holidays.

## ladder

A **ladder** is used to climb up and down. It is made of wood, metal, or rope. Carpenters use **ladders** to work on high places.

◆ ladder

## ladybug

A **ladybug** is a kind of beetle. **Ladybugs** are red or orange with black spots.

## laid

**Laid** is a form of **lay.** The carpenter **laid** some boards on the ground. Then he put nails in them.

## lain

**Lain** is a form of **lie.** Kurt likes to lie on his bed. When he has **lain** there for a few minutes, he usually falls asleep.

## lake

A **lake** is a large amount of water that is all in one place. A **lake** has land all around it. **Lakes** are much smaller than oceans.

> The water in a **lake** is fresh because it does not have salt in it. Water from an **ocean** is very salty.

## lamb

A **lamb** is a young sheep. Wool from **lambs** is very soft.

◆ lamb

## lamp

A **lamp** is a machine used to make light. Most **lamps** use electricity. Matthew turned on the **lamp** when he wanted to read a book.

◆ lamp

## land

**1. Land** is the part of the world that is not covered by water. **Land** is usually made of rocks and dirt. People live on **land**. **2.** A **land** is a country. You can collect stamps from many different **lands**. **3.** The **land** is the earth or ground that someone uses. The farmers planted potatoes on their **land**. **4.** To **land** is to come down to the ground. The airplane **landed** in a field.

## language

**Language** is what people use when they speak or write to each other. Some people can speak several **languages.**

A **language** has many thousands of words. People put words together to make sentences.

## lantern

A **lantern** is a container for holding a candle or a lamp to light up dark places. You can carry some **lanterns**. Other **lanterns** hang from the ceiling.

## large

To be **large** is to fill a lot of space. Elephants are **large** animals.

The opposite of **large** is **small.**

## last

**1. Last** means that there are not any more. The letter **Z** is the **last** letter in the alphabet. **2. Last** also means the one before. **Last** night it was so cold that there is frost on the ground this morning. **3.** To **last** means to stay. The ice on the roof **lasted** for a week.

## late

**1. Late** means after the time when something is expected to happen. We got to the movie after it started. We were **late** for the movie. **2. Late** also means near the end. The big storm started **late** in the night.

## later

**Later** means after more time. We can't come now, but we will see you **later.**

## laugh

To **laugh** is to make a sound that shows that something is funny. Emmy and her sister always **laugh** when they hear a good joke.

> The sound of **laughing** is called **laughter**. The **laughter** of the audience filled the theater during the funny movie.

## laundry

**Laundry** is dirty clothes that are ready to be washed. **Laundry** is also clean clothes that have just been washed.

◆ laundry

## law

A **law** is a rule that people agree to. **Laws** are made to tell people what is right for them to do. Governments try to make sure that people follow the **laws.**

## lawn

A **lawn** is an area of grass near a house or other building. On hot, sunny days, our neighbors water their **lawns.**

◆ lawn

## lay

**1.** To **lay** means to put something down. When it was time for lunch, the carpenter **laid** down his tools. **2. Lay** is also a form of **lie.** Sylvie was tired. She **lay** down on her bed and went to sleep. ■ **laid**

## lazy

To be **lazy** is to want to do nothing. Yesterday was so nice that Clark did not want to cut the grass. He felt too **lazy** to work. ■ **lazier, laziest**

(A) (B) (C) (D) (E) (F) (G) (H) (I) (J) (K) (L) (M)

## lead

**1. Lead** is a kind of metal. It is soft and gray. **Lead** is very heavy. **2. Lead** is the part of a pencil that makes marks on paper. Pencil **leads** are made from a special powder that is pressed together. **3.** To **lead** means to go first and show the way. The man **led** his camel through the desert. I **led** my cousin to the park when she came to visit. **4.** To **lead** also means to be the person who decides. Our teacher **leads** the class. **5.** To **lead** also means to go in the direction of. This road **leads** into the forest. ■ **led**

> When **lead** means metal or a part of a pencil, it rhymes with **head**. When **lead** means to be first, it rhymes with **seed**.

## leaf

A **leaf** is part of a plant. **Leaves** are usually green. In the fall, some leaves change color to red, orange, or yellow. They are the part that makes food for the plant. **Leaves** come in many different shapes. ■ **leaves**

◆ leaf

## leak

To **leak** means to let a liquid come out of something when it shouldn't. Our roof **leaked** when it rained, but then we had the roof fixed.

## lean

**1.** To **lean** is to rest against something. Amalia **leaned** against the tree in her front yard and watched the cars go by. **2.** To **lean** also means to be not straight up and down. That tower **leans** to the right.

◆ lean

## leap

To **leap** means to jump up quickly. The dolphins **leaped** above the water. I **leaped** out of my seat and clapped when my sister made the goal that won the game.

## learn

To **learn** is to get to know something. Josephine **learned** how to play the guitar last summer.

## leash

A **leash** is a rope or strip used to hold an animal or lead it from one place to another. There are many dogs on **leashes** at the park.

◆ **leash**

## least

**Least** means less than any other. A car makes some noise. A bicycle makes less noise. Walking makes the **least** noise.

## leather

**Leather** is the skin of some animals. It is made into boots, shoes, and gloves.

## leave

**1.** To **leave** is to go away. We have to **leave** at five o'clock. **2.** To **leave** also means to put something somewhere and then go away. I **left** my books in my room while we had dinner. **3.** To **leave** something out means to not put it in or to forget to put it in. The cook **left** the salt out of the soup. ■ **left**

## leaves

**Leaves** means more than one **leaf.** Some **leaves** change color in the fall.

## led

**Led** is a form of **lead.** Abby **led** her sister by the hand. The path **led** up the mountain and down the other side.

## left

**1. Left** is a direction. It is the opposite of **right.** We read words on a page from **left** to right. **2. Left** is also a form of **leave.** I went to Rolf's house on the way to school, but he had already **left.** Allison cannot remember where she **left** her shoes.

## leg

**1.** A **leg** is a part of the body. Animals and people use their **legs** to walk. Ants have six **legs.** Spiders have eight **legs.** Dogs and cats have four **legs.** **2.** A **leg** is also a piece that holds something up. Most furniture has **legs.**

## legend

A **legend** is a very old story that people believe but may not be true. The **legends** about King Arthur and his knights have been told for many hundreds of years.

## lemon

A **lemon** is a kind of fruit. It is yellow. **Lemons** have a sour taste.

If you squeeze a **lemon,** juice will come out. You can mix the juice with water and sugar to make **lemonade.**

## lend

To **lend** means to let someone borrow something. I **lent** my new helmet to my sister. ■ **lent**

## length

**Length** is how long something is. Our cat's tail is ten inches long. Its **length** is ten inches.

## lent

**Lent** is a form of **lend.** Mom **lent** our mop to our neighbor.

## leopard

A **leopard** is a large animal. It is a kind of wild cat. **Leopards** usually have brown or yellow fur with groups of black spots.

◆ **leopard**

## less

**Less** means not as much. A quart of milk is **less** than a gallon of milk.

The opposite of **less** is **more.** I wish this sandwich had **less** lettuce and **more** cheese.

## lesson

To have a **lesson** is to meet with a teacher to learn something. Cassie practices hard for her piano **lessons.**

## let

**1.** To **let** means not to stop something. Lily's mother **lets** her have a glass of juice before supper. When Deborah threw an apple to her brother, he didn't catch it. He **let** it fall on the ground. **2.** To **let** also means to cause something to happen. My new glasses **let** me see the boats on the ocean that are far away from the shore.

## let's

**Let's** is a short way to say **let us.** "**Let's** go to a movie," Connie said to her mother when she came home from school.

## letter

**1.** A **letter** is one of the symbols people use to write words. The **letters** of our alphabet are A, B, C, D, E, F, G, H, I, J, K, L, M, N, O, P, Q, R, S, T, U, V, W, X, Y, and Z. **2.** A **letter** is also a message you write on paper. Eli wrote **letters** to his friends.

> Every **letter** can be capital or small. The **letter E** is a capital **letter**. The **letter e** is a small **letter**.

## lettuce

**Lettuce** is a kind of vegetable. It has large, green leaves.

## library

A **library** is a place where many books are kept. People borrow books from **libraries** to take home and read. ■ **libraries**

◆ library

> A person who works in a **library** is called a **librarian**. A **librarian** helps you find the books that you want.

## lick

To **lick** means to move your tongue over something. Ella **licked** her ice cream. The puppy **licked** my face.

◆ lick

## lie

**1.** To **lie** is to say something that is not true. When Cheyenne broke the window playing baseball, she did not want to get into trouble. So she **lied** and said she had not broken the window. **2.** A **lie** is something you say that is not true. Nathaniel told his mother a **lie,** but later he decided to tell her the truth. **3.** To **lie** is to be in a place and not move. Cameron **lay** on her bed yesterday when she was tired. The cat has **lain** on the sofa all day. ■ **lay, lain**

## life

**1.** **Life** is what people, animals, and plants have when they are alive. There is **life** on earth, but there is no **life** on the moon. **2.** A **life** is the time something is alive. Insects have short **lives.** Some trees have very long **lives.** ■ **lives**

Ⓐ Ⓑ Ⓒ Ⓓ Ⓔ Ⓕ Ⓖ Ⓗ Ⓘ Ⓙ Ⓚ Ⓛ Ⓜ

## lift

To **lift** is to pick up. The rock was so heavy that two people together could not **lift** it. The mother **lifts** her baby up into the air.

◆ **lift**

## light

**1. Light** is energy that we can see. The sun, stars, lamps, flashlights, and candles make **light**. **2.** To be **light** is to have light. During the day it is **light** outside. **3.** To **light** is to make something burn. Cara's aunt **lighted** a fire in the fireplace. **4. Light** also means easy to lift. It is the opposite of **heavy**. Feathers are **light**. Paper is also **light**.

A **lighthouse** is a tall building with a **light** at the top. **Lighthouses** stand near the shore of the ocean. Their **lights** guide ships in fog and at night.

## lightning

**Lightning** is a big flash of light in the sky. It is a form of electricity. **Lightning** can come from the sky to the ground during storms.

◆ **lightning**

## like

**1.** To **like** something means that it makes you feel good. Rafael and his friends **like** pizza. **2. Like** means the same as. Luke and Logan are twin brothers. They look **like** each other. **3. Like** also means in the same way as. The kids pretended to walk **like** elephants. **4. Like** also means for example. Clare loves team sports **like** soccer and basketball.

## lime

A **lime** is a kind of fruit. It is green and looks like a small lemon. **Limes** have a sour taste.

## line

**1.** A **line** is a long, thin mark. **Lines** can be straight, curved, or crooked. **2.** A **line** is a group of people where each person stands behind another. Dawn and Lin stood in a **line** to buy tickets to a movie. They were waiting in **line**. **3.** A **line** is also something an actor says in a play or a movie. When Kayla was in the school play, she had to learn her **lines**.

> You can make shapes by drawing **lines** in a special way. A square is made from four **lines**. A triangle is made from three **lines**.

## lion

A **lion** is a large animal. It is a kind of wild cat. Male **lions** have long, thick hair around their heads. Female **lions** are smaller than male **lions**. They do not have long hair around their heads.

◆ lion

## lip

A **lip** is a part of the face. It is around the outside of your mouth. People have two **lips**. Your **lips** and your tongue help you speak.

## liquid

A **liquid** is something that you can pour. **Liquid** in a bottle will take the shape of the bottle. Water, milk, and juice are **liquids**.

> You can turn a **liquid** into something that is hard. If you put water in a very cold place, it will freeze and become ice. Ice is a **solid**.

## list

A **list** is a group of words that you write down. Patrick's father gave him a **list** of things to buy at the store.

Buy:
eggs
carrots
bread
milk
tomatoes

◆ list

## listen

To **listen** is to hear and pay attention to something. When she is riding in a car, Marlene likes to **listen** to music. Students should **listen** to their teachers.

(A) (B) (C) (D) (E) (F) (G) (H) (I) (J) (K) **L** (M)

## little

**1. Little** means small. Only two people can fit into our **little** car. **2.** A **little** means not very much. I ate a **little** soup.

> The opposite of **little** is **big.**

## live

**1.** To **live** means to grow and change. Some turtles **live** for more than a hundred years. **2.** To **live** means to have a home. Many people **live** in cities. Fish **live** in the water.

## lives

**Lives** means more than one **life.** Insects have short **lives.** Some people have long **lives.**

## load

**1.** A **load** is something to be carried. My aunt brought two **loads** of wood into the house. **2.** To **load** is to put something in a place where it can be carried away. The man **loaded** the boxes into the van.

◆ load

## loaf

A **loaf** is an amount of bread. It is baked in one piece. **Loaves** of bread come in different shapes.
■ **loaves**

◆ loaf

## loaves

**Loaves** means more than one **loaf. Loaves** of bread in the store are often cut into slices.

## lobster

A **lobster** is a small animal. It lives on the bottom of the ocean. **Lobsters** have hard shells and big claws and tails.

## lock

**1.** A **lock** is an object used to keep something shut. You can open the **lock** only if you have a key. **2.** To **lock** means to put the key in the lock and turn it. Arthur **locked** all the doors to his house before he went away.

> A **locker** is a place that can be **locked** to keep things safe. My older sister has a **locker** at school.

## locket

A **locket** is a small piece of jewelry that can hold a picture inside of it. I keep a picture of my parents in my **locket.**

## log

A **log** is a large, round piece of wood. **Logs** are cut from trees. Some **logs** are used in fireplaces. Other **logs** are cut up into boards.

◆ log

## lollipop

A **lollipop** is a piece of hard candy that is stuck to the top of a small stick. **Lollipops** are usually round and taste sweet.

## long

**1. Long** is the opposite of **short.** Swans and giraffes have **long** necks. **2. Long** means how much time something takes. This television show is one hour **long.**

◆ long

## look

**1.** To **look** means to see and pay attention to. Glen and Kirsten **looked** at all the animals in the zoo. **2.** To **look** also means to be the way that something is or how it makes you feel when you look at it. Naomi **looks** nice in her new dress. It **looks** like it's going to rain tomorrow. **3.** To **look** for something is to try to find it. Evelyn is **looking** for her backpack. Have you seen it?

## loose

**Loose** is the opposite of **tight.** Marla tried to walk in her mother's shoes, but they were so big that they fell off her feet. The shoes were too **loose** for her.

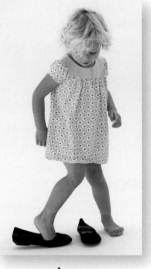

◆ loose

## lose

**1.** To **lose** something is to forget where it is. Howie often **loses** his gloves. Last winter he **lost** three pairs. **2.** To **lose** a race or game means that someone else wins. Ava and Zoe ran to the corner in a race. Zoe **lost** the race because she tripped. ■ **lost**

(A) (B) (C) (D) (E) (F) (G) (H) (I) (J) (K) **(L)** (M)

## lot

A **lot** means that something has many things to count or measure. There are a **lot** of things to do in the summer. A hippopotamus eats a **lot** of food. We had a **lot** of fun at the party.

## loud

To be **loud** means to make a lot of noise. Thunder in a storm is heard for many miles. Thunder is a **loud** noise. When you yell, you use a **loud** voice.

> The word **loudly** means in a **loud** way. The band played so **loudly** that the sound hurt my ears.

## love

To **love** means to like something or someone very much. Evangeline **loves** swimming in the ocean. Demetrius **loves** to eat sandwiches for lunch. Harrison **loves** his little sister.

> **Love** rhymes with **glove.** Can you think of another word that rhymes with **love?**

## low

**1. Low** means close to the ground or bottom. My grandfather and I ate dinner at a **low** table. **2. Low** also means less than usual. Sometimes vegetables do not cost very much in the summer. Then they have a **low** price.

◆ low

## luck

**Luck** is something that you do not plan. If you have good **luck,** you may find a quarter on the street. If your **luck** is bad, it rains when you go outside to play.

## lucky

To be **lucky** means that you have good luck. One **lucky** person will win two tickets to the basketball game.

> The opposite of **lucky** is **unlucky.** It was **unlucky** that it started to rain while Patrick was riding his bicycle home.

## lullaby

A **lullaby** is a song that helps a child go to sleep. When we were babies, my grandmother sang **lullabies** to my brother and me every night before we went to sleep. ■ **lullabies**

## lumber

**Lumber** is wood that has been cut into boards. **Lumber** comes from large trees. It is used to build things such as houses and boats.

## lump

A **lump** is a piece of something that has a rough shape. The artist formed the **lump** of clay into a bowl.

## lunch

**Lunch** is a meal that people eat in the middle of the day. Many people make **lunch** at home and bring it to school or work.

◆ lunch

A **lunchbox** is a special box that holds your **lunch.**

## lung

A **lung** is a part of the body. You have two **lungs** inside your chest. Air goes in and out of your **lungs** when you breathe.

# M

## macaroni

**Macaroni** is a kind of food. It is made from flour and comes in the shape of little hollow tubes.

## machine

A **machine** is an object that does work for people. It may be large or small and may have many parts. Airplanes, computers, and windmills are all **machines.**

◆ machine

There are many **machines** in your house or apartment. A refrigerator, a toaster, and a clock are all **machines.** A group of **machines** is called **machinery.**

## mad

**Mad** means angry. Will slept too late this morning. Now he is **mad** at himself because he missed the bus to school.
■ **madder, maddest**

## made

**Made** is a form of **make.** Emmaline and Kaitlyn **made** a snowman. Playing in the snow **made** them happy.

◆ made

## magazine

A **magazine** is something that people read. **Magazines** are usually printed every week or every month. They can have stories, poems, photographs, drawings, and cartoons.

## magic

**Magic** is the power to make impossible things seem real. In the story, the wizard changed the prince into a frog by **magic.** I learned to do **magic** tricks.

> A **magician** is a person who does **magic. Magicians** often pull rabbits out of hats, make things disappear, and do other kinds of tricks.

## magnet

A **magnet** is a piece of metal that iron will stick to. **Magnets** are used in many machines. Andre stuck a picture on the refrigerator with a **magnet.**

◆ magnet

## magnifying glass

A **magnifying glass** is a piece of glass that makes things look bigger. We looked at the paper through a **magnifying glass.**

◆ magnifying glass

## mail

**1.** The **mail** is the way we send letters and packages from one place to another. I sent some pictures to my cousin Ava by **mail. 2.** The **mail** is also the letters and packages that are sent to people in the mail. When we came back after vacation, there was a lot of **mail** at our house. **3.** To **mail** something is to send it through the mail. Alex's parents **mailed** her a package at camp last week.

> You can also send letters on a computer. **Mail** that you send on a computer is called **email.**

## mailbox

A **mailbox** is a container that you put letters in to send them by mail. People also pick up mail that has been sent to them from **mailboxes.** ▪ **mailboxes**

◆ mailbox

## main

**Main** means most important. A **main** street is large and holds many cars.

(A) (B) (C) (D) (E) (F) (G) (H) (I) (J) (K) (L) (M)

## make

**1.** To **make** means to cause to be. Wes can use flour, water, butter, and apples to **make** a pie. Good music **makes** Franco feel happy. **2.** To **make** up means to imagine. Gilbert **makes** up great stories about unicorns and giants. **3.** To **make** a bed means to make the sheets and blanket smooth. Melanie **makes** her bed every morning. **4.** To **make** money is to earn money. Roz **made** a dollar helping her father. ■ **made**

◆ make

## male

**Male** is a kind of person or animal. It is the opposite of **female.** Boys and men are **male** people.

## mall

A **mall** is a large shopping area with many stores. Some **malls** also have restaurants, banks, or theaters.

## mammal

A **mammal** is a kind of animal. **Mammals** have hair or fur, and the females make milk to feed their babies. Whales are **mammals** that live in the ocean, but most **mammals** live on land.

## man

A **man** is a grown, male person. My father and uncles are **men.** ■ **men**

## manners

**Manners** are ways of acting and speaking with other people. It is good **manners** to say "please" when you ask for something.

## many

**Many** is a large number or amount. There are **many** penguins on the island.

The opposite of **many** is **few.**

◆ many

## map

A **map** is a picture that shows where places are. **Maps** can show countries, cities, towns, roads, rivers, lakes, mountains, and many other things.

## maple

A **maple** is a kind of tree. **Maple** trees turn beautiful colors in the fall.

◆ maple

People collect a sweet liquid from inside **maple** trees and make **maple syrup.** It tastes good on pancakes!

## marble

**1. Marble** is a kind of stone. It is used to make statues and buildings. Most **marble** is white, but it can also be pink, gray, or other colors. **2.** A **marble** is a small, glass ball. **Marbles** are used in several games.

◆ marble

## march

To **march** with someone means to take the same size steps at the same time. Bethany and Jeremiah **marched** with the school band during the parade on Saturday.

## March

**March** is the third month of the year. It has 31 days. **March** comes after February and before April.

## mark

**1.** A **mark** is a spot you can see on something. Pens and pencils leave **marks** on paper. **2.** To **mark** is to put a mark on something. The teacher **marked** the right and wrong answers on our tests.

## marry

To **marry** means to join with someone as husband or wife. Men who are **married** are husbands, and women who are **married** are wives. ■ **marries, married**

## marsh

A **marsh** is an area of land that is soft and wet. Frogs, mosquitoes, and some kinds of birds, such as cranes, live in **marshes.**

(A) (B) (C) (D) (E) (F) (G) (H) (I) (J) (K) (L) (M)

## marshmallow

A **marshmallow** is a kind of candy. It is soft and white. People sometimes roast **marshmallows** over a fire.

## mask

A **mask** is something that covers your face. It can be made of paper, cloth, plastic, or rubber. Rose made a green **mask** for the school play.

◆ mask

## match

**1.** To **match** is to be the same. Riley and Leah both have yellow coats. Their coats **match**. **2.** A **match** is a short, thin piece of paper or wood used to start a fire. Playing with **matches** is dangerous. **3.** A **match** is also a game or contest between two or more people or teams. My sister won her tennis **match** yesterday.

◆ match

## math

**Math** is what people know about numbers and shapes. When we add or subtract, we do **math**.

## mattress

A **mattress** is the soft, top part of a bed. People sleep on **mattresses**.

## may

**1. May** means that there is a chance something will happen. It **may** snow today. It **might** have snowed yesterday, but it didn't. **2. May** also means that you are allowed to do something. Jon's mom says he **may** go to the movies. ■ **might**

## May

**May** is a month of the year. It has 31 days. **May** comes after April and before June.

## maybe

**Maybe** means that something may happen. **Maybe** Jamie will come to visit us this afternoon.

## mayor

A **mayor** is a person who leads the government of a city or a town. My parents voted for our **mayor** in an election last year. Our town has had three **mayors** in the past six years.

## me

**Me** is a word I use when I speak about myself. After I bought the kite, it belonged to **me**. My grandmother sent **me** a puzzle when I finished first grade.

## meadow

A **meadow** is an area of land that is covered with long grass. Mice, rabbits, and butterflies live in **meadows.** Jaylen and Tabbie like to play in the **meadow.**

◆ meadow

## meal

A **meal** is an amount of food that people eat at one time. Breakfast, lunch, and dinner are **meals.**

◆ meal

You can eat a **meal** at a table in your house or in a restaurant. You can also eat a **meal** outside when you have a picnic. Where do you like to eat your **meals**?

## mean

**1.** To **mean** is to say the same thing in different words. Large **means** big. When I said yes, I **meant** that I agree with you. **2.** To **mean** is also to have a message that people understand. A green light **means** "Go." A red light **means** "Stop." **3.** To **mean** is also to be important. Alison wants very much to go to the movies. It **means** a lot to her. It **meant** a lot to her brother to go last week. **4.** To be **mean** is to not be friendly or kind. **Mean** people are not nice to be with.
■ meant

**Meaning** is what something **means.** Dictionaries tell us the **meanings** of many words.

## measure

To **measure** is to find out how big something is. You can **measure** height in inches, feet, or meters. Liquids can be **measured** in quarts or gallons.

◆ measure

(A) (B) (C) (D) (E) (F) (G) (H) (I) (J) (K) (L) (M)

## meat

**Meat** is a kind of food. It comes from animals. Chicken, beef, and ham are all **meats.**

## medicine

**Medicine** helps sick people get well. Many **medicines** are made from plants. Usually a doctor tells you what kind of **medicine** to take.

## meet

**1.** To **meet** is to get to know someone. You **meet** many new people on the first day of school. **2.** To **meet** also means to be at the same place at the same time. Darrin and Gordon **met** at the corner at three o'clock. ■ **met**

When people **meet** together to talk about something, they are in a **meeting.** People sometimes have to go to **meetings** when they are at work.

## melody

A **melody** is a group of pleasant sounds that are sung or played on an instrument one after the other. Gavin's grandmother plays beautiful **melodies** on the piano after dinner. ■ **melodies**

## melt

To **melt** is to change from something solid into a liquid. The butter in the pan began to **melt** as we heated it.

◆ melt

## memory

**Memory** is what makes people able to remember. **Memory** helps you learn. People who have good **memories** can remember a lot of things. ■ **memories**

## men

**Men** means more than one **man.** Three **men** are planting a tree in the yard.

## merry-go-round

A **merry-go-round** is a kind of ride you see at a park or a fair. It is sometimes called a **carousel. Merry-go-rounds** have horses and other animals made of wood or plastic. People sit on the animals as they go around in a circle.

## mess

A **mess** is something that is not neat. Dennis left clothes, toys, and books on the floor in his room. The room was a **mess.** His little sister makes **messes** when she paints.

◆ mess

If a place has a **mess** in it, or if something is a **mess,** we say that it is **messy.** Tino has to clean his room because it is **messy.**

## message

A **message** is a group of words that is sent from one person to another. Many people send **messages** through the mail.

## met

**Met** is a form of **meet.** Pia **met** six new friends at the school picnic. Samantha and Alyssa **met** to have lunch at a restaurant.

## metal

A **metal** is something hard that is made from rocks in the ground. **Metals** can bend and not break. Iron, gold, silver, and lead are all kinds of **metal.**

## meter

A **meter** is an amount of length. One **meter** is a little more than a yard. There are one thousand **meters** in a kilometer.

## mice

**Mice** means more than one **mouse.** Our cat chases **mice.**

## microscope

A **microscope** is used to see things that are too small to see with our eyes alone. **Microscopes** can make tiny things look big.

◆ microscope

Scientists and doctors use **microscopes** to see very small living things that make people and animals sick.

## middle

The **middle** of something is the inside. It is not close to the end. My friends and I stand together. Kylie, who is tallest, stands in the **middle.**

◆ middle

## midnight

**Midnight** means 12 o'clock at night. It is dark outside at **midnight.**

## might

**Might** is a form of **may.** Our friends **might** have come to see us last night, but we don't know because we were not home.

## mile

A **mile** is an amount of distance. There are 5,280 feet in a **mile.** It takes a person about 20 minutes to walk a **mile.**

## milk

**Milk** is a kind of food. It is a liquid that comes from cows, goats, and other animals. **Milk** can be made into butter and cheese.

## million

A **million** is a number. It is written **1,000,000.** There are a thousand thousands in a **million.** The sun is **millions** of miles away from the earth.

## mind

**1.** The **mind** is the part of a person that thinks, feels, learns, remembers, wishes, and imagines. If it rains, we might change our **minds** about going to the zoo. **2.** To **mind** means to have bad feelings about something. If we **mind** something, we are sad or angry about it. Melinda doesn't really **mind** when her little brother plays with us. **3.** To **mind** also means to do what you are asked to. Jack **minds** his parents most of the time.

**Mind** rhymes with **kind.**

## mine

**Mine** means belonging to me. After I bought the book, it was **mine.**

## mint

**Mint** is a kind of plant with leaves that smell and taste nice. The flavor of **mint** is used in some foods and in toothpaste.

## minus

**Minus** means you subtract something. If you subtract two from six, you have four. Six **minus** two is four. Six **minus** two can also be written 6 - 2.

> The opposite of **minus** is **plus.**

## minute

A **minute** is an amount of time. One **minute** has 60 seconds in it. There are 60 **minutes** in one hour.

## mirror

A **mirror** is a piece of glass you can see yourself in. Connor combed his hair in front of the **mirror.**

◆ mirror

## miss

**1.** To **miss** means not to hit or catch. Wyatt swung his bat, but he **missed** the ball. **2.** To **miss** also means to wish something was there when it is not. Sheena had fun on her vacation, but she **missed** her friends.

## mistake

A **mistake** is something you do that is wrong. I made a **mistake** and counted 20 pencils when there were only 18. When I hurry, I make more **mistakes.**

## mitten

A **mitten** fits over your hand to keep it warm. **Mittens** have one part for your fingers and another for your thumb. Kara's aunt made her pink **mittens** for her birthday.

◆ mitten

## mix

To **mix** is to put two or more things together. Cameron and Alex **mixed** flour, eggs, butter, sugar, and chocolate together in a bowl. Then they baked cookies.

## moat

A **moat** is a deep, wide hole that goes all the way around a town or castle to protect it. Sometimes, **moats** are filled with water.

## multiply

To **multiply** is to add a number to itself one or more times. × is the symbol for **multiply**. 2 × 4 is the same as 2 + 2 + 2 + 2.
■ **multiplies, multiplied**

## muscle

A **muscle** is a part of the body. **Muscles** are under the skin. People and animals use **muscles** to move around.

## museum

A **museum** is a place where things are collected so that people can go to look at them. **Museums** can have art, machines, models of animals, and many other things.

## mushroom

A **mushroom** is a living thing. It grows from the ground in damp places. **Mushrooms** often have a narrow stem and a larger, round top. Some **mushrooms** are good to eat, but others make you sick.

◆ mushroom

## music

**Music** is sounds that people make with instruments or their voices. There are many kinds of **music** all over the world.

A person whose job is singing or playing a **musical** instrument is called a **musician**. An orchestra is made up of many **musicians.**

## must

**1. Must** means that you have to do something. We **must** leave at noon, or we will be late. **2. Must** also means something is probably true. That saw **must** be on the bench. I left it there yesterday.

## mustard

**Mustard** is a kind of food. It is yellow or brown and has a strong, hot taste. People like **mustard** on hot dogs and sandwiches.

◆ mustard

Do you like **mustard** or ketchup on your sandwiches?

## my

**My** means that something belongs to me. This is **my** bicycle. It was given to me for **my** birthday. **My** hair is brown and **my** eyes are blue.

## myself

**Myself** means me and nobody else. I planted a garden all by **myself.**

## mystery

A **mystery** is something that you do not understand. I do not know how my cap got lost. It is a **mystery** to me. Nature is full of **mysteries.** ■ **mysteries**

## myth

A **myth** is a story that people made up a long time ago. **Myths** often have heroes and try to explain why things happen in the world.

(A) (B) (C) (D) (E) (F) (G) (H) (I) (J) (K) (L) (M)

# N

## nail

**1.** A **nail** is a piece of metal with a point at one end. **Nails** are usually used to hold two pieces of wood together. **2.** A **nail** is also a part of the body. It is the hard part at the end of your fingers and toes. Chelsea had dirt under her **nails** when she worked in the yard.

◆ **nail**

## name

A **name** is a word that people use to call someone or something by. My parents' **names** are Beatrice and Zachary.

## nap

To **nap** means to sleep for a short time. People usually **nap** during the day. ▪ **napped**

## napkin

A **napkin** is a piece of paper or cloth that you use to clean your face and fingers when you eat. **Napkins** also protect your clothes.

## napped

**Napped** is a form of **nap.** The children **napped** during the long ride home.

## narrow

**Narrow** is the opposite of **wide.** Some city streets are very **narrow.** The buildings on opposite sides are close to each other. The street was so **narrow** that Tanya could touch the building on her left and the building on her right at the same time.

◆ **narrow**

## nation

A **nation** is a group of people who live in one country. Sometimes people from different **nations** meet to talk about problems in the world.

> Our **nation** celebrates its birthday on July 4. We became an independent country on that day.

## nature

**Nature** is everything in the world that is not made by people. Animals, plants, the land, the ocean, the sky, and the weather are all parts of **nature.**

## near

To be **near** means to be a small distance away. Natalie can walk from her house to school in two minutes. Her house is **near** the school.

## neat

**Neat** means clean and with everything in order. Lorraine likes to keep her room **neat.**

> The opposite of **neat** is **messy.** Dillon's room is **neat,** but it was **messy** before he cleaned it.

## neck

The **neck** is a part of the body. It is between your head and your shoulders. **Necks** let people turn their heads.

◆ neck

## need

To **need** means that you must have something. Plants cannot live without water. They **need** water to live.

## needle

**1.** A **needle** is a kind of tool. It is a very thin piece of metal with a sharp point. **Needles** and thread are used to sew cloth. **2.** A **needle** is a kind of leaf. It is thin and shaped like a sewing needle. Pine trees have **needles.**

## neighbor

A **neighbor** is someone who lives near you. Many **neighbors** are friends.

> A **neighborhood** is an area where **neighbors** live. Kimo knows almost everyone in his **neighborhood.**

## neither

**Neither** means not either. Teresa went **neither** left nor right. She kept walking straight up the street.

## nest

A **nest** is what birds build. Birds lay eggs and feed their babies in **nests. Nests** are made from grass, mud, sticks, string, and other things.

◆ nest

## net

A **net** is pieces of string or rope tied across each other with holes in between. Fishermen often use large **nets** to catch fish. **Nets** are also used in sports. Jessica hit the tennis ball over the **net.**

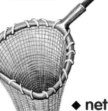

◆ net

## never

**Never** means not ever. The sun always rises in the east. It **never** rises in the west.

**Never** is the opposite of **always.**

## new

**1. New** means never used or worn before. Alisa's radio came from the store. Nobody ever owned it before. It is a **new** radio. **2. New** also means that something was not there before. The **new** drugstore is across the street.

**New** is the opposite of **old.**

## news

The **news** is stories about things that are happening. Many people watch the **news** on television. Other people read the **news** in a newspaper or on a computer.

## newspaper

A **newspaper** is many large pieces of paper with stories and photographs printed on them. People read the news in a **newspaper. Many newspapers** are printed every day.

A **newspaper** is one way to learn about things in the world. You can read about what is happening in other countries. You can see how well your favorite sports team is playing.

## next

**Next** means the one after this one. This summer Eduardo stayed at home. **Next** summer he will go to camp.

## nice

To be **nice** is to make people feel good. Our neighbors are **nice,** friendly people.

## nickel

A **nickel** is a kind of coin. One **nickel** is the same as five pennies. Five **nickels** are the same as a quarter.

## night

**Night** is the time when it is dark outside. The buildings in the city are lit up at **night.**

> The opposite of **night** is **day.** You can see stars in the sky at **night.** The sun shines during the **day.**

◆ night

## nightmare

A **nightmare** is a dream that scares you. Courtney had **nightmares** after she saw a movie about monsters.

## nine

**Nine** is a number. **Nine** is written **9.** $8 + 1 = 9.$

## no

**1. No** means that someone does not agree. Avery asked if she could have another dessert. Her mother said, "No." **2. No** also means not any. There is **no** snow during the summer. Sonny was sick yesterday, and he is still sick today. He feels **no** better today than he did yesterday.

## nobody

**Nobody** means no person. **Nobody** can fly like a bird.

## nod

To **nod** is to move your head up and down. People often **nod** to show that they agree. ■ **nodded**

## noise

A **noise** is a sound. Machines make many different kinds of **noises.**

## none

**None** means that there is not one. **None** of the lunch bags had apples inside.

Ⓐ Ⓑ Ⓒ Ⓓ Ⓔ Ⓕ Ⓖ Ⓗ Ⓘ Ⓙ Ⓚ Ⓛ Ⓜ

## noon

**Noon** is twelve o'clock during the day. People usually eat lunch around **noon.**

## north

**North** is a direction. If you look where the sun rises, **north** is on your left.

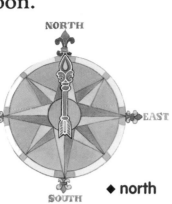

◆ north

## nose

The **nose** is a part of the face. It is below your eyes and above your mouth. People and animals smell with their **noses.** They can also breathe air through their **noses.**

◆ nose

## not

**Not** means there is no way that something can happen. The sun shines during the day. It does **not** shine at night. Julia is **not** going to school today because she is still sick.

## note

**1.** A **note** is one sound in music. Music is made of many **notes.** The **notes** are written down so that people can read them and play or sing the music. **2.** A **note** is also a short message that you write down. My father put a **note** in my backpack.

◆ note

## nothing

**Nothing** means no thing. An empty box has **nothing** in it.

## notice

**1.** To **notice** is to see or hear something. Lin **noticed** that her brother looked tired yesterday. **2.** A **notice** is a message that gives people information. The teacher gave the class several **notices** to take home.

## November

**November** is a month of the year. It has 30 days. **November** comes after October and before December.

## now

**Now** means at this time. You are reading these words **now.**

## numb

**Numb** means that a part of your body can't feel anything. If you play outside in the snow for too long, your fingers might become **numb.**

## number

**1.** A **number** is a symbol people use when they count things. 12, 52, and 100 are all **numbers**.
**2.** A **number** is also what you use to call people on the telephone. Kyle's **number** is 312-555-1324.

There is a way to spell every **number** by using letters. The number **6** is the same as the word **six.** The number **10** is the same as the word **ten.**

## nurse

A **nurse** is a person who takes care of sick people. **Nurses** work with doctors. Many **nurses** have jobs in hospitals. Some **nurses** have jobs in schools. The **nurse** took care of the baby.

◆ nurse

## nut

A **nut** is a seed that grows inside a hard shell. Many **nuts** grow on trees.

The shell that covers a **nut** is called a **nutshell.**

(A) (B) (C) (D) (E) (F) (G) (H) (I) (J) (K) (L) (M)

# O

## oak

An **oak** is a kind of tree. Acorns grow on **oak** trees.

◆ oak

## obey

To **obey** means to do what someone tells you to do. Our dog **obeys** me. When I call his name, he comes over.

## object

An **object** is anything that people can see or touch and is not alive. Buildings, tables, chairs, books, scissors, pens, and pencils are all **objects.**

## ocean

An **ocean** is a very large area of water. **Ocean** water has salt in it. **Oceans** cover almost three quarters of the earth.

> Many kinds of animals live in the **ocean.** Some are very big, like whales. Others are small, like lobsters.

## o'clock

**O'clock** is a word people use to say what time it is. Nikos gets up at seven **o'clock** in the morning and gets ready for school. School is over at three **o'clock** in the afternoon.

## October

**October** is a month of the year. It has 31 days. **October** comes after September and before November.

## octopus

An **octopus** is a kind of animal. It lives in the ocean. **Octopuses** have a large head and eight body parts that act like arms.

■ octopuses, octopi

◆ octopus

## odd

**1.** An **odd** number is a number that you cannot get to when you start at zero and count by twos. One, three, five, seven, and nine are **odd** numbers. **2. Odd** means strange. Jack noticed an **odd** smell in the yard. He could not tell what was making it.

> When we talk about numbers, the opposite of **odd** is **even.** Five is an **odd** number. Six is an **even** number.

## of

**1. Of** means that something belongs to something else. The walls **of** my room are white. **2. Of** also tells what is used to make something. Most tables are made **of** wood. **3. Of** also tells what something has in it. Hilary was carrying a pail **of** water. **4.** When you tell time, **of** means before. The time is ten minutes **of** four. **5. Of** also means at a distance from. The science museum is seven miles east **of** here.

## off

**1. Off** means away from. Please take your books **off** the table before supper. **2. Off** also means not working. Our house is dark when the lights are **off.**

## offer

To **offer** is to say you will give or do something. I **offered** to help my father rake the leaves.

## office

An **office** is a place where people work. Many people have jobs in **offices.**

◆ office

## often

**Often** means many times. It **often** rains in April.

## oil

**Oil** is a liquid. It floats on water. **Oils** from vegetables are used in foods. **Oil** from the ground is used in cars and machines.

◆ oil

> If something has **oil** on it, or if something feels like **oil,** we say that it is **oily.** My hair felt **oily** after I played outside all afternoon.

(A) (B) (C) (D) (E) (F) (G) (H) (I) (J) (K) (L) (M)

## old

**1. Old** is the opposite of **new.** Travis puts on his **old** jacket when he goes out to play football. **2.** To be **old** means to have been alive a long time. **Old** is the opposite of **young.** My grandmother is **old,** but she still walks several miles every day. **3. Old** also tells how long something has been alive. Some trees are hundreds of years **old.**

## on

**1. On** tells where something is. The dishes are **on** the table. **2. On** means that something is working. The room is bright when the light is **on. 3. On** means about. Thea has a book **on** dinosaurs. **4. On** also tells what day something happens. We play ball **on** Sundays.

## once

**1. Once** means one time. Birthdays only come **once** every year. **2. Once** also means after. **Once** Al started the third grade, he learned how to multiply.

## one

**1. One** is a number. **One** is written **1. One** is the first number when you count. **2. One** is used for something you have already talked about. Nia likes green grapes, but she doesn't like purple **ones.**

## onion

An **onion** is a kind of vegetable. It is round and has a strong smell and taste. **Onions** grow in the ground.

◆ onion

## only

**Only** means a certain amount and no more. There is **only** one piece of pie left.

## open

**1. Open** means that something can move in or out of a space or container. The breeze came in through the **open** window. **2.** To **open** means to take off the cover. Maggie **opened** a jar to get the peanut butter out. **3.** To **open** also means to allow people to enter. The factory **opens** at nine o'clock.

> **Open** is the opposite of **close.** I'll **open** the door for you. Remember to **close** it!

## opposite

**1. Opposite** means different in every way. Tall is the **opposite** of short. **2.** To be **opposite** also means to be on the other side of something. The players stood on **opposite** sides of the field.

## or

Or shows that one thing out of two or more things can happen. You can have a turkey sandwich **or** a peanut butter and jelly sandwich. We can watch a movie, read a book, **or** play a board game.

## orange

**1.** An **orange** is a kind of fruit. It is about the size of a tennis ball. **Oranges** grow on orange trees. **2. Orange** is a color. Pumpkins and oranges are **orange.**

◆ orange

## orchestra

An **orchestra** is a large group of people who play instruments together. **Orchestras** can have more than a hundred people. Sandy and DeMarcus play the violin in the school **orchestra.**

During a concert an **orchestra** performs for an audience. People buy tickets so they can go to the concert. Many musicians work for **orchestras.**

## order

**1. Order** is the way one thing follows another. The letters of the alphabet always come in the same **order. 2.** To **order** means to ask for something that you will pay for. Ashley **ordered** a hamburger at the restaurant. **3.** To **order** also means to tell someone what to do. The firefighters **ordered** everyone to leave the building. **4.** In **order** means everything is the way it should be. Tabitha always keeps her room in **order.**

## ostrich

An **ostrich** is a very large bird. It has long legs and a long neck. **Ostriches** cannot fly.

◆ ostrich

## other

**1. Other** means one of two. One of Vicki's socks has a hole in it. The **other** one has no holes. **2. Other** also means different. Keiko has no time to play today. She will have time some **other** day.

## ounce

An **ounce** is an amount of weight. There are 16 **ounces** in one pound.

(A) (B) (C) (D) (E) (F) (G) (H) (I) (J) (K) (L) (M)

## our

**Our** means belonging to us. These are **our** clothes. The people who live next door are **our** neighbors.

## ours

**Ours** means belonging to us. Those are your books and crayons. These books and crayons are **ours**.

## ourselves

**Ourselves** means us and nobody else. Because Ahmed and Alana were not there, Tiana and I had to finish the painting **ourselves**.

## out

**1. Out** tells where something is or is going. **Out** is the opposite of **in**. A bird flew in one window and **out** the other. Jose went **out** the door. **2. Out** also means that something stops making light. The lights were **out** in the kitchen, so we used flashlights to help us see while we made sandwiches. I blew **out** the candle before I went to sleep.

When you are **out of** something, there is no more of it. We are going to the store because we are **out of** milk.

## outgrow

To **outgrow** something means that you have grown too big for it. The baby **outgrows** her clothing and shoes quickly.
■ **outgrew, outgrown**

## outside

**1. Outside** is the opposite of **inside**. Leonardo and his sister Tabitha played **outside** until it was dark. Then they went into the house. **2.** The **outside** of something is the part that goes around things on the inside. The **outside** of an apple is the skin. Eggs are smooth on the **outside**. I wrote my friend's address on the **outside** of the package that I was mailing to him.

## oval

An **oval** is a shape. It looks like a circle that has been stretched. Hens' eggs are shaped like **ovals**.

◆ oval

## oven

An **oven** is a metal box that uses heat to cook food. **Ovens** can become very hot. Talia and her mother baked cookies in the **oven**.

## over

**1. Over** means above. A helicopter flew **over** our house.
**2. Over** also means on top of. Jacqueline wore a sweater **over** her shirt.
**3. Over** can also mean more than. Caroline's father is **over** six feet tall.
**4. Over** can also mean down. Paulette knocked **over** a glass of milk.
**5. Over** also means again. The band played a song. Then they played it **over** because everyone liked it. **6. Over** can mean finished. After our basketball game was **over,** everyone on the team went home.

◆ over

## owe

To **owe** means that you must give someone something. Timothy **owes** the store a quarter for his apple.

## owl

An **owl** is a kind of bird. It has a large head and large, round eyes that look straight ahead. **Owls** can see well at night.

◆ owl

## own

**1.** To **own** means to have and keep something. Janie **owns** a lot of books and toys. **2. Own** also means that something belongs only to you. Like the other kids, I brought my **own** snack on the field trip.

An **owner** is someone who **owns** something. The **owner** of the store let us enter early.

◆ ox

## ox

An **ox** is a large animal that is used to pull heavy loads. **Oxen** are usually male cattle.
■ **oxen**

(A) (B) (C) (D) (E) (F) (G) (H) (I) (J) (K) (L) (M)

# P

## pack

**1.** To **pack** is to put something in a suitcase or a box to take with you. Walter **packed** his clothes and some books for his vacation. **2.** A **pack** is another word for bag. We put bottles of water and food in a **pack.** We took the **pack** with us when we went camping.

## package

A **package** is a box that you put something in and send through the mail. People bring **packages** to the post office to mail.

## page

A **page** is a piece of paper. There are words on both sides of this **page.** Books are made of many **pages** held together.

◆ page

## paid

**Paid** is a form of **pay.** Milo **paid** twelve dollars for a movie ticket.

## pail

A **pail** is used to hold things. It is made of metal or plastic and has a flat, round bottom. **Pail** is another word for **bucket.**

◆ pail

**Pails** are useful for many things. You can make castles from sand when you take a **pail** and a small shovel to the beach. When farmers get milk from a cow, they put the milk in a **pail.**

## pain

**Pain** is what you feel when you are hurt. When I fell on the ice, I had **pains** in my leg.

## paint

**1. Paint** is a liquid with color in it. People put **paint** on things to make them look new. Artists make pictures with **paints**.
**2.** To **paint** is to cover with paint. April and her mother **painted** one room pink and one room blue. **3.** To **paint** is also to use paints to make a picture. The artist **painted** a picture of a mountain.

> A **painting** is a picture that is made with **paint.** Many art museums have **paintings** you can look at.

## pair

A **pair** is two things that match each other. Shoes, socks, and boots come in **pairs**.

◆ pair

## pajamas

**Pajamas** are a kind of clothes. People wear them when they sleep. Most **pajamas** are warm and soft.

## palace

A **palace** is a huge building where kings and queens live. Some **palaces** have more than one hundred rooms.

## palm

**1.** A **palm** is the flat part of your hand that your fingers touch when you bend them. There are many lines on the **palms** of our hands.
**2.** A **palm** is also a kind of tree. **Palm** trees grow in warm climates.

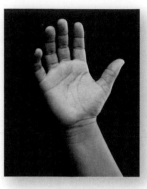

◆ palm

## pan

A **pan** is something to cook in. It is made of metal. My father used two **pans** to make pancakes and eggs for our breakfast.

## pancake

A **pancake** is a kind of food. It is a thin, flat cake that is cooked in a hot pan. You have to flip a **pancake** to cook both sides. **Pancakes** are made of flour, eggs, and milk.

◆ pancake

A B C D E F G H I J K L M

## panda

A **panda** is a large animal that looks like a bear. **Pandas** have thick fur that is black and white.

◆ panda

Pandas usually live in forests. There are only a few kinds of plants that **pandas** like to eat. There are not many **pandas** in the world, so scientists are trying to save them.

## pants

**Pants** are a kind of clothes. People wear **pants** over their legs. Most **pants** have pockets in the sides. Pete is wearing orange **pants.**

◆ pants

## paper

**Paper** is something people use to write on. It is made from wood. My aunt's desk has lots of **papers** on it.

**Paper towels** are **towels** that are made of **paper.** They can be used only once.

## parachute

A **parachute** is something that a person can use to help them fall slowly to the ground. **Parachutes** are made of cloth.

## parade

A **parade** is a group of people who march together down the street. Most **parades** have bands that play music as they march. **Parades** often happen on holidays.

## parent

A **parent** is a mother or father. Men and women who have children are **parents.**

## park

**1.** A **park** is a place where people go to enjoy being outside. Most **parks** are full of grass and trees. **2.** To **park** is to put a car somewhere and leave it there. Cheng's father **parks** the car in the garage every night.

## parrot

A **parrot** is a kind of bird. It has a large beak and feathers in bright colors. **Parrots** usually live in warm places. Some **parrots** can learn to say a few words.

◆ parrot

Can you think of a word that rhymes with **parrot**?

## part

**1.** A **part** is one piece of something. Leaves, branches, roots, and the trunk are **parts** of a tree. Bread, lettuce, and turkey are **parts** of a sandwich. **2.** A **part** is also the person that someone pretends to be in a movie or play. Alma got a big **part** in the school play this year. She is going to play the **part** of the queen. **3.** To **part** means to leave someone. Vincent didn't like **parting** from his family when he went to camp.

## partner

A **partner** is someone who works or plays with another person or with a group of people. During dance class, Deb is my **partner.** Everyone in the first grade has two **partners** in his or her reading group.

## party

A **party** is a time when people get together to have fun. Maggie invites many friends to her birthday **parties.** ■ parties

## pass

**1.** To **pass** means to go past. My teacher **passes** my house when he walks to school. **2.** To **pass** also means to give to someone with your hands. I **passed** the salad to my father at the table. **3.** To **pass** also means to get a score on a test that is good enough. You have to **pass** a test to drive a car.

◆ pass

## passenger

A **passenger** is a person who travels in a car, boat, train, or airplane. The **passengers** slept on the train.

## past

**1.** The **past** is the part of time that has already happened. Yesterday is in the **past. 2.** To go **past** means to go beside. A big river goes **past** many towns.

(A) (B) (C) (D) (E) (F) (G) (H) (I) (J) (K) (L) (M)

## paste

**Paste** is something used to stick paper or light cloth together. **Paste** is not as strong as glue.

## pasture

A **pasture** is a field of grass where animals eat. Horses and cows eat grass in **pastures.**

## pat

To **pat** means to touch in a gentle way with your hand. Anton **patted** his dog when he came home from school.
- **patted**

## patch

**1.** A **patch** is a small piece of cloth. People sew **patches** on clothes to cover up holes. **2.** A **patch** also means an area of ground. Carrots and potatoes are growing in a **patch** behind the barn.

## path

A **path** is a place where you can walk through a field or a forest. There is a **path** to the lake through the woods.

◆ path

## paw

A **paw** is the foot of some animals. Dogs, cats, bears, and rabbits all have four **paws.** The kitten raised his **paw.**

◆ paw

Paw rhymes with **claw, law,** and **saw.**

## pay

**1.** To **pay** is to give money for something. Louise **paid** five dollars for a book. **2.** To **pay** attention means to look and listen carefully. Philippe **pays** attention when his teacher talks to the class. ■ **paid**

## pea

A **pea** is a kind of vegetable. It is small, round, and green. **Peas** are the seeds of **pea** plants.

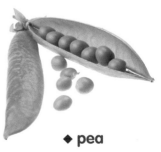

◆ pea

## peace

**Peace** is a time when people are not fighting. When the war was over, everyone was glad to have **peace.**

## peach

A **peach** is a kind of fruit. It is yellow and red and has a lot of juice inside. **Peaches** grow on peach trees.

## peacock

A **peacock** is a very large, male bird. It has blue and green feathers on its head and body. **Peacocks** have long back feathers that can spread out like a large fan. These feathers have spots that look like eyes.

◆ peacock

## peak

A **peak** is the top of a mountain. Some mountain **peaks** are covered with snow.

◆ peak

## peanut

A **peanut** is a kind of food. It comes in a shell and looks and tastes like a nut. **Peanuts** grow in the ground.

◆ peanut

**Peanut butter** is made by breaking **peanuts** into very small pieces and making them soft. There is no real **butter** in **peanut butter,** but it is soft and smooth like **butter.** Many people like to put **peanut butter** on sandwiches.

## pear

A **pear** is a kind of fruit. **Pears** are yellow, green, brown, or red. They are round at both ends, but one end is smaller than the other.

## pebble

A **pebble** is a small rock. Savannah likes to look for smooth, pretty **pebbles** when she goes to the beach.

(A) (B) (C) (D) (E) (F) (G) (H) (I) (J) (K) (L) (M)

## peek

To **peek** is to look at something quickly. After my mother told me to cover my eyes, I **peeked** and saw my birthday cake.

**Peek** and **peak** sound alike. Both words rhyme with **cheek**. Can you think of another word that rhymes with **peek** and **peak**?

## peel

**1.** A **peel** is the skin of some fruits or vegetables. Carrots, bananas, and oranges have **peels**. **2.** To **peel** means to take the skin off a fruit or vegetable. My sister and I help my father **peel** potatoes for dinner.

◆ peel

## pen

A **pen** is a tool to write with. **Pens** are filled with ink. They are usually made of plastic or metal.

## pencil

A **pencil** is a tool to write with. **Pencils** are made of wood or plastic. The part that writes on paper is called the lead.

## penguin

A **penguin** is a kind of bird. It lives near the ocean in places where it is very cold. **Penguins** cannot fly. They use their wings to swim in the water.

◆ penguin

**Penguins** can swim for a long time under the water, but they need to come up for air. **Fish** do not need to breathe air.

## penny

A **penny** is a coin. One **penny** is one cent. There are 5 **pennies** in a nickel, 10 **pennies** in a dime, 25 **pennies** in a quarter, and 100 **pennies** in one dollar. ■ **pennies**

## people

**People** means more than one **person**. No two **people** are the same. There were a lot of **people** at the beach yesterday because it was very hot and sunny.

## pepper

**1. Pepper** is a kind of food called a spice. It is a black powder that is made from a tiny fruit. **2.** A **pepper** is also a vegetable. **Peppers** are usually red, yellow, or green.

◆ pepper

## perfect

**Perfect** means that everything is just right. Miles did a **perfect** job cleaning his room.

## perform

To **perform** means to do something in front of an audience. My piano teacher **performs** twice each year.

## perhaps

**Perhaps** means maybe. **Perhaps** we will have time for a walk after dinner.

## period

A **period** is a dot that is at the end of a sentence. **Periods** are not used after sentences that are questions.

## person

A **person** is a man, woman, boy, or girl. A horse can carry a **person** on its back.

## pet

A **pet** is an animal that lives with people. Many people have dogs, cats, or birds as **pets.**

## phone

**Phone** is another word for **telephone.** Ayumi called her friend Jacob on the **phone.** We turned off our **phones** during the movie.

## photograph

A **photograph** is a picture that cameras make. People like to have **photographs** of special times like vacations and holidays.

**Photo** is a short way of saying **photograph.** Mom took a lot of **photos** at my birthday party.

## piano

A **piano** is an instrument. **Pianos** have 88 black and white keys. You push down on the keys with your fingers to make music.

◆ piano

A B C D E F G H I J K L M

## pick

**1.** To **pick** means to take something off a tree or another plant. Cooper **picked** the highest apple he could reach. **2.** To **pick** also means to choose. Stu **picked** out a tie to go with his shirt.

◆ pick

## picnic

A **picnic** is a meal that people eat outside. We have **picnics** at the lake on summer afternoons.

## picture

**1.** A **picture** is something you draw or paint. Harris drew a **picture** of his house. **2.** A **picture** can also be a photograph. Many people like to take **pictures** of their pets.

## pie

A **pie** is a kind of food. **Pies** are baked in an oven. The outside of a **pie** is often made with flour and butter. The inside can be fruit, cheese, meat, or other things.

◆ pie

## piece

**1.** A **piece** of something is less than the whole thing. Carrie gave Deirdre a **piece** of her peach. When the baseball hit the window, the glass broke into many **pieces**. **2.** A **piece** is also something that is one of a group of things used together. We picked up all of the **pieces** of the game after we finished playing.

## pig

A **pig** is a kind of animal. It is short and fat and has a flat nose. **Pigs** are raised for their meat.

◆ pig

A young **pig** is called a **piglet**.

## pile

A **pile** is a lot of something all in one place. Zachary and I dug a hole at the beach. We left big **piles** of sand.

## pill

A **pill** is a solid piece of medicine that you swallow. When my brother was sick, he took **pills** every day.

## pillow

A **pillow** is a cloth cover filled with feathers or something else that is soft. People put their heads on **pillows** when they sleep or rest.

## pilot

A **pilot** is a person who flies an airplane or a helicopter. **Pilots** have to practice many hours before they can fly alone.

## pin

A **pin** is a short, thin piece of metal with a sharp point. **Pins** are used to hold clothes together while they are being sewn.

## pine

A **pine** is a kind of tree. **Pines** have needles on their branches. **Pine** needles stay green all winter.

## pineapple

A **pineapple** is a large fruit. It has thick skin and long leaves. The inside is yellow and sweet. **Pineapples** grow in warm places.

◆ pineapple

## pink

**Pink** is a color. You can mix red paint and white paint to make **pink** paint.

## pint

A **pint** is an amount of liquid. Two **pints** are the same as one quart.

## pipe

A **pipe** is a tube made of metal, plastic, or glass. **Pipes** are used to carry liquids from one place to another.

## pirate

A **pirate** is a person who robs people on ships. Hundreds of years ago, **pirates** sailed all over the world.

## pit

**1.** A **pit** is a hard seed in the center of some fruits. Peaches and cherries have **pits**. **2.** A **pit** is also a hole in the ground. Sometimes people cook food in **pits**.

◆ pit

## pitch

To **pitch** means to throw. In baseball, a player from one team **pitches** the ball. A player from the other team tries to hit the ball with a bat.

A B C D E F G H I J K L M

## pitcher

**1.** A **pitcher** is a container that is used to hold and pour liquids. **Pitchers** usually have a handle. There was a **pitcher** of juice at breakfast. **2.** A **pitcher** is also a person on a baseball team who pitches a ball. The **pitchers** on my brother's team can throw the ball very fast.

◆ pitcher

## pizza

**Pizza** is a kind of food. It is flat bread with tomatoes, cheese, and other foods on top. The tomatoes on **pizza** are usually made into a sauce. **Pizzas** are baked in an oven.

## place

**1.** A **place** is somewhere for something to be. Rooms, fields, stores, houses, schools, and countries are all **places**. **2.** To **place** something is to put it somewhere. Shannon **placed** the forks and spoons on the table.

> Some words that rhyme with **place** are **base, chase, face,** and **race.**

## plain

**1. Plain** means simple. I bought a **plain** white dress for the concert. **2.** A **plain** is a large, flat area of land with few trees. **Plains** often have grass that cows can eat.

## plan

**1.** A **plan** is an idea or information about how to do something. Our vacation **plans** are to travel and to ski. **2.** To **plan** is to have a plan to do something. Our family **plans** to go to the beach this summer.
■ **planned**

## plane

**Plane** is another word for **airplane.** Robby's father knows how to fly a **plane.**

## planet

A **planet** is a very large object in space that moves around a star. There are eight **planets** that move around the Sun.

◆ planet

## planned

**Planned** is a form of **plan.** We **planned** to go to the baseball game, but when it started raining, we decided not to go.

## plant

**1.** A **plant** is a living thing that is not an animal and can make its own food. Most **plants** grow in the ground. Flowers, trees, and vegetables are all **plants**. **2.** To **plant** means to put seeds or small plants in the ground. Jacob helped his mother **plant** a tree in the yard.

◆ plant

## plastic

**Plastic** is something that things are made of. Some kinds of **plastic** are easy to bend, and some are very hard. **Plastic** can be any color. It is less easy to break than glass.

**Plastic** is not something that you can find in nature. Instead, people make **plastic** from oil found in the ground.

## plate

A **plate** is a thin, flat dish that you put food on. Paige put **plates,** glasses, forks, and spoons on the table before dinner.

## play

**1.** To **play** is to have fun. Most people like to **play** games. You can **play** alone or with other people. **2.** To **play** is also to make music with an instrument. Larry can **play** the trombone. **3.** A **play** is a kind of story. People act in **plays** while other people watch them. **Plays** are seen in theaters and on television.

A **player** is someone who **plays.** There are nine **players** on a baseball team. Chess is a game for only two **players.**

## playful

To be **playful** is to be happy and to have a lot of energy. The puppy was very **playful.**

## playground

A **playground** is a place to play outside. **Playgrounds** usually have swings, seesaws, and other objects for people to play on. Most schools have **playgrounds.**

## pleasant

**Pleasant** means nice. The picnic we went to was **pleasant.** Ms. Greenberg is always **pleasant** when we give her our money for lunch.

## please

**1. Please** is a word people use when they ask for something. Paco asked, "May I have an apple, **please**?" **2.** To **please** means to make someone happy. The students **pleased** their teacher when they behaved so well.

## plum

A **plum** is a kind of fruit. **Plums** are usually purple and grow on small trees.

◆ plum

## plural

A **plural** is the form of a word that means more than one person or thing. "Cats" is the **plural** of "cat." Most **plurals** are made by adding the letter **s** to a word.

## plus

**Plus** means added to. If you add two and three, you get five. Two **plus** three is five. Two **plus** three can also be written 2 + 3.

## pocket

A **pocket** is a small bag of cloth. **Pockets** are sewn into jackets, coats, shirts, and pants. You can carry all kinds of things in your **pockets.**

◆ pocket

## poem

A **poem** is a group of words that are put together in a special way. People write **poems** to say things that can be hard to say with usual language. The words in many **poems** rhyme.

Another word for a **poem** or a group of **poems** is **poetry**. **Poets** write **poetry**.

## point

**1.** A **point** is a sharp end. Pins, needles, and arrows have **points**. **2.** To **point** is to show where something is. Shona **pointed** to the map to show where she was born.

◆ point

## poison

A **poison** is something that can hurt people or animals if they swallow or breathe it. Some medicines that you put on your skin are **poisons** if you eat or drink them.

## pole

A **pole** is a long piece of wood or metal. Telephone **poles** hold wires up in the air.

## police

The **police** are people whose job is to protect other people. But if people break the law, the **police** can put them in jail.

> The people who are part of the **police** are called **police officers.**

## polite

**Polite** means acting kind and pleasant to other people. People who are **polite** have good manners.

## pollution

**Pollution** is bad things that people put into the environment. **Pollution** can make people, animals, and plants sick. There is a lot of **pollution** at that beach.

◆ pollution

## pond

A **pond** is a large amount of water that is all in one place. Some **ponds** are big enough to swim in. A **pond** is smaller than a lake.

◆ pond

## pony

A **pony** is a kind of horse. **Ponies** are not as big as most horses. ■ **ponies**

## pool

A **pool** is a container filled with water that you can swim in. Some **pools** are large holes that are dug into the ground. Others are made of plastic and sit on top of the ground. Our neighbors have a **pool** in their backyard.

## poor

**Poor** is the opposite of **rich**. **Poor** people do not have much money.

Ⓐ Ⓑ Ⓒ Ⓓ Ⓔ Ⓕ Ⓖ Ⓗ Ⓘ Ⓙ Ⓚ Ⓛ Ⓜ

## popcorn

**Popcorn** is a kind of food made from the seeds of corn. Pieces of **popcorn** get big and soft when they are cooked. They make a loud sound when they get hot.

◆ popcorn

## porch

A **porch** is a covered area at an entrance to a building. People like to sit on their **porches** and rest during the summer.

## port

A **port** is a harbor or a city that has a harbor. Boats and ships come and go at **ports.**

## possible

**Possible** means that something can happen. It is **possible** that it will rain tomorrow.

> The opposite of **possible** is **impossible.** It is **possible** to teach dogs to sit, but it is **impossible** for dogs to fly.

## post office

A **post office** is a building. When you mail a letter, it goes to the **post office.** From there, it goes to the person you are sending it to.

## pot

A **pot** is a deep, round pan to cook food in. **Pots** are made of metal, glass, or clay. Most **pots** have handles.

## potato

A **potato** is a kind of vegetable. **Potatoes** grow in the ground.
■ potatoes

◆ potato

> Can you think of another food whose name rhymes with **potato**?

## pound

A **pound** is an amount of weight. One **pound** is 16 ounces. Three apples weigh about one **pound.** Makayla's new baby sister weighs seven **pounds.**

## pour

To **pour** is to make liquid go from one place to another. Could you **pour** me a cup of tea?

◆ pour

## powder

A **powder** is a lot of very tiny pieces of something. Flour is a kind of **powder.** Some spices are crushed until they become **powder.**

◆ powder

## power

**1. Power** is being able to do work. A bulldozer has enough **power** to move big piles of dirt. **2.** To have **power** means to be able to decide things. The president of our country has a lot of **power. 3. Power** is another word for **electricity.** Our house had no **power** after the storm.

## practice

To **practice** is to do something many times so that you can do it well. People who play music well have to **practice** a lot.

## prepare

To **prepare** is to get ready. Ernie **prepared** to go to camp by packing his clothes in a suitcase.

## present

**1.** A **present** is a gift. People often get **presents** on their birthdays. **2.** The **present** is the part of time that is here now. This minute is part of the **present. 3.** To be **present** means to be somewhere. My parents were **present** when I won the race.

◆ present

The opposite of **present** is **absent.** Only ten students were **present,** and the rest were **absent** because they were sick.

## president

A **president** is a person who leads a group of people. The people in our country elect a **president** every four years. Some **presidents** have monuments made for them.

◆ president

(A) (B) (C) (D) (E) (F) (G) (H) (I) (J) (K) (L) (M)

# pretend

To **pretend** is to act in a way that is not real. When Katherine acted in the school play, she **pretended** to be an astronaut who traveled to another planet.

# pretty

**Pretty** means nice to look at. Everyone likes **pretty** flowers.
■ **prettier, prettiest**

# pretzel

A **pretzel** is a kind of salty food that is usually shaped like a knot. **Pretzels** can be soft or hard.

◆ **pretzel**

# prevent

To **prevent** means to stop something from happening. The rain will **prevent** us from having our picnic today. Taking that medicine **prevented** them from getting sick.

# price

A **price** is how much money you have to pay for something. The **price** of Vickie's skirt was twenty dollars.

# prince

A **prince** is the son of a king or a queen. Some **princes** become kings.

# princess

A **princess** is the daughter of a king or a queen. Some **princesses** become queens.

# principal

**1.** A **principal** is a person who leads a school. School **principals** work with teachers to help students learn.
**2. Principal** also means something that is most important. The **principal** problem in our building is noise.

# print

**1.** To **print** means to write with care so that none of the letters touch each other. Deval **printed** his name at the top of his paper.
**2.** To **print** also means to put letters on paper with a machine. Large machines are used to **print** books and newspapers.
**3.** A **print** is a mark that is made on a surface by pushing into it. I like to leave **prints** in the sand with my feet.

◆ **print**

## prize

A **prize** is something that you win. **Prizes** can be cups, ribbons, money, or many other things. When I won the spelling bee, I got a blue ribbon as a **prize.**

◆ prize

## probably

**Probably** means that something is expected to happen. Roland comes to my house every Saturday to play games. He will **probably** come this Saturday too.

## problem

**1.** A **problem** is something that you have trouble with. My brother had **problems** with reading last year. **2.** A **problem** is also a question that you need to solve. Yesterday Alex had five math **problems** to do for homework.

## project

A **project** is something you do or make that shows what you have learned. Students often work on special **projects** at school. This year Andrea's science **project** is about magnets.

## promise

**1.** To **promise** is to say you will do something. When Les borrowed Josh's baseball glove, he **promised** to return it the next day. **2.** A **promise** is something that you say you will do. People should always keep their **promises.**

## pronounce

To **pronounce** means to speak the sounds of letters or words. Cameron's baby sister is learning how to **pronounce** her name.

## propeller

A **propeller** is a part of a machine. It is made of wood or metal. **Propellers** make planes and boats move by spinning in the air or water.

◆ propeller

## protect

To **protect** means to keep safe. An umbrella **protects** you from the rain or the sun. A helmet **protects** your head when you ride a bicycle.

(A) (B) (C) (D) (E) (F) (G) (H) (I) (J) (K) (L) (M)

## proud

To be **proud** is to be glad to have people see what you have or what you have done. Alice was **proud** of the picture she made.

When you feel **proud** of something, you have **pride** in it. We say "**proud** as a peacock" because some people think peacocks have **pride** in their fancy tails.

## pudding

**Pudding** is a kind of food. **Pudding** is sweet and smooth. You can eat it with a spoon. Tamara's family likes vanilla **pudding** for dessert.

## puddle

A **puddle** is a small amount of water that has collected in one place. Rain makes **puddles** in the street. I think it's fun to step in **puddles.**

◆ puddle

## pull

To **pull** is to make something move toward you. My dog and I **pulled** on opposite ends of the rope.

◆ pull

## pumpkin

A **pumpkin** is a very large fruit. It is yellow or orange and grows on a vine. We place **pumpkins** on our porch in the fall.

◆ pumpkin

## punch

To **punch** means to hit hard with your fist. At the gym, I learned how to **punch** the ball over the net.

## puppet

A **puppet** is a toy that looks like a small person or animal. Some **puppets** fit on your hand. Others are moved by strings from above.

## puppy

A **puppy** is
a young dog.
**Puppies** have
soft fur and big
feet. They like
to play with
everything.
■ **puppies**

◆ puppy

Another word for **puppy** is
**pup.**

## purchase

To **purchase** means to buy. Our
teacher **purchased** new books
for our class this year.

## purple

**Purple** is a color. Grape juice
and grape jelly are usually
**purple.**

## purse

A **purse** is a bag that
you hold in your hand
or carry over your
shoulder. You can
keep keys, money,
pens, and other
things in a **purse.**

◆ purse

## push

To **push** is to make something
go ahead of you. Sophia **pushed**
the basket across the room.

◆ push

## put

**1.** To **put** is to find a place for
something and leave it there.
Diana **put** a sandwich in her
lunch box to take to school.
**2.** To **put** out a fire means that
you stop the fire from burning.
My mother **put** out the candles.
**3.** To **put** on clothes means to
cover your body with them.
Josie **put** on a new vest. ■ **put**

## puzzle

**1.** A **puzzle** is a game. **Puzzles**
are pieces of paper or wood
that you have to put together
to make pictures. **2.** A **puzzle**
is also something that is hard
to understand. It was a **puzzle**
to Tess how her sister got home
before she did.

**A B C D E F G H I J K L M**

# Q

## quart

A **quart** is an amount of liquid. There are four **quarts** in one gallon.

## quarter

**1.** A **quarter** is a kind of coin. One **quarter** is the same as five nickels. Four **quarters** is the same as one dollar. **2.** A **quarter** is one of four pieces that are the same size. You can cut a pie into **quarters.**

## queen

A **queen** is a woman who rules a country. **Queens** usually rule for as long as they live. A **queen** can also be the wife of a king.

## question

A **question** is a group of words that ask something. Sometimes the teacher asks **questions** that nobody can answer.

When a **question** is asked, there is usually an **answer.** The teacher asked the **question** "What is 2 plus 2?" The correct **answer** is "4."

## quick

**Quick** means fast. Mice are **quick.**

## quiet

To be **quiet** means to make very little sound. Our neighborhood is very **quiet** at night.

**Quietly** means in a **quiet** way. I spoke **quietly** in the library.

## quilt

A **quilt** is a kind of blanket. **Quilts** are made by sewing pieces of cloth together.

◆ quilt

## quit

To **quit** means to stop doing something. Al **quit** the swim team to play soccer. ■ **quit**

## quite

**Quite** means very. It was **quite** hot at the beach.

## rabbit

A **rabbit** is a small animal. It has long ears and soft fur. **Rabbits** hop using their long back legs.

> A **rabbit** is sometimes called a **bunny**. The farmer let us pet the **bunnies**.

## raccoon

A **raccoon** is a small animal. It has short legs and dark marks like a mask over its eyes. **Raccoons** live in forests.

◆ raccoon

## race

A **race** is a contest to find out who is fastest. People have **races** on foot, in cars, on horses, and in many other ways.

## radio

A **radio** is a machine that uses electricity to make sounds. A **radio** station uses electricity to send the sounds to **radios** in homes and cars. You can hear music or news on the **radio.** My parents like to listen to the **radio** when they work in the yard.

## raft

A **raft** is a kind of flat boat. **Rafts** are made of logs, boards, rubber, or plastic.

◆ raft

## rag

A **rag** is a piece of cloth used for cleaning, washing, or dusting. My mother uses **rags** to wash the car.

(A) (B) (C) (D) (E) (F) (G) (H) (I) (J) (K) (L) (M)

## railroad

A **railroad** is the metal path that trains ride on. **Railroads** can go across bridges, through tunnels, and over mountains.

## rain

**1. Rain** is water that falls in drops from clouds. Plants need **rain** to grow. **2.** To **rain** means to fall as drops of water. When it **rains,** everything gets wet.

## rainbow

A **rainbow** looks like a ribbon of many colors curving across the sky. **Rainbows** appear when the sun is shining but there is rain nearby.

> The color red is on the top of a **rainbow.** The color purple is at the bottom. The colors orange, yellow, green, and blue are in the middle.

◆ rainbow

## raise

**1.** To **raise** is to lift up. Caleb **raised** his hand to answer the question. **2.** To **raise** means to take care of something while it grows. Farmers **raise** vegetables. Parents **raise** children.

◆ raise

## rake

**1.** A **rake** is a tool. It is made of a row of stiff, thin strips fastened at the end of a long handle. The strips are spread apart so there is space between them. **Rakes** are used to gather grass and leaves into piles. **2.** To **rake** is to gather into a pile with a rake. Geraldo helps his father **rake** the leaves in the fall.

◆ rake

## ran

**Ran** is a form of **run.** Michele **ran** to school yesterday morning.

## rang

**Rang** is a form of **ring.** The bell **rang** at the end of the day.

### rat

A **rat** is a kind of animal. It has a long tail, short fur, and sharp teeth. **Rats** are bigger than mice.

> **Rat** rhymes with **bat, cat,** and **that.**

### reach

**1.** To **reach** means to put your hand out toward something. Jasmine **reached** up to take a book off the shelf. **2.** To **reach** also means to get all the way to. The big storm did not **reach** our part of the country.

◆ **reach**

### read

To **read** means to look at words and know what they mean. June is learning to **read.** She often **reads** stories with her friends. ■ **read**

> A **reader** is someone who **reads.** The teacher is happy that the students are good **readers.** A **reader** is also a book that helps people learn how to **read.** There is a story about a rabbit and a turtle in our **reader.**

### ready

**1.** When something is **ready,** people can use it. "Dinner will be **ready** when the food is cooked." **2.** When people get **ready,** they are prepared to do something. After we packed, we were **ready** to go on vacation. ■ **readier, readiest**

### real

**Real** means the way the world is. When something is **real,** people did not make it up.

### really

**Really** means that something is actually true. Pine needles do not look like other leaves. But they **really** are leaves.

### reason

A **reason** is why something is so. There are many **reasons** why I like chocolate better than vanilla.

### recipe

A **recipe** is a set of directions for making food. My uncle borrowed my mother's **recipe** for tomato sauce.

### rectangle

A **rectangle** is a shape. **Rectangles** have four sides and four corners.

◆ **rectangle**

(A) (B) (C) (D) (E) (F) (G) (H) (I) (J) (K) (L) (M)

## recycle

To **recycle** means to make trash into something that can be used again. Our city **recycles** old newspapers, cans, and glass.

## red

**Red** is a color. Some apples and fire engines are **red**. ■ **redder, reddest**

**Redden** means to become **red**. The sky **reddens** as the sun sets.

## refrigerator

A **refrigerator** is a kind of machine. It is a box that is cold inside. **Refrigerators** keep food and drinks cold. Kitchens usually have **refrigerators**.

## remember

To **remember** is to be able to think of something again. Laurie **remembers** the phone numbers of all her friends.

## remind

To **remind** means to cause someone to remember something. My mother **reminded** me to bring an umbrella to school.

## repeat

To **repeat** is to do or say again. "I did not hear you. Would you please **repeat** what you said?"

## reptile

A **reptile** is a kind of animal. Snakes, turtles, and alligators are **reptiles**.

◆ reptile

## research

To **research** is to study something. People **research** things to learn about them. Our teacher asked us to go to the library so we could **research** the history of our state.

## rest

**1.** To **rest** is to be still. People and animals need to **rest** when they are tired. **2.** The **rest** of something is what has not been used. Louis ate half of his sandwich for lunch. He saved the **rest** for after school.

The word **rest** rhymes with **best, nest, test,** and **west.**

## restaurant

A **restaurant** is a place where people pay for meals. Most **restaurants** have many different kinds of food. All **restaurants** have kitchens where cooks make the food.

## return

**1.** To **return** is to come back. Birds that have gone south in the fall **return** every spring.
**2.** To **return** also means to bring back. Megan **returned** the books to the library after she read them.

## rhinoceros

A **rhinoceros** is a very large animal. It has short legs and gray skin. **Rhinoceroses** have one or two horns on their faces.

◆ rhinoceros

## rhyme

To **rhyme** means to end with the same sounds. Cook **rhymes** with book. Group **rhymes** with soup. Tall **rhymes** with small. Many poems use words that **rhyme.**

## ribbon

A **ribbon** is a long, thin piece of cloth or paper. **Ribbons** come in many colors. Presents are often wrapped in paper and tied with a **ribbon.**

◆ ribbon

## rice

**Rice** is a kind of food. Grains of **rice** are soft when they are cooked. **Rice** is the seeds of a kind of grass.

◆ rice

## rich

To be **rich** means to have a lot of money. The author became **rich** when her book was made into a movie.

The opposite of **rich** is **poor.** The **rich** king rode in a carriage past the **poor** farmers.

## ridden

**Ridden** is a form of **ride.** Katrina likes to ride her bicycle. She has **ridden** it every day this week. Have you ever **ridden** a horse?

(A) (B) (C) (D) (E) (F) (G) (H) (I) (J) (K) (L) (M)

## riddle

A **riddle** is a kind of joke. **Riddles** are questions that have funny answers. "When does Thursday come before Wednesday?" is a **riddle**. The answer is "In a dictionary."

## ride

**1.** To **ride** is to sit in or on something that moves. Cowboys **ride** horses. At the playground, Haley and her friends **rode** around in a circle. **2.** A **ride** is a time when you ride in something. Every Sunday our family goes for a **ride** in the country. **3.** A **ride** is also a kind of machine at a carnival or a fair. **Rides** turn people around or upside-down or carry them through the air.
■ **rode, ridden**

◆ ride

## ridiculous

To be **ridiculous** means to be silly. The movie made us laugh because it had a **ridiculous** story.

## right

**1.** **Right** means correct. Robin usually knows the **right** answer. **2.** **Right** also means the way something should be. **Right** is the opposite of **wrong**. It is always **right** to tell the truth. **3.** **Right** is the opposite of **left**. In this country, people drive cars on the **right** side of the road. **4.** A **right** is something that the law allows a person to do. Every citizen has the **right** to vote.

## ring

**1.** A **ring** is a metal circle that people wear on their fingers. Many **rings** are made of gold or silver. Some **rings** have jewels on them. **2.** To **ring** is to make the sound of a bell. The school bell **rings** every morning when school starts.
■ **rang, rung**

◆ ring

## rink

A **rink** is a place where you skate. There are **rinks** for ice skating, roller skating, and ice hockey.

## rip

To **rip** means to pull something into pieces. Jake **ripped** the paper in half before he threw it away. ■ **ripped**

### ripe

**Ripe** means that a piece of fruit has grown enough that you can eat it. Bananas are yellow when they are **ripe.**

### rise

**1.** To **rise** is to go up. The sun **rises** in the east every morning. I like to watch bubbles **rise** to the top of my glass. **2.** To **rise** is also to become more in amount. The temperature outside **rises** on hot days. It has **risen** every day this week. **3.** To **rise** also means to stand up. We **rose** when the parade passed by. ■ **rose, risen**

### river

A **river** is a wide path of water that has land on both sides. Some **rivers** are hundreds of miles long.

◆ river

### road

A **road** is a wide path. **Roads** can go through fields, forests, and towns. People travel over **roads** in cars, trucks, and buses.

### roast

To **roast** is to cook with hot air in an oven or over a fire. Shari and her friends **roasted** marshmallows on Sunday.

### rob

To **rob** means to take from someone something that doesn't belong to you. Three people **robbed** the bank on Tuesday. They took all the money. ■ **robbed**

A **robber** is a person who **robs** someone. The police caught the **robbers** and put them in jail.

### robin

A **robin** is a kind of bird. **Robins** are red in front.

◆ robin

### robot

A **robot** is a machine that does a job. Many **robots** do the same jobs over and over again.

(A) (B) (C) (D) (E) (F) (G) (H) (I) (J) (K) (L) (M)

## rock

A **rock** is a hard object that comes from under the ground. Some **rocks** have metal in them. There are a lot of **rocks** in the river.

◆ rock

## rocket

A **rocket** is a kind of machine. It is a tube that flies up when something inside burns very fast. Astronauts are carried into space on large **rockets**.

## rode

**Rode** is a form of **ride**. Lawrence **rode** to school on the bus this morning, but he walked home.

> The word **rode** sounds the same as the word **road**.

## roll

**1.** To **roll** is to keep turning over and over. When you kick a ball, it **rolls** away. **2.** A **roll** is a kind of round or curved bread. People usually eat hamburgers and hot dogs in **rolls**.

## roof

A **roof** is the top of a building. Some **roofs** are flat. Others have sides that join at the top.

## room

**1.** A **room** is an area in a building. **Rooms** usually have four walls, but they can be many different shapes or sizes. **2.** **Room** means space. There is **room** for one more person to sit on the couch.

## rooster

A **rooster** is a male chicken. **Roosters** make a lot of noise early in the morning.

## root

A **root** is a part of a plant. It usually grows under the ground. Plants get water and food from the ground through their **roots**.

◆ rooster

◆ root

## rope

**Rope** is made of several pieces of string twisted together. **Rope** can be tied in knots and used to hold things together.

## rose

**1.** A **rose** is a kind of flower. **Roses** are usually red, pink, yellow, or white. They grow on bushes and have a wonderful smell. **2. Rose** is a form of **rise**. The sun **rose** this morning at six o'clock.

## rotate

To **rotate** means to turn in a circle. The earth **rotates** in space. The picture was upside-down, so we **rotated** it.

## rough

Something that is **rough** does not feel even. The bark of most trees is **rough.**

◆ rough

The opposite of **rough** is **smooth.** The edge of the rock was **rough.** The front of the mirror is shiny and **smooth.**

## round

**Round** means having the shape of a circle. A **round** object has no points or corners. Balls, wheels, and coins are **round.**

## route

A **route** is the area that you go through to go from one place to another. There are two different bus **routes** from the library to my house.

## row

A **row** is a group of things that are in a line. The plants on the farm are growing in long **rows.**

◆ row

## rub

To **rub** means to press against something with your hand and move back and forth. Pat **rubbed** the window with a cloth to clean the dirt off.
■ **rubbed**

## rubber

**Rubber** is something that is strong and easy to stretch. Tires for cars are made of **rubber.**

(A) (B) (C) (D) (E) (F) (G) (H) (I) (J) (K) (L) (M)

## ruby

A **ruby** is a kind of jewel. **Rubies** are red. ▪ **rubies**

## rude

To be **rude** is to say or do something in a way that is not kind or pleasant to other people. It is **rude** to stare at people.

## rug

A **rug** is used to cover all or part of a floor. It is made of cloth or yarn. **Rugs** can be one color or many colors. We have a red and blue **rug** at the bottom of the stairs.

◆ rug

## rule

**1.** A **rule** tells how people must behave. To play a game right, you have to follow the **rules.**
**2.** To **rule** is to make laws and decide things. Sometimes wars are fought about who will **rule** a country.

## ruler

**1.** A **ruler** is a strip of wood, metal, or plastic used to measure lengths or to draw straight lines. We measured our books with **rulers.** My book was eight inches long. **2.** A **ruler** is also a person who rules. Kings and queens are **rulers.**

## run

**1.** To **run** is to go somewhere by moving your legs quickly. Rudy has **run** in races with her friends. **2.** To **run** also means to work. The washing machine makes a noise when it is **running.** ▪ **ran, run**

◆ run

## rung

**Rung** is a form of **ring.** We are late for school. The bell has already **rung.**

## rush

To **rush** means to hurry. I **rushed** home because I did not have much time to get dressed for the party.

# S

## sack

A **sack** is a bag made of cloth, plastic, paper, or string. How much rice is in that **sack**? We bought two **sacks** of flour.

◆ sack

## sad

**Sad** means not happy. Jonah is **sad** because his best friend moved to another town. Everybody feels **sad** sometimes.
■ **sadder, saddest**

## safe

**1. Safe** means not in danger. There was a terrible storm outside, but inside the house everyone was **safe**. **2. Safe** also means not dangerous. Are these berries **safe** to eat?

## said

**Said** is a form of **say.** When Emerson called his friend Michelle on the phone, the first thing Emerson **said** was, "Hello!"

## sail

**1.** A **sail** is a large piece of cloth on a boat. Boats move when the wind hits their **sails**. **2.** To **sail** is to move over water. The boat **sailed** to a small island. **3.** To **sail** also means to make something sail. The captain **sailed** the ship in the ocean.

◆ sail

A **sailor** is a person who **sails** a boat. **Sailors** know a lot about wind and water.

## salad

A **salad** is something you can eat. **Salads** are made from different kinds of vegetables that are cut into pieces and mixed together.

◆ salad

## sale

A **sale** is an offer to sell something for less money than usual. Many stores have **sales** the day after Thanksgiving.

> Something is **for sale** if you can buy it. If something is **on sale**, you can buy it for less money than usual.

## salt

**Salt** is something people put on food. It looks like white sand. Ocean water has **salt** in it.

> **Salty** means something has a lot of salt in it. My soup tastes too **salty.**

## same

To be the **same** means to be alike in every way. **Same** is the opposite of **different.** The boats are all white and red. The colors are the **same.**

◆ same

## sand

**Sand** is made of tiny grains of rock. It covers beaches at the edge of lakes or oceans. **Sand** can feel rough or soft. Tovah and Leonardo's mother helped them build a castle made of **sand.**

◆ sand

## sandwich

A **sandwich** is a kind of food. It is two pieces of bread with meat, cheese, peanut butter, or other foods in between. Many students in our class eat **sandwiches** for lunch.

◆ sandwich

## sang

**Sang** is a form of **sing.** Elizabeth learned a new song yesterday. She **sang** it all day long. Her friends liked it so much they **sang** it too.

## sank

Sank is a form of sink. The divers explored the ship that sank hundreds of years ago.

## sat

Sat is a form of sit. Perry sat on the floor while he played with marbles.

## Saturday

Saturday is a day of the week. Saturday comes after Friday and before Sunday.

## sauce

Sauce is a thick liquid that is put on food to make it taste better. Cheese sauce tastes good on macaroni. Other sauces are made from tomatoes and apples.

## saucer

A saucer is a small dish that isn't very deep. It usually fits under a cup. People sometimes put milk into saucers for cats to drink.

◆ saucer

## save

1. To save means to make someone or something safe. Firefighters often save people's lives. 2. To save also means to keep and not use. Lila saves a little money every week. She has saved enough to buy a kite.

## saw

◆ saw

1. A saw is a tool. It is made of a flat piece of metal with a handle at one end. The edge of the metal piece has sharp points that are called teeth. Saws are used to cut wood, metal, and plastic.
2. Saw is a form of see. Erin looked out the window and saw two squirrels in the front yard.

## say

1. To say means to speak words. When Jacob answers the telephone, he says, "Hello!"
2. To say also means to tell us something that is not spoken. The sign says the store opens at 8:00. The recipe says to add salt. ■ said

## scale

A scale is an object that weighs people or things. The scales at the supermarket are for weighing fruits and vegetables.

◆ scale

## scare

To **scare** means to make afraid. The thunder **scared** the cat.

## scarecrow

A **scarecrow** is something outside that looks like a person wearing old clothes. **Scarecrows** are put in fields or gardens to scare birds away from the plants.

◆ scarecrow

## scarf

A **scarf** is a piece of cloth that you wear around your neck or head. The teacher helped the children put on their coats and **scarves** before they went outside to play. ■ **scarves**

## school

**School** is a place where students learn from teachers. Most **schools** are open from September until June.

A **schoolyard** is the area around a **school** where children can play.

## science

**Science** is what people know about nature and about how things in the world work. Facts about the earth, oceans, weather, stars, plants, and electricity are all parts of **science.**

A **scientist** is a person whose job is to learn about **science.** **Scientists** do experiments to find out what is true.

## scissors

**Scissors** are a kind of tool. They are used to cut paper or cloth. Two pieces of metal are joined to make one pair of **scissors.** Each piece has a sharp edge and a hole for your fingers.

◆ scissors

## score

A **score** is a number that tells how well you perform at a game or on a test. Our football team had the winning **score** at the end of the game.

A **scoreboard** is a large sign that shows the **score** of a game.

## scrap

A **scrap** is a small piece of something. There were **scraps** of paper on the floor after we used scissors to make paper stars.

## scratch

**1.** To **scratch** means to make marks with something hard. A rock can **scratch** a piece of glass. **2.** To **scratch** also means to rub hard with fingernails or claws. Ariel **scratched** her skin when it itched. The cat is **scratching** herself with her claws.

## scrub

To **scrub** means to clean by rubbing hard. My parents **scrubbed** the plastic pool before we could use it.
■ **scrubbed**

## sea

**Sea** is another word for **ocean.** Many years ago, pirates sailed the **seas** looking for adventure and treasure.

The **seashore** is the land that is at the edge of an ocean or **sea.** Some **seashores** are covered with rocks, and others are covered with sand.

## seal

**1.** A **seal** is a kind of animal. It has smooth fur. **Seals** swim in the ocean and eat fish. **2.** To **seal** means to close tight. My mom **sealed** the bag so that the cereal inside would stay fresh.

◆ seal

## search

To **search** for something is to look for it in many places. We **searched** for the ball in the tall grass beside the field.

## season

A **season** is a part of the year. There are four **seasons** that come every year. They are winter, spring, summer, and fall.

## seat

A **seat** is anywhere you can sit. Matthew found a **seat** at the back of the room.

Chairs, benches, and sofas are all kinds of **seats.** What are some other kinds of **seats?**

(A) (B) (C) (D) (E) (F) (G) (H) (I) (J) (K) (L) (M)

## second

**1.** A **second** is a very short amount of time. Lightning flashes in about a **second.** There are 60 **seconds** in one minute. **2. Second** is next after first. The **second** letter of the alphabet is **B.**

## secret

A **secret** is something nobody else knows. Jordana kept the **secret** about who won the class election. It is hard for me to keep **secrets.**

## see

**1.** To **see** is to know what something is like by using your eyes. Did you **see** the beautiful sunset yesterday? Have you **seen** the new movie? **2.** To **see** also means to understand. I **see** why my teacher said the test would be hard. ■ **saw, seen**

See sounds the same as **sea.**

## seed

A **seed** is a hard part of a plant. New plants grow from **seeds.** Many fruits have **seeds** inside them.

◆ seed

## seem

To **seem** means to be the way that something is or how it makes you feel. This spot by the lake **seems** like a good place to have a picnic.

## seen

**Seen** is a form of **see.** Danielle likes to look at birds. She has **seen** several dozen different kinds of birds.

## seesaw

A **seesaw** is something to play on. **Seesaws** are long boards with one person sitting on each end. When one end goes up, the other end goes down.

◆ seesaw

## sell

To **sell** means to give something for money. Donald **sells** glasses of juice outside his house on hot days. ■ **sold**

The opposite of **sell** is **buy.** When my friends **sell** lemonade, my mother **buys** some for me.

## send

To **send** means to make someone or something go somewhere. Hasreet likes to **send** letters to her friends. Frank's mother **sent** him to the store to buy some bread. ■ **sent**

## sentence

A **sentence** is a group of words. Books are usually written in **sentences.**

## separate

To **separate** means to put things apart. Ezra **separated** the white clothes from the colored clothes in the drawer.

## September

**September** is a month of the year. It has 30 days. **September** comes after August and before October.

## serious

**1. Serious** means that you are not being funny. Brett was **serious** when he said I couldn't borrow his new book. **2. Serious** also means being very interested in something. Kayla is a **serious** student who always does well in school.

## serve

To **serve** means to give food or drinks to someone. Please **serve** me a slice of pie.

## set

**1.** A **set** is a group of things that go together. Casey's mother has one **set** of blue dishes and two **sets** of white ones. **2.** To **set** means to put somewhere. Rafi **set** the plate on the table. **3.** To **set** also means to go below the part of the sky that you see. It was such a fine evening that everyone went out to watch the sun **set.**

## settler

A **settler** is one of the first people to live in an area. The **settlers** liked the land because it was good for farming.

## seven

**Seven** is one more than six. **Seven** is written **7.** $6 + 1 = 7.$

## several

**Several** means more than two or three. Stacey has **several** hobbies.

## sew

To **sew** is to use a needle and thread to join cloth with another piece of cloth or a button. Joey **sewed** a button on his shirt. May has **sewn** a patch on her pants. ■ **sewn**

◆ sew

## shack

A **shack** is a very small building. We keep tools in a **shack** in our backyard.

## shade

**1. Shade** is a place that is not in the sun's light. It is usually cooler in the **shade**. **2.** A **shade** is a cover for a window that keeps light out. When we go to sleep, we pull down the **shades** in our room.

> When a place is in the **shade,** it is called **shady.** I sat under the trees in the park because it was **shady** there.

## shadow

A **shadow** is a dark area where the sun cannot shine. When there is a light behind you, you see your **shadow** in front. When the light is in front of you, your **shadow** is behind. On the beach, we could see the **shadows** of our umbrella and chairs.

◆ shadow

## shake

**1.** To **shake** means to make something go up and down or from side to side very quickly. Sid **shakes** the bottle to mix up the orange juice. After he has **shaken** the bottle, he pours the juice into a glass. **2.** To **shake** your head is to move your head from side to side or up and down. People **shake** their heads from side to side to say no.

■ **shook, shaken**

> A **saltshaker** is a small container that holds **salt** and has small holes on top. When you turn it upside-down and **shake** it, salt falls out.

## shall

**Shall** is another word for **will**. We **shall** play tennis tomorrow.

## shallow

**Shallow** means that there is little space between the top and bottom of something. I like to swim in **shallow** water.

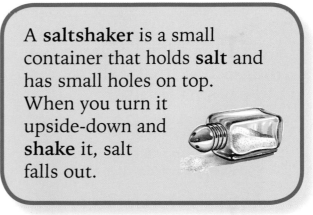

◆ shallow

## shape

**1.** The **shape** of something is what it is like on the outside. Baseballs and basketballs have round **shapes.** A box has the **shape** of a square or rectangle. **2.** To **shape** is to give a shape to something. Alejandro **shaped** a piece of clay into a ball.

## share

To **share** means to let someone have or use something. Rick **shared** his crayons with me.

## shark

A **shark** is a kind of large fish. **Sharks** have many sharp teeth and eat smaller fish.

◆ shark

## sharp

To be **sharp** is to have a point or a thin edge that cuts. Some knives have **sharp** edges.

## she

**She** means a female person. Ms. Perez lives on our block. **She** is our neighbor.

## shed

A **shed** is a small building used to store things. Many people keep shovels and other tools in **sheds** in their yards.

## sheep

A **sheep** is a kind of animal. It is covered with wool. **Sheep** are raised for their wool and their meat. ▪ **sheep**

## sheet

**1.** A **sheet** is a large cloth shaped like a rectangle that you put on a bed. I have green cotton **sheets** on my bed. **2.** A **sheet** is also a single piece of paper. We need ten **sheets** of white paper for our writing project.

## shell

A **shell** is a hard cover on the outside of something. Eggs, nuts, and turtles all have **shells.**

A **seashell** is a **shell** that you find on the beach. **Seashells** were once part of small animals.

## shelter

A **shelter** is a safe place for a person or an animal to stay. **Shelters** protect us from rain and other kinds of bad weather.

A B C D E F G H I J K L M

## shine

To **shine** is to send out a bright light. The sun **shines** every day when there are no clouds.
- **shone**

## ship

A **ship** is a big boat. It sails in deep water. Large **ships** can carry many people across the ocean.

## shirt

A **shirt** is a kind of clothing. People wear **shirts** on the top part of their bodies. Many **shirts** have buttons.

◆ shirt

## shoe

A **shoe** is something that covers a foot. It may be made of leather, cloth, or plastic. **Shoes** come in pairs.

◆ shoe

A **shoelace** is a string that helps a **shoe** fit on your foot. Allegra knows how to tie her **shoelaces.**

## shone

**Shone** is a form of **shine.** The moon **shone** in the sky all night.

## shook

**Shook** is a form of **shake.** Catalina **shook** the bottle until the juice was all mixed up. When she asked Stan if he wanted any of the juice, he **shook** his head to say no.

## shoot

**1.** To **shoot** is to go up or out quickly. Rockets **shoot** up into the air. **2.** To **shoot** also means to make something go quickly toward something else. Ross **shoots** a basketball at the basket. ■ **shot**

## shop

**1.** A **shop** is a small store. There are book **shops,** flower **shops,** hat **shops,** barber **shops,** and many other kinds of **shops.**
**2.** To **shop** is to go to a store to buy things. My uncle **shops** at the supermarket for food.
- **shopped**

A **shopper** is a person who **shops.** Cho was one of the first **shoppers** at the new mall.

## shore

The **shore** is the land at the edge of the water. Oceans, lakes, ponds, and rivers all have **shores**.

## short

**1. Short** is the opposite of **tall**. Ponies are **short** horses.
**2. Short** is also the opposite of **long**. I have **short** hair.
**3. Short** means a small amount when we talk about time. It only took Jo a **short** time to do her homework.

## shot

**1. Shot** is a form of **shoot**. I **shot** the ball into the basket.
**2.** A **shot** is something you shoot. The player tried three **shots** before he got one in the basket.

## should

**Should** means that people want something to happen. Everyone **should** be in the room when class starts.

## shoulder

A **shoulder** is a part of the body. It is between your neck and your arm. My father put the jacket over his **shoulders**.

◆ shore

## shout

To **shout** is to talk in a loud voice. Ken **shouted** so that his friend could hear him across the street.

The opposite of **shout** is **whisper**. Jim **shouted** in the library, and his teacher asked him to **whisper** instead.

◆ shot

## shovel

A **shovel** is a tool. It is made of a wide piece of metal or plastic joined to a long handle. **Shovels** are used to dig holes and to move dirt and snow. Zac lifted a big ball of snow with his **shovel**.

◆ shovel

A B C D E F G H I J K L M

## show

**1.** To **show** means to let someone see. Meredith **showed** Rina her books. **2.** To **show** also means to teach. Lizzie **showed** Edwin how to skate. **3.** A **show** is a story that you see or hear on television or radio, at the movies, or in a theater. I watch my favorite television **shows** on Friday afternoons. ▪ **shown**

> **Show** rhymes with **throw.**

## shut

To **shut** means to close. Marina opened the door and came into the house. Then she **shut** the door behind her. ▪ **shut**

## shy

To be **shy** means to find it hard to talk to people. **Shy** people are often quiet.

## sick

To be **sick** is to have something wrong with you. Sometimes when you are **sick,** your head or your stomach hurts. Doctors and nurses take care of **sick** people.

## side

A **side** is a flat part of the outside of something. A piece of paper has two **sides.** A square has four **sides.**

## sidewalk

A **sidewalk** is a narrow path or road where people can walk. Usually there are **sidewalks** along the sides of streets. Kayla likes to take her dog for walks on the **sidewalk** in her neighborhood.

◆ sidewalk

## sign

**1.** A **sign** is a symbol. The **signs** for plus and minus are + and –. **2.** A **sign** is also a flat piece of metal, wood, or plastic with a message printed on it. Road **signs** are placed where people who are driving can see them.

◆ sign

> There are many **signs** that you can make with your arms and hands. One kind is called **sign language.** **Sign language** is sometimes used by people who are deaf.

## silent

To be **silent** is to make no sound at all. Nat tried to stay **silent** so his sister would not find him hiding behind the door.

> **Silent** letters are letters in words that are written but not spoken. The **g** in the word **sign** is **silent.**

## silk

**Silk** is a soft, fancy kind of cloth. Becca has a **silk** shirt that she only wears on special days.

## silly

To be **silly** means to act funny. Raj and his friends were giggling and running around the room. They were acting **silly.**
■ **sillier, silliest**

## silver

**Silver** is a kind of metal. **Silver** is used to make coins, jewelry, and other things.

## simple

**Simple** means not fancy. Helen can make a **simple** drawing of a person with only lines and circles.

◆ simple

## since

**Since** means after. We have not had any rain **since** last month. The weather has been dry **since** then.

## sing

To **sing** is to make music with your voice. Blair likes to **sing** lullabies to her little sister. Yesterday in the car I **sang** along to the radio. ■ **sang, sung**

> A **singer** is a person who **sings.** Most bands have **singers** and people who play instruments.

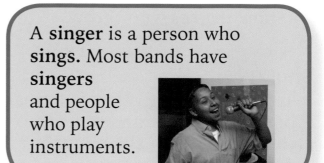

## single

**Single** means only one. Our class walked in a **single** line when we entered the gym. Jordan ate a **single** slice of pizza for lunch.

◆ single

(A) (B) (C) (D) (E) (F) (G) (H) (I) (J) (K) (L) (M)

## sink

**1.** To **sink** is to go under the surface of a liquid. Alex's toy boat has a hole in it. It has started to **sink**. **2.** A **sink** is a container that has pipes that water can come out of. You can wash things at a **sink**. I washed my hands at the **sink** before we ate dinner. ■ **sank, sunk**

## sip

To **sip** means to drink in small amounts. I **sip** hot drinks so that I don't burn my mouth. ■ **sipped**

## sister

A **sister** is a girl who has the same parent or parents as somebody else. Alec and his **sisters** made supper for their parents.

## sit

To **sit** is to rest your weight on something. Shawn has his own chair to **sit** on at his desk. Last night he **sat** there so he could use his computer. ■ **sat**

## six

**Six** is one more than five. **Six** is written **6.** 5 + 1 = **6.**

## size

The **size** of something is how big it is. All tennis balls are the same **size.** People and clothes come in many different **sizes.**

## skate

**1.** A **skate** is a kind of shoe. It has a long piece of metal or small wheels on the bottom. People wear **skates** to go fast on ice, on the sidewalk, or on the floor. **2.** To **skate** is to move on skates. Ruth is learning how to **skate.**

◆ skate

A **roller skate** is a **skate** with wheels that is used to **skate** on floors or sidewalks. **Ice skates** have a sharp edge for **skating** on ice.

## ski

**1.** A **ski** is a long, narrow piece of wood, metal, or plastic. People wear **skis** on their feet to go fast on snow. **2.** To **ski** means to move over the snow on skis. Connor **skied** down a hill.

◆ ski

## skin

The **skin** is the outside part of people, animals, and many plants. The **skin** protects what is inside. Banana **skins** are yellow.

## skip

**1.** To **skip** means to move by hopping on one foot and then the other. We like to **skip** to the playground after school.
**2.** To **skip** also means not to do something that you usually do. I **skipped** the school picnic because I visited my cousins.
■ **skipped**

## skirt

A **skirt** is a kind of clothing that hangs down from the middle of the body. Rosa wore a **skirt** when she danced in the school play.

◆ skirt

## skunk

A **skunk** is a small animal. It has a big tail and a white stripe on its back. **Skunks** can make a very strong smell that protects them from other animals.

◆ skunk

## sky

The **sky** is the space far above the ground. It is blue during the day when there are no clouds. We see the sun, the moon, and the stars in the **sky.** ■ **skies**

## skyscraper

A **skyscraper** is a very tall building. Most big cities have many **skyscrapers.**

◆ skyscraper

## sled

A **sled** is something you ride on to go over the snow. **Sleds** are made of wood, metal, or plastic.

## sleep

**Sleep** is a time when your body is resting. Most people **sleep** in beds at night. Angela **sleeps** under a warm quilt. ■ **slept**

When you are **sleepy,** you are awake but very tired.

Ⓐ Ⓑ Ⓒ Ⓓ Ⓔ Ⓕ Ⓖ Ⓗ Ⓘ Ⓙ Ⓚ Ⓛ Ⓜ

## sleeve

A **sleeve** is a part of a shirt, sweater, or coat that covers your arm. In the winter Christopher wears shirts with long **sleeves,** but in the summer he likes to wear shirts with short **sleeves.**

◆ sleeve

## slept

**Slept** is a form of **sleep.** Ginny and Miranda **slept** at their friend's house last night.

## slice

**1.** A **slice** is a piece that you cut from something. Alejandro likes to eat **slices** of apple as a snack. **2.** To **slice** is to cut something into pieces. Please **slice** the pumpkin pie so we can eat it!

◆ slice

## slide

**1.** To **slide** is to move in a smooth way across something slippery. We **slid** down the hill on our sled. **2.** A **slide** is also an object made for playing on by sliding down it. The playground has three **slides.** ■ slid

◆ slide

## slip

To **slip** means to slide by accident. People often fall down after they **slip.** My father **slipped** and fell because the floor was wet. ■ **slipped**

> When something can make you **slip,** we say that it is **slippery.**

## slipper

A **slipper** is a kind of shoe. **Slippers** are usually worn inside the house.

## slow

To be **slow** means to take a long time. Turtles move very **slow.**

> **Slow** is the opposite of **fast.**

## small

**1. Small** means filling not much space. We would like two **small** jars instead of one big one. Mice are **small** animals. **2. Small** also means letters of the alphabet that are not capital letters. The letters **a** and **b** are **small** letters. The letters **A** and **B** are capital letters.

> **Small** is the opposite of **big.** Bees and spiders are **small.** Elephants and rhinoceroses are **big.**

## smell

**1.** To **smell** is to know what something is like by using your nose. Billy **smelled** the smoke in the kitchen when the food burned in the oven. **2.** A **smell** is what something is like when you smell it. Flowers often have a pleasant **smell.** Many nice **smells** come from my garden. **3.** To **smell** also means to have a smell. The bread that we bake in the oven **smells** wonderful.

## smile

**1.** A **smile** is a happy look on a person's face. The ends of the mouth turn up, and the skin near the eyes wrinkles. When I told the jokes, there were a lot of **smiles** in the room. **2.** To **smile** is to put a smile on your face. Fatima **smiled** when I took her picture.

◆ smile

## smoke

**Smoke** is something made by things that burn. It looks like a cloud. **Smoke** can be white, gray, or black. When we start a fire in our fireplace, **smoke** comes out of the chimney.

> A room that is full of **smoke** is called **smoky.** It is hard to breathe in a **smoky** room.

## smooth

To be **smooth** is to feel even and have no rough spots. A piece of glass in a window is **smooth.** The top of our kitchen table is **smooth.**

(A) (B) (C) (D) (E) (F) (G) (H) (I) (J) (K) (L) (M)

## snack

A **snack** is something you eat sometimes between meals. My favorite **snacks** are carrots and peanuts.

## snail

A **snail** is a very small animal. It has a soft body and a hard shell. **Snails** can live on land or on the bottom of the sea. They are very slow.

◆ snail

## snake

A **snake** is a kind of reptile. It has a long, narrow body and no arms or legs. Most **snakes** are short, but some can be very long.

## sneaker

A **sneaker** is a kind of shoe. It has rubber on the bottom and cloth on the top. People wear **sneakers** when they run or play sports.

◆ sneaker

## sneeze

**1.** A **sneeze** happens when your nose itches. The air comes out of your nose and mouth very fast. Some people have three or four **sneezes** at a time. **2.** To **sneeze** is to make a sneeze. Ava **sneezed** because she has a cold.

## snow

**1. Snow** is tiny pieces of frozen water that fall from the clouds. In some places, **snow** covers the ground in winter. **2.** To **snow** means to fall as pieces of frozen water. When it **snows,** we like to go skiing.

When there is **snow,** it is fun to build a **snowman.** The **snowman** will look funny when it begins to melt.

## so

**1. So** means very. Yasir thought of a joke. It was **so** funny that he could not stop laughing for several minutes. **2. So** can mean also. Isabel and Patty read the same book. Isabel liked it, and **so** did Patty. **3. So** also means that one thing causes another thing to happen. Tanya forgot her umbrella, **so** she got wet when it rained.

## soap

**Soap** helps take dirt off things when it is mixed with water. Rochelle uses **soap** and water to wash her hands.

## soar

To **soar** is to fly or glide in the air. Jack likes to watch birds **soar** in the sky.

**Soar** sounds the same as **sore**.

## soccer

**Soccer** is a sport. In **soccer** two teams kick a ball up and down a field. They may not touch the ball with their hands. Katie and Jenna play **soccer** on different teams.

◆ soccer

## sock

A **sock** is a kind of clothing. People wear **socks** on their feet, inside their shoes.

## sofa

A **sofa** is a kind of furniture that you sit on. **Sofas** are wider than chairs. **Sofa** is another word for **couch**.

◆ sock

## soft

**1.** When something is **soft,** it is easy to change its shape with your fingers, and it does not scratch other things. **Soft** is the opposite of **hard.** Fur and cotton are **soft. 2. Soft** also means quiet. **Soft** is the opposite of **loud.** When Harrison is in the library, he tries to be quiet. He speaks in a **soft** voice.

**Soften** means to become **soft**. The clay **softened** when we added water to it.

## soil

**Soil** is the top part of the ground. Most plants grow in **soil.**

## sold

**Sold** is a form of **sell.** Chico's father sells cars. Last week he **sold** four cars.

## solid

**1. Solid** means hard. Things that are **solid** always have a shape of some kind. Things made of wood and steel are **solid. 2.** A **solid** is something that is hard. Ice is a **solid,** but water is a liquid, and air is a gas.

(A) (B) (C) (D) (E) (F) (G) (H) (I) (J) (K) (L) (M)

## solve

To **solve** means to find the answer. After a few minutes we **solved** the mystery of my lost glasses. I had left them in the car.

## some

**Some** means an amount that is more than a little but less than a lot. Brenda has not read most of the books in the library. But she has read **some** of them. The high mountains have **some** snow on them.

◆ some

## somebody

**Somebody** means a person, but you don't know or don't say who it is. **Somebody** from our school won first prize.

## somehow

**Somehow** means in some way or another. **Somehow** I found the glove I lost last week. Rain is getting through the roof **somehow**.

## someone

**Someone** is another word for **somebody**. **Someone** turned on the radio in my room while I was outside.

## something

**Something** means a thing, but you don't know or don't say what it is. The baby is hungry. She wants **something** to eat. **Something** is making a noise outside.

## sometimes

**Sometimes** means at some times but not all times. **Sometimes** it rains during the winter, and **sometimes** it snows.

## somewhere

**Somewhere** means a place, but you don't know or don't say where it is. I left my jacket **somewhere** in the park. We want to go **somewhere** that is warm for vacation.

## son

A **son** is a person's male child. Harun's parents have two **sons**. One is Harun, and the other is Fareed.

**Son** sounds the same as **sun**.

## song

A **song** is what someone sings or the music that someone plays with an instrument. Some **songs** are written for a lot of voices singing together. Other **songs** are written only for instruments to play.

## soon

**Soon** means in a short time. It is almost time for supper. We will be eating **soon.**

## sore

To be **sore** means to feel pain in part of your body. My legs were **sore** after walking all day.

## sorry

To be **sorry** is to feel sad about something. Maryam was **sorry** that Nathaniel was sick.

■ **sorrier, sorriest**

## sound

**Sound** is anything that you hear. Wind, thunder, dogs, and trains all make different **sounds.**

Words have **sounds** when you say them. When two words **sound** the same, they have the same **sound.** To **sound out** a word means to say the **sounds** of the letters slowly.

## soup

**Soup** is a kind of food. It is made with water and pieces of vegetables, meat, or other things. Usually, **soup** is hot when you eat it. You eat **soup** from a bowl with a spoon.

◆ soup

## sour

**Sour** is a kind of taste. Lemon juice tastes **sour.** Those apples aren't ripe yet. They are too **sour** to eat.

## south

**South** is a direction. It is the opposite of **north.** If you look at where the sun rises, **south** is to your right.

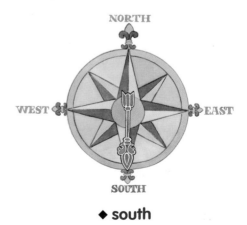

◆ south

(A) (B) (C) (D) (E) (F) (G) (H) (I) (J) (K) (L) (M)

## space

1. A **space** is a place where nothing is. There are **spaces** between the words on this page.
2. **Space** is everywhere outside of the earth. The sun, moon, and stars are in **space**.

◆ space

## speak

To **speak** is to make the sounds of words with your mouth. Sometimes Phil **speaks** in a soft voice. Other times he **speaks** loudly. ■ **spoke, spoken**

## special

**Special** means important and not like all the rest. Holidays and birthdays are **special** days.

## spell

To **spell** is to put letters together to make words. Nan knows how to **spell** most of the words in this book.

> A **spelling bee** is a contest where people take turns **spelling** words.

## spend

To **spend** means to pay money to buy things. Andreas often **spends** his money on books. Irene **spent** most of her money on gifts. ■ **spent**

## spice

A **spice** is something that adds flavor to food. Ginger and pepper are **spices**.

> Something that has lots of **spice** in it is called **spicy**.

## spider

A **spider** is a very small animal with eight legs. **Spiders** are not insects. But they catch insects in the webs they make.

◆ spider

## spill

To **spill** means to let something fall from a container by accident. I **spilled** some juice when I dropped the cup.

◆ spill

(N) (O) (P) (Q) (R) (S) (T) (U) (V) (W) (X) (Y) (Z) **213**

## spin

**1.** To **spin** means to turn around in a circle. The wheels of my bicycle were still **spinning** when it fell on the street. **2.** To **spin** also means to make a web or cocoon. The spider **spun** a big web near the shed. ▪ **spun**

## splash

To **splash** means to hit a liquid and make it fly through the air. Leo **splashed** in the pool.

◆ **splash**

## spoke

**Spoke** is a form of **speak.** We could not hear the teacher in the back of the room, so he **spoke** louder.

## spoken

**Spoken** is a form of **speak.** Eleni has **spoken** with a lot of people about the winter concert today.

## spoon

A **spoon** is a tool to eat with. It looks like a tiny bowl with a handle. People eat soup and cereal with **spoons.**

## sport

A **sport** is a kind of game. Baseball, football, hockey, tennis, basketball, and soccer are all different **sports.**

## spot

**1.** A **spot** is a small mark that is a different color from the area around it. Some animals are covered with **spots.**
**2.** A **spot** is also a place. Lance found a very nice **spot** to sit down.

◆ **spot**

## spread

**1.** To **spread** means to put something over a wide area. My uncle **spread** the blanket on the sand. **2. Spread** also means to put over a surface in a smooth and even way. My sister used the knife to **spread** jelly on her bread. ▪ **spread**

## spring

**Spring** is a season. It comes after winter and before summer. The weather gets warmer and flowers begin to grow in the **spring.**

The days of **spring** are called **springtime.**

(A) (B) (C) (D) (E) (F) (G) (H) (I) (J) (K) (L) (M)

## spun

**Spun** is a form of **spin**. The propeller of the helicopter **spun** while the helicopter flew.

## square

A **square** is a shape. All four sides of a **square** are the same length.

◆ square

## squeeze

To **squeeze** means to push on the outside of something. Callie **squeezed** the tube until toothpaste came out.

## squirrel

A **squirrel** is a small animal. It has gray or red fur and a big tail. **Squirrels** live in trees.

## stable

**1.** A **stable** is a building on a farm where horses, cows, or other animals are kept. Sometimes animals sleep in the **stable**. **2. Stable** means that something will not fall down. The shed we built is strong and **stable**. We will have it for many years.

## stack

A **stack** is a pile of things, one on top of another. We put the books in **stacks** on the desk.

◆ stack

## stairs

**Stairs** are a group of steps. People walk up and down **stairs** to get from one floor of a building to another.

## stamp

A **stamp** is a small piece of paper with words and numbers and a picture on it. People buy **stamps** to stick on letters and packages they send through the mail.

## stand

To **stand** is to keep your body straight and rest all your weight on your feet. Objects can **stand** on their legs or bases. Nate's desk **stands** by the door.
■ **stood**

## star

**1.** A **star** is a large amount of burning gas that is very far away. It looks like a tiny dot of light in the sky at night. There are millions and millions of **stars**. Our sun is a **star**, too. **2.** A **star** is also a shape. It has five or six points. Our country's flag has 50 **stars**. **3.** A **star** can also be an important person in movies, plays, or shows. **Stars** are people that almost everybody knows about.

## stare

To **stare** is to look for a long time at something. Felix **stared** at the rainbow.

## start

**1.** To **start** is to do something when you have not been doing it before. Graham **started** to walk home from the library at three o'clock. **2.** To **start** also means to begin working. The engine in a car **starts** when you turn a key.

> The opposite of **start** is **finish**. I **started** my project yesterday and **finished** it today.

## state

**1.** A **state** is a part of a country. Our country is divided into 50 **states**. **2.** To **state** means to say. The mayor **stated** that the roads would be closed after the storm.

## station

A **station** is a special place or building. A train **station** is a place where trains stop so that people can get on and off. A gas **station** is where people buy gasoline for their cars. Television shows are made at television **stations**. The police can be found at a police **station**.

## statue

A **statue** is an object that is a kind of art. **Statues** usually look like people or animals. **Statues** are made from stone, clay, wood, or metal and can be small or large.

◆ statue

## stay

To **stay** means to be in a place and not go away. Isabella, Michael, and Charlotte **stayed** at school in the afternoon to play baseball with some other children.

## steady

**Steady** means not shaking. Benjamin's father held the ladder **steady** while Benjamin and his friends climbed up to the tree house. ■ **steadier, steadiest**

## steak

A **steak** is a piece of meat. Most **steaks** are made of beef. They are often cooked over a fire outside or in the oven.

> **Steak** rhymes with **lake**.

(A) (B) (C) (D) (E) (F) (G) (H) (I) (J) (K) (L) (M)

## steal

To **steal** means to take something that belongs to someone else without asking first and without meaning to give it back. Somebody **stole** Emma's lunch from her locker.
■ **stole, stolen**

## steam

**Steam** is water that has become a gas. Water changes into **steam** when it becomes hot. There was **steam** coming out of the kettle when the water boiled.

◆ steam

> A place that is full of **steam** is called **steamy.**

## steel

**Steel** is a metal. It is made from melted iron. **Steel** is hard and strong. It is used to make bridges, buildings, and other things.

## stem

A **stem** is a part of a plant that usually grows up from the ground. **Stems** are long and thin. They let water go up to the leaves.

## step

**1.** A **step** is lifting one foot and putting it down. Tall people with long legs can take big **steps. 2.** A **step** is also a flat place where you can put your foot to go up or down. Carla walks down the **steps** to the basement. **3.** To **step** is to move one foot in front of the other and walk. Erik **stepped** forward and raised his hand. ■ **stepped**

## stick

**1.** A **stick** is a piece of wood. Many **sticks** are old, dry branches of trees. Bob's dog likes to play with **sticks. 2.** To **stick** is to push into. Ellie **sticks** her foot into the water to see how cold it is. **3.** To **stick** out means not to be in all the way. The branches **stick** out from the trunk of a tree. **4.** To **stick** together means to put two things against each other so they do not come apart. Ricardo used glue to **stick** two pieces of paper together. ■ **stuck**

◆ stick

## still

**1. Still** means that something has not stopped. My sister was mad at me yesterday. She is **still** mad at me today. **2. Still** also means not moving. When there is no wind, the water in the lake is very **still**. Please stand **still** while your picture is being taken.

## sting

To **sting** means to use a sharp point to hurt someone. If you go near a hive, a bee may **sting** you. ■ **stung**

> The part of a bee or other insect that stings is called a **stinger**.

## stir

To **stir** means to mix something by placing an object in it and moving that object in a circle. Kayla **stirred** the flour and sugar together. ■ **stirred**

◆ stir

## stomach

A **stomach** is a part of the body. The food we eat goes into our **stomachs**.

## stone

A **stone** is a small piece of rock. When the water in the river gets low, we can see a lot of **stones**.

◆ stone

## stood

**Stood** is a form of **stand**. Athena's mother **stood** on a chair to reach some dishes.

## stop

**1.** To **stop** means not to move. Buses **stop** at different places to let people get on and off. **2.** To **stop** something means that you were doing it, but you don't do it now. We **stopped** playing tennis when it started to rain. **3.** To **stop** also means to not let someone do something. The teacher **stopped** us before we put more food in the aquarium. ■ **stopped**

## store

**1.** A **store** is a place where things are sold. You can buy toys in a toy **store**. Some **stores** are very big and have all kinds of things to buy. **2.** To **store** something is to put it away and save it. We **store** furniture in our attic.

A B C D E F G H I J K L M

## storm

A **storm** is a strong wind. **Storms** usually bring rain or snow. Some also have thunder and lightning.

◆ storm

After a **snowstorm,** there is a lot of **snow** on the ground. After **rainstorms,** there are many puddles.

## story

A **story** is a group of words that tell what happened to people and places. **Stories** can be real or they can be made up. I like to hear **stories** about how my parents met. When Dave and his family went camping, they sat by the fire and told scary **stories** about monsters.

■ **stories**

## stove

A **stove** is a machine that makes heat. Food is cooked in pots or pans on top of some **stoves.**

## straight

To be **straight** is to have no turns or curves. The opposite of **straight** is **crooked.** We drove all the way to Sara's house on a **straight** road.

◆ straight

## strange

**Strange** means different and hard to understand. New things often feel **strange** to us until we learn more about them.

## stranger

A **stranger** is someone you do not know. Julie's family moved to a new town. They were **strangers** there until they met some neighbors.

## straw

A **straw** is a long tube made of plastic. People can drink beverages through **straws.** Katy drinks orange juice through a **straw.**

◆ straw

## stream

A **stream** is a narrow path of water. It moves in one direction. **Streams** are not as big as rivers. Our dog loves to play in the **streams** in the park.

## street

A **street** is a road in a city or a town. Large cities have many **streets.** Eamon lives on the same **street** as his friend Angela.

> A **streetlight** is a **light** at the top of a pole outside. **Streetlights** are usually on during the night.

## stretch

**1.** To **stretch** is to change the shape of something by pulling it. Rubber and some kinds of plastic are easy to **stretch.**
**2.** To **stretch** also means to reach with your arms or legs. I had to **stretch** to reach the cabinet. Maddie **stretches** one leg out to the side.

◆ stretch

## string

**String** is used to tie things. It is made from a plant or from a special kind of plastic. **String** comes in many different sizes and colors. Rope is made of many **strings** that are twisted together.

◆ string

## strip

A **strip** is a narrow piece of something. Ribbons are made from **strips** of cloth or paper.

## stripe

A **stripe** is a line of color. The umbrella is covered with **stripes.**

◆ stripe

## strong

**1.** To be **strong** is to have a lot of power. Morty is so **strong** that he can lift two full suitcases.
**2. Strong** also means hard to break. Things made from steel are very **strong.**

> The opposite of **strong** is **weak.** If you exercise, you can turn **weak** muscles into **strong** ones.

(A) (B) (C) (D) (E) (F) (G) (H) (I) (J) (K) (L) (M)

## stuck

**Stuck** is a form of **stick.** Brianne **stuck** a pin into the cushion by accident. Omar **stuck** two pieces of paper together with paste.

## student

A **student** is a person who goes to school to learn. **Students** learn from teachers in classes.

## study

To **study** means to try to learn. People usually read when they **study.** Francie is **studying** for a test. My mother **studied** medicine so that she could become a doctor. ▪ **studies, studied**

## stuff

**Stuff** is any kind of object that is needed or used by people. There is a lot of **stuff** in our classroom to help us learn.

## submarine

A **submarine** is a kind of boat that can travel underwater. **Submarines** are long and narrow.

## subtract

To **subtract** is to take away one number from another number. When you **subtract** four from nine, you get five. – is the symbol for **subtract.** 9 – 4 = 5.

## subway

A **subway** is a train that travels through tunnels underground. **Subways** carry people through large cities.

◆ subway

## such

**1. Such** means so much. Rod went to see his sister dance. He did not know she was **such** a good dancer. **2. Such** as means for example. I like places that have rides, **such** as fairs and carnivals.

## sudden

To be **sudden** is to happen quickly without anyone expecting it. The **sudden** noise was a surprise to us.

> **Suddenly** means that something happens in a **sudden** way. We were having a good time at the picnic, when **suddenly** it began to rain.

## suds

**Suds** are many tiny bubbles made by soap and water. Margie likes to have a lot of **suds** when she washes her hands.

◆ suds

## sugar

**Sugar** is something people put on or in food. It is made of small white or brown grains that are sweet. Many desserts are made with **sugar.**

**Sugar** looks like **salt,** but it tastes very different. **Salt** comes from the earth or the ocean, and **sugar** comes from plants.

## suit

A **suit** is a set of clothes that match. A jacket and pants or a jacket and a skirt made from the same cloth are a **suit.** Some people wear **suits** on special days.

◆ suit

## suitcase

A **suitcase** is a kind of box to carry clothes in when you travel. All **suitcases** have handles, and many have small wheels.

◆ suitcase

## sum

A **sum** is a number that you get when you add two other numbers together. The **sum** of 11 and 9 is 20. We made **sums** of the numbers the teacher gave us.

## summer

**Summer** is a season. It comes after spring and before fall. The weather is often hot during the **summer.** Many schools are closed in **summer.**

## sun

The **sun** is a yellow star. It shines in the sky during the day. The **sun** gives us heat and light.

A **sunny** day is a day when the **sun** is shining. We went on a picnic because it was **sunny** outside.

(A) (B) (C) (D) (E) (F) (G) (H) (I) (J) (K) (L) (M)

## Sunday

**Sunday** is a day of the week. **Sunday** comes after Saturday and before Monday.

## sung

**Sung** is a form of **sing.** Hala has been singing all morning. She has **sung** the songs she knows from many shows.

## sunk

**Sunk** is a form of **sink.** The ship was **sunk** by a terrible storm.

## sunlight

**Sunlight** is light from the sun. **Sunlight** is good for plants and animals.

## sunrise

A **sunrise** is what happens when the sun comes up. There is a **sunrise** every morning, but we can't see it if there are too many clouds.

◆ sunrise

## sunset

A **sunset** is what happens when the sun goes down. During a **sunset**, the sky can change colors. Many people like to go out to watch a beautiful **sunset.**

## supermarket

A **supermarket** is a very big store where food is sold. **Supermarkets** sell all kinds of food.

## supper

**Supper** is a meal. People eat **supper** in the evening.

## suppose

To **suppose** means to think when you do not know for sure. When eleven students were late, we **supposed** it was because the school bus broke down.

## sure

To be **sure** is to know. Addie was **sure** she had time to take the dog for a walk before dinner.

## surface

A **surface** is the outside or top part of something. Boats sail on the **surface** of the ocean. The **surfaces** of a desk and table are smooth. The **surface** of a bed is soft.

## surprise

**1.** A **surprise** is something you do not expect. We thought it would rain today. It was a **surprise** to see the sun in the sky. Mia loves **surprises**. **2.** To **surprise** someone is to do something he or she did not expect. Joe's friends **surprised** him with flowers when he was sick.

If you give someone a **surprise party,** that person does not know about the **party.** We had a **surprise party** for my father on his birthday. When he entered the room, we yelled **"Surprise!"**

## swallow

To **swallow** is to make food go from your mouth to your stomach. Bart's mother tells him to chew his food before he **swallows** it.

## swam

**Swam** is a form of **swim.** Rusty **swam** all the way across the pool. Then he **swam** back.

## swamp

A **swamp** is an area of land that is soft and wet. Frogs, mosquitoes, snakes, and alligators live in **swamps.**

◆ swamp

## swan

A **swan** is a large bird. It is usually white and has a long neck. People like to watch **swans** swimming on ponds and lakes.

◆ swan

## sweater

A **sweater** is a kind of clothing. People wear **sweaters** over their shirts when it is cold outside. **Sweaters** are often made of wool or cotton.

(A) (B) (C) (D) (E) (F) (G) (H) (I) (J) (K) (L) (M)

## sweet

**Sweet** is a kind of taste. Apple juice and cake are **sweet.**

## swim

To **swim** is to go through the water by moving your arms and legs. Tina **swims** in races every month. Some people can **swim** long distances. ■ **swam, swum**

## swing

**1.** To **swing** something is to move it from one side to the other while holding it at one end. Phoebe **swings** her bat to hit the ball. **2.** A **swing** is a seat held up by ropes or chains. Children play on **swings** in playgrounds. ■ **swung**

## swum

**Swum** is a form of **swim.** Asher has been swimming all morning. He must have **swum** about a mile.

## swung

**Swung** is a form of **swing.** Howie and Kat **swung** the rope and Mariana jumped over it.

## symbol

A **symbol** is a mark or design that means something. Letters of the alphabet are **symbols** for sounds. Words are **symbols** for things.

The colors of a traffic light are **symbols.** Red means "stop" and green means "go."

## syrup

**Syrup** is a thick, sweet liquid. It is made from sugar or the juice from some plants. **Syrup** is good to eat on pancakes and waffles.

◆ syrup

# T

## table

A **table** is a kind of furniture. It has a flat top and legs. My family sits at the **table** to eat dinner.

> A **cloth** that covers a **table** is called a **tablecloth.**

## tadpole

A **tadpole** is a young frog. **Tadpoles** hatch from eggs. They are tiny and have tails. Some are black, and some are clear.

◆ tadpole

## tail

A **tail** is a part of the body of some animals. **Tails** can be long or short. An animal's **tail** is at the opposite end from its head.

◆ tail

## take

**1.** To **take** means to move something with your hand. Katherine **takes** an apple out of the refrigerator and eats it. My aunt **took** the sock away from the dog. **2.** To **take** also means to bring with you. Avi **takes** books home from the library to read. **3.** To **take** can also mean to ride. Brayden **takes** the bus to school in the morning. **4.** To **take** a picture means to use a camera to make a photograph. Dahlia has **taken** three pictures of her brother with her new camera. **5.** To **take** also means that something is needed. It **takes** a lot of practice to play the piano well. It **takes** two hours to drive to my cousin's house. **6.** To **take** medicine means to swallow it. The medicine didn't taste good, but I **took** it anyway.
■ **took, taken**

## tale

A **tale** is another word for a story. Graham loves to read **tales** about adventure and magic.

## talent

A talent is something that is easy for you to do well. Raymond has a **talent** for drawing. My **talent** is playing the flute.

> When people have a **talent,** we say they are **talented.** Maia is a **talented** artist.

## talk

To **talk** is to speak to someone. Nicole and Jorge **talked** about the chapter we read.

## tall

To be **tall** means to stand high above the ground. **Tall** is the opposite of **short.** Luis hopes to grow as **tall** as his father.

◆ tall

## tame

To be **tame** means for an animal to do what people want. **Tame** animals make good pets.

## tape

**Tape** is a piece of plastic or paper that has one side that can stick to things. My brother stuck pictures on his wall with **tape.**

## taste

**1.** To **taste** is to use your mouth to find out what something is like. Sally's mother **tasted** the sauce that she made. **2.** To **taste** also means to make your tongue feel some way. Foods **taste** sweet, sour, salty, and bitter. **3.** A **taste** is what something is like when you taste it. Lemons and grapefruits have a sour **taste.** Honey has a sweet **taste.**

## taught

**Taught** is a form of **teach.** Jinko's parents **taught** him how to take photographs.

## taxi

A **taxi** is a car that people pay to ride in. People take **taxis** to go from one place to another.

## teach

To **teach** is to give information so that someone can learn. Nadia **taught** me how to whistle. ■ **taught**

## teacher

A **teacher** is a person who teaches other people. Most **teachers** work in schools.

## team

A **team** is a group of people who work or play together. In many sports two **teams** play against each other.

◆ **team**

A person who is on your **team** is your **teammate**. **Teammates** work together to play the game.

## tear

**1.** A **tear** is a drop of salty liquid that your body makes. **Tears** come out of people's eyes when they cry. **2.** To **tear** is to pull something apart. Lenny **tears** the napkin and gives half of it to Mike. My mother **tore** the cloth to make patches for my pants. **3.** A **tear** is a space you can see after something becomes torn. I had to change clothes because there were **tears** in my dress.

■ **tore, torn**

The **tear** in your eye rhymes with **hear** and **near**. The **tear** in your pants rhymes with **hair** and **pear**.

## teddy bear

A **teddy bear** is a kind of toy. It is soft and looks like a bear. **Teddy bears** can be large or small.

◆ **teddy bear**

## teeth

**Teeth** means more than one **tooth**. People chew food with their **teeth**. When Xavier smiles, you can see his **teeth**.

◆ **teeth**

## telephone

A **telephone** is a small machine that lets people talk from far away. Many **telephones** can be carried with you.

## telescope

A **telescope** is a tool that helps people see things that are far away. **Telescopes** are made of curved pieces of glass or mirrors inside a tube. People use **telescopes** to look at the moon and stars.

## television

A **television** is a machine that uses electricity to show pictures with sounds. A **television** station uses electricity to send the pictures and sounds to **televisions** in people's homes.

> A short way of saying **television** is **TV**. Teddy's favorite movie is on **TV** tonight.

## tell

**1.** To **tell** is to talk about something. After Curtis did a magic trick, he **told** his friends how he did it. **2.** To **tell** also means to know. Susana can **tell** that winter is coming because the days are getting shorter. **3.** To **tell** also means to give information without talking. The clock **tells** the time. This map **tells** us where your street is. ▪ **told**

## temperature

The **temperature** of something is how much heat it has. The inside of an oven has a high **temperature.** Ice and snow have low **temperatures.**

## ten

**Ten** is one more than nine. **Ten** is written **10. 9 + 1 = 10.**

## tennis

**Tennis** is a sport. In **tennis,** people hit a ball back and forth across a wide net.

◆ tennis

## tent

A **tent** is a place to sleep when you camp. **Tents** are large pieces of cloth held up by poles.

◆ tent

## terrible

**Terrible** means very bad. Many trees were broken in the **terrible** storm.

## test

**1.** A **test** is a way to find out how well someone can do something. Teachers often give **tests** in school. **2.** To **test** something is to see if it works well. My parents **tested** the computer in the store before they bought it.

## than

**Than** means that something is being compared to something else. Denny likes summer weather more **than** he likes winter weather.

## thank

To **thank** means to tell someone you are glad they did something for you or gave something to you. Ana **thanked** her friends for the cards they gave her when she was sick.

> People say **"thank you"** or **"thanks"** when they want to **thank** someone. **"Thank you for the birthday present!"**

## Thanksgiving

**Thanksgiving** is a holiday that comes in November. People eat dinner with their families on **Thanksgiving.**

## that

**1. That** means one thing you are looking at or talking about and not something else. Ilene put the blue cotton quilt on her bed. She loves **that** quilt.
**2. That** is also used to put two parts of a sentence together. I told my mother **that** the shed was locked.

## the

**The** tells which one. Ramon is very happy. He won **the** school prize for helping his community.

## theater

A **theater** is a building where people watch movies or plays. Some **theaters** are very large.

## their

**Their** means belonging to them. My sisters couldn't finish **their** homework because they forgot **their** books.

> The word **their** sounds the same as the words **there** and **they're.**

## theirs

**Theirs** means belonging to them. The students all bought some fish for an aquarium. The fish are **theirs.**

## them

**Them** means more than one person, animal, or thing. There are some birds in Angel's yard. He feeds **them** seeds and bread.

## themselves

**Themselves** means them and nobody else. The students wrote the song **themselves.**

(A) (B) (C) (D) (E) (F) (G) (H) (I) (J) (K) (L) (M)

## then

**1. Then** means at that time. It is cold now. But it was not cold last summer. The weather was warm **then**. **2. Then** also means next. Paul pulled his sled up the hill. **Then** he rode back down.

## there

**1. There** means at that place. "Where should I put these logs?" Talia asked her father. He pointed to the fireplace. "Please put them **there**," he said.
**2. There is** and **there are** mean that something can be found. "**There is** a bee in the car!" Steve shouted.

## thermometer

A **thermometer** is a tool that is used to measure temperature. Some **thermometers** show how hot or cold it is outside. Others are used to show the temperatures of people who might be sick.

◆ thermometer

## these

**These** means more than one of **this**. If you will carry those chairs, I will carry **these**.

## they

**They** means more than one. Darcy and Penny ran on the beach. Then **they** dug holes in the sand.

## they're

**They're** is a short way to say **they are**. Chris and Alec are not here yet. **They're** coming later.

## thick

**1. Thick** means big and heavy. Felix found a board so **thick** he could not hit a nail through it. **Thick** is the opposite of **thin**.
**2.** To be **thick** also means to be hard to pour. Honey is **thick**.

◆ thick

If something becomes **thick,** we say that it **thickens.** The tomato sauce **thickened** when my dad added flour to it.

## thin

**1. Thin** means having the top and bottom close together. A piece of paper is **thin**. **Thin** is the opposite of **thick**. **2. Thin** also means the opposite of **fat**. My uncle lost weight. He is **thin** now. ■ **thinner, thinnest**

◆ thin

## thing

**1.** A **thing** is an object, animal, or plant. You can see many interesting **things** in a museum. **2.** A **thing** can also be what someone does. Patty gave Shelby some of her snack. That was a nice **thing** for her to do.

## think

**1.** To **think** means to use your mind. Sunil **thinks** about the book he is reading. My family **thought** about where we would like to go on vacation. **2.** To **think** also means to believe. Eileen **thinks** she will go to the library on Saturday. Cameron **thought** the movie was funny.
■ **thought**

## third

**Third** is next after second. The **third** letter of the alphabet is **C**.

## thirsty

To be **thirsty** is to need to drink. When you are **thirsty,** your mouth feels dry.
■ **thirstier, thirstiest**

## this

**This** means one thing and not something else. It is often something that is near you. Sean likes the hat he is wearing. "**This** is my favorite hat," he says.

## thorn

A **thorn** is a sharp part that grows on the branch or stem of some plants. Roses have **thorns.**

◆ thorn

## those

**Those** means more than one of **that.** I have read these books on the table but not **those** on the couch.

## thought

**1. Thought** is a form of **think**. When the teacher asked a question, Spencer **thought** about his answer before he spoke. **2.** A **thought** is also something a person thinks about. Noor had many happy **thoughts** about her trip to the country last fall.

## thousand

A **thousand** is a number. It is written **1,000**. There are ten hundreds in a **thousand**. **Thousands** of people went to watch the football game.

(A) (B) (C) (D) (E) (F) (G) (H) (I) (J) (K) (L) (M)

## thread

**Thread** is very thin string. It comes in many different colors. People sew clothes with a needle and **thread**.

◆ thread

## three

**Three** is one more than two. **Three** is written **3.** 2 + 1 = **3.**

## threw

**Threw** is a form of **throw**. Tad **threw** a tennis ball against the barn until his arm got tired.

## throat

**1.** The **throat** is a part of the body. In the inside of your body, the **throat** is past the inside of your mouth. When you swallow food, it goes through your **throat**. **2.** On the outside of your body, the **throat** is the front part of your neck. When the weather is cold, you can cover your **throat** with a scarf.

## throne

A **throne** is a special chair that a king or queen sits on. **Thrones** are usually big and fancy.

**Throne** sounds the same as **thrown**.

## through

**Through** means from one side to the other. Jess walked **through** a field to get to school. A bird flew into our house **through** an open window.

**Through** sounds the same as **threw**.

## throw

To **throw** is to make something go through the air. The baseball player **throws** the ball. ▪ **threw, thrown**

◆ throw

## thumb

A **thumb** is a part of the hand. **Thumbs** are short, strong fingers. People have one **thumb** on each hand.

◆ thumb

## thunder

**Thunder** is a loud noise in the air. It is made when lightning flashes.

## Thursday

**Thursday** is a day of the week. **Thursday** comes after Wednesday and before Friday.

## ticket

A **ticket** is a small piece of paper that lets you enter a place. When Lauren and Zoya went to the theater, they bought two **tickets** to see the movie.

## tie

**1.** To **tie** is to keep things together with string or rope. Arun keeps his boat **tied** to the dock. **2.** To **tie** also means to make knots in string, rope, or ribbon. Joy **ties** her shoelaces to keep her shoes on. **3.** A **tie** is a kind of clothing. It is a narrow piece of cloth that people wear around their necks. **Ties** come in many different colors.

◆ tie

A **bow tie** is a **tie** that has the shape of a **bow.** People wear **bow ties** at the top of their shirts.

## tiger

A **tiger** is a large, wild cat. **Tigers** often have brown or orange fur with black stripes.

◆ tiger

## tight

To be **tight** means to be hard to take off or take apart. Doug's boots were **tight** because they were too small for him. **Tight** is the opposite of **loose.**

## time

**1. Time** is how long it takes for something to happen. The past, the present, and the future are all parts of **time.** I live close to school. It only takes a short **time** for me to walk there. If I have **time,** I stop at my friend's house on the way. **2. Time** is also the hour on the clock when something happens. "What **time** does the show start?" "It starts at eight o'clock." **3.** A **time** is how often something is done. We sang the song once. Then we sang it again. We sang the song two **times.**

(A) (B) (C) (D) (E) (F) (G) (H) (I) (J) (K) (L) (M)

## tin

Tin is a kind of metal. It is used to make cans, toys, and other things.

## tiny

Tiny means very, very small. Ants are tiny insects. We use a microscope to look at things that are too tiny to see. ■ tinier, tiniest

## tire

A tire is a round object made of rubber. It covers the outside of a wheel. Cars have four wheels with four tires.

◆ tire

## tired

To be tired is to need rest. Crystal has played basketball all afternoon. Now she is tired.

## tissue

A tissue is a piece of soft, thin paper. You use tissues to wipe your eyes and nose when you are crying or when you have a cold.

## title

A title is the name of something you read or see. Books, poems, plays, and paintings all have titles. The title of the book I am reading now is "Stuart Little."

## to

1. To tells where something goes. Astronauts have flown to the moon. 2. To also means until. The store opens at nine o'clock. It closes at six o'clock. It is open from nine to six. 3. To also tells how something changes. Elijah colored the white page with a blue crayon. He changed the color from white to blue. 4. To is also used to show things that people do. Aurora likes to swim in the ocean.

## toad

A toad is an animal that is like a frog. Toads have skin that is rough and dry. Frogs like to live in water, but toads like to live on land.

## toast

Toast is bread that has been sliced and heated. Toast is brown on both sides. I like toast with butter and strawberry jam.

A toaster is a machine that makes toast from bread. My father uses our toaster at breakfast every morning.

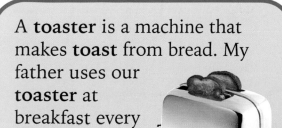

## today

Today means this day. Yesterday came before today. Tomorrow comes after today.

## toe

A toe is a thin part at the front of the foot. People have five toes on each foot.

## together

1. Together means with each other. Nina and Jasper walked to school together. 2. Together also means that two or more parts touch each other or are joined. I sewed the pieces of cloth together.

◆ together

The opposite of together is apart. Davy put the pieces of the puzzle together. Then Jana took them apart.

## told

Told is a form of tell. Marissa told us about her visit to the museum yesterday.

## tomato

A tomato is a kind of fruit. It is round and red. Ketchup is made from tomatoes.

■ tomatoes

◆ tomato

## tomorrow

Tomorrow is the day after today. Tomorrow is in the future. If today is Monday, then tomorrow will be Tuesday.

## tongue

The tongue is a part of the mouth. People use their tongues to help them eat and speak. Animals have tongues too.

◆ tongue

## tonight

Tonight is the night between today and tomorrow. Mindy does her homework this afternoon so she can watch television tonight.

## too

1. Too means also. Whitney can play two instruments. She plays the violin, and she plays the harp, too. 2. Too also means more than what is good. It is too hot to work outside today.

(A) (B) (C) (D) (E) (F) (G) (H) (I) (J) (K) (L) (M)

## took

**Took** is a form of **take**. Val **took** her books off the table. Destiny and Jon **took** the bus to school. Chase **took** pictures of his family with his camera. It **took** the artist months to make that statue.

## tool

A **tool** is something people use to help them work. Rakes, hammers, knives, and shovels are all **tools**.

◆ tool

A **toolbox** is a container for carrying or storing small tools and other things. Many **toolboxes** have hammers, nails, and scissors in them.

## tooth

A **tooth** is a part of your mouth. A **tooth** is hard and white. People chew food with their **teeth**. ▪ **teeth**

A **toothbrush** is a small brush with a handle. **Toothpaste** is something gooey and thick. People put **toothpaste** on **toothbrushes** to clean their teeth.

## top

**1.** The **top** is the highest part of something. Josie stored her old toys in a box at the **top** of her closet. **2.** A **top** is also a kind of toy. People play with **tops** by making them spin on a surface.

**Top** is the opposite of **bottom**.

## tore

**Tore** is a form of **tear**. Zoe **tore** her jacket on a fence on the way home from school.

## torn

**Torn** is a form of **tear**. The cat has **torn** the curtain. There is a tear there now.

## tornado

A **tornado** is a very strong wind. It is shaped like a cone that twists in the air. **Tornadoes** can knock down houses and pull trees out of the ground. ▪ **tornadoes**

◆ tornado

## touch

**1.** To **touch** is to feel something with your body. The pillow felt soft when Carrie **touched** it.
**2.** To **touch** also means for one thing to be against another so that there is no space between them. The two bowls are **touching.** I will move them apart.

## toward

**Toward** means in the direction of. The ship seemed to grow bigger as it sailed **toward** us. The wind is blowing **toward** the front of the house.

## towel

A **towel** is a soft piece of cloth. People use **towels** to dry off after they take a bath or go swimming.

◆ towel

## tower

A **tower** is a building or part of a building that rises very high. Castles often have many **towers.**

## town

A **town** is a place where people live and work. Most **towns** are smaller than cities.

## toy

A **toy** is an object that people play with. Wood blocks, dolls, and kites are **toys.**

> **Toy** rhymes with **boy.**

## tractor

A **tractor** is a large machine with big wheels and a strong engine. Farmers use **tractors** to help prepare the ground to plant vegetables.

## traffic

**Traffic** means cars, trucks, and buses on streets or roads. At some times of the day there is a lot of **traffic.**

◆ traffic

> A **traffic light** is a machine that tells you what to do when you are driving. A green light means you can go. A red light means you have to stop.

(A) (B) (C) (D) (E) (F) (G) (H) (I) (J) (K) (L) (M)

## trail

**1.** A **trail** is a path through a field or forest or across mountains. People walk on **trails** for fun and exercise. **2.** To **trail** is to follow behind someone or something. The baby ducks **trailed** their mother.

◆ trail

## trailer

A **trailer** is a large, metal box on wheels. **Trailers** can be pulled by tractors and trucks to carry things. Some people use **trailers** as houses or offices.

## train

**1.** A **train** is a group of railroad cars. **Trains** carry people or heavy loads from one place to another. **2.** To **train** means to teach a person or an animal how to do something. Lucy **trained** her dog to sit. My violin teacher was **trained** at a large music school.

## transportation

**Transportation** is the way you get from one place to another. Cars, trains, airplanes, and boats are all kinds of **transportation.**

## trap

**1.** A **trap** is a way to catch wild animals. Some **traps** are like cages. Other **traps** are nets or holes in the ground. **2.** To **trap** is to catch an animal in a trap. Spiders **trap** insects in their webs. ■ **trapped**

## trash

**Trash** is something people do not want to keep. A lot of **trash** can be recycled.

◆ trash

A **trash can** is something that you put **trash** in. There were pieces of paper on the floor. I picked them up and put them in the **trash can.**

## travel

To **travel** means to go and visit another place. Every year Lori's family likes to **travel** to some place they have never seen before.

## tray

A **tray** is a flat, shallow container used to carry or hold things. Allen and his friends carry their lunches on **trays**.

◆ tray

## treasure

**Treasure** is a lot of gold, silver, and jewels. Hundreds of years ago, pirates gathered **treasure** from all over the world.

■ treasure

## treat

**1.** A **treat** is something special that you enjoy. One of my favorite **treats** is going to the movies. **2.** To **treat** means to pay for someone else. My uncle **treated** my sisters and me to lunch. **3.** To **treat** also means to act in some way toward a person or animal. The boy across the street **treats** his dog well.

## tree

A **tree** is a kind of plant. It has branches and leaves. **Trees** can grow to be very tall. Wood comes from **trees**. Oaks, pines, and palms are different kinds of **trees**.

## triangle

A **triangle** is a shape. **Triangles** have three straight sides. Malcolm drew lines between three dots to make a **triangle**.

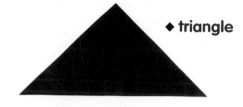

◆ triangle

A **triangle** has three sides. Rectangles and squares have four sides.

## trick

**1.** A **trick** is something that seems to happen but really does not. The magician seemed to make a rabbit disappear, but it was just a **trick**. The magician's **tricks** are fun to watch. **2.** To **trick** is to get someone to do something he or she does not want to do. Wayne **tricked** the dog into taking the bitter medicine by hiding it in her food.

## tried

**Tried** is a form of **try**. I **tried** to find the book at the library, but someone had borrowed it. Last night my baby brother **tried** cake for the first time. He got some all over his fingers and face!

## trip

**1.** A **trip** is a time when you travel somewhere. Our family went on two **trips** to the mountains last year. **2.** To **trip** means to bump into something with your foot and fall down. Penelope **tripped** on a rock as she was climbing the hill.
- **tripped**

## trombone

A **trombone** is an instrument. It is a kind of horn. **Trombones** are made of long, metal tubes that fit together. Cole plays the **trombone** in the school band.

◆ trombone

## trophy

A **trophy** is a cup, statue, or other prize that you get as an award. Sarah swam faster than anyone else in that race. She won a **trophy**.
- **trophies**

◆ trophy

## trot

To **trot** means to run in a slow way. The horses **trotted** around the pasture.
- **trotted**

## trouble

**1. Trouble** is something that makes someone sad, angry, or confused. My little brother had **trouble** learning how to tie his shoelaces. **2.** To be in **trouble** means that someone is angry at you. Genevieve woke up too late. She knew she would be in **trouble** with her teacher when she got to school.

## trousers

**Trousers** are a kind of clothes. People wear **trousers** over their legs. Most **trousers** have pockets in them.

> Another word for **trousers** is **pants**.

## truck

A **truck** is a machine. It is like a very large car that is used to carry heavy loads. Theodore's father has a job driving **trucks** across the country.

◆ truck

## true

To be **true** means that something matches the facts that we know. It is **true** that the world is round. It is not **true** that snow is purple.

> The opposite of **true** is **false**. It is **true** that water turns into ice when it gets very cold. It is **false** that 2 + 2 = 5.

## trumpet

A **trumpet** is an instrument. It is a kind of horn. **Trumpets** are made of metal tubes. The sound of a **trumpet** can be very loud.

## trunk

**1.** A **trunk** is the thick middle part of a tree. The **trunk** of a tree grows up from the ground. Branches grow out of it. Most tree **trunks** are covered with bark. **2.** A **trunk** is also part of an elephant. It is like a very long nose. Elephants can pick up things with their **trunks**. **3.** A **trunk** is also a large box. People often store clothes and other things in **trunks**.

◆ trunk

## trust

To **trust** someone is to believe they will do as they say. Sasha and Valerie are best friends. They **trust** each other not to tell their secrets to anyone else.

## truth

The **truth** is what is true. If people do not tell the **truth**, you cannot trust them.

## try

**1.** To **try** is to work to make something happen. Cheryl **tries** to carry the watermelon. **2.** To **try** means to do something you never have before. Lou has **tried** different hobbies, but he still likes painting the best.
■ tries, tried

## tuba

A **tuba** is an instrument. It is a kind of horn. A **tuba** is made of a metal tube that is curved. **Tubas** are very large.

## tube

**1.** A **tube** is a long, hollow piece of metal, glass, rubber, or plastic. Most **tubes** are used to carry liquids or gases from one place to another. **2.** A **tube** is also a container that is sealed at one end and has a cap on the other end. There are many **tubes** of toothpaste at the store.

(A) (B) (C) (D) (E) (F) (G) (H) (I) (J) (K) (L) (M)

## Tuesday

**Tuesday** is a day of the week. **Tuesday** comes after Monday and before Wednesday.

## tug

To **tug** is to pull something for a short time. Paulo **tugs** at his mother's coat when he wants to go home. ■ **tugged**

> A **tugboat** is a kind of boat. It has a very strong engine for pulling and pushing large ships. **Tugboats** are used in harbors where there is not enough room for big ships to move by themselves.

## tulip

A **tulip** is a kind of flower. It is shaped like a cup. **Tulips** come in many colors.

## tumble

To **tumble** means to fall quickly. My sister **tumbled** off her bed last night and hurt her elbow. Be careful not to **tumble** down the stairs!

◆ tulip

## tuna

A **tuna** is a kind of fish that lives in the ocean. People eat **tuna**. Milo ate a **tuna** sandwich for lunch.

## tunnel

A **tunnel** is a long hole under the ground or under water. Some **tunnels** go through mountains so that people can travel from one side of the mountain to the other. Some animals will make **tunnels** in the ground and live in them.

◆ tunnel

## turkey

**1.** A **turkey** is a kind of bird. It has a long neck. Some **turkeys** are wild. **2. Turkey** is a kind of meat that comes from a turkey. People often eat **turkey** on Thanksgiving and other holidays. People also buy **turkey** in thin slices and put it on sandwiches.

◆ turkey

## turn

**1.** To **turn** is to move in a circle. The wheels on an automobile **turn** when the automobile moves. **2.** To **turn** is also to move something from being in one direction to being in another direction. I **turned** my head to see who had come into the room. **3.** To **turn** also means to fold, bend, or twist. I **turned** my cap inside out. **4.** To **turn** a page is to move it so you can see the other side. **5.** To take **turns** means that one goes, and then the other. Pearl and Meg played checkers. First, Pearl moved a piece. Then Meg did. They took **turns**.

> To **turn on** something makes it have electricity. To **turn off** something stops it from having electricity.

## turtle

A **turtle** is a kind of reptile. Turtles can live both in the water and on the land. A **turtle** can pull its head, legs, and tail inside its shell.

◆ turtle

## twice

**Twice** means two times. Ashanti liked the movie so much she saw it **twice**.

## twig

A **twig** is a small branch. We put **twigs** through our marshmallows so we could roast them in the fire.

## twin

A **twin** is one of two children born at the same time to the same parents. Some **twins** look alike.

◆ twin

## twist

To **twist** is to turn around and around. Rope is made of pieces of string that are **twisted** together.

> A **twister** is another name for a **tornado**. **Tornadoes** look like windy cones that **twist** in the air.

## two

**Two** is one more than one. It is the second number when you count. **Two** is written **2**. $1 + 1 = 2$.

# U

## ugly

**Ugly** means not nice to look at. Lauren found some old **ugly** coats in the attic. ■ **uglier, ugliest**

## umbrella

An **umbrella** is something you use to protect yourself from rain or sun. **Umbrellas** are shaped like upside-down bowls and have long handles.

◆ **umbrella**

## umpire

An **umpire** is someone who makes sure that baseball players follow the rules. Kyle's father was the **umpire** during our game yesterday.

## uncle

An **uncle** is the brother of a parent. An **uncle** is also the husband of a sister or brother of a parent. Fritz and Kara have six **uncles.**

## under

**1. Under** means lower than the bottom of something. The cat sat **under** a bench to stay out of the rain.
**2. Under** also means lower than the surface of something. The roots of a plant grow **under** the ground.

◆ **under**

The opposite of **under** is **over.** The ball flew **over** my head and went **under** the porch.

## underground

**Underground** means under the ground. Worms live **underground.**

## underline

To **underline** is to draw a line under something. Leon **underlines** his name on the page. People often **underline** things that are important.

## understand

To **understand** something means to know it well. Charlotte knows how to read. She **understands** all the words on this page. Riley **understood** the rules of the game after Lucas explained them to him.
- **understood**

## underwater

**Underwater** means below the surface of the water. Fish live **underwater.** Anna knows how to swim **underwater.**

◆ underwater

## uneasy

**Uneasy** means not feeling safe. Madeline was a little bit afraid to go to school for the first time. She was **uneasy** about it.
- **uneasier, uneasiest**

## uneven

**Uneven** means not smooth or straight. It was hard for us to walk in the field. The ground was very **uneven** there.

## unhappy

**Unhappy** means sad. The passengers were **unhappy** when the train arrived late.

> When **un-** is placed in front of a word, it often means **not.** **Unhappy** means not happy. **Unfair** means not fair.

## unicorn

A **unicorn** is an animal in stories. **Unicorns** are not real. A **unicorn** looks like a horse with one long horn on its head.

◆ unicorn

## uniform

A **uniform** is a special kind of clothing. People wear **uniforms** to show that they belong to a group. Police officers, firefighters, nurses, and people who are on the same sports team wear **uniforms.**

## universe

The **universe** is everything in our world and in space put together. The earth, the sun, the moon, and the stars are all part of the **universe.**

## wear

**1.** To **wear** something means to have it on your body to cover or protect you. When it is cold outside, Jade **wears** a coat, a hat, boots, and gloves. Baseball players **wear** a special glove to help them catch the ball. **2.** To **wear** out means to get old and not work well. The tires on our car **wore** out, so we had to buy new ones. ■ **wore, worn**

## weather

**Weather** is what it is like outside. When the **weather** is warm, Bud likes to go to the lake. When the **weather** is cold, he likes to ski.

## web

A **web** is a group of threads that a spider makes. Spiders make **webs** to catch insects to eat.

◆ web

## wedding

A **wedding** is a time when two people marry. My sister carried flowers at two **weddings** last summer.

## Wednesday

**Wednesday** is a day of the week. **Wednesday** comes after Tuesday and before Thursday.

## weed

A **weed** is a plant that grows where it is not wanted. My grandmother pulls **weeds** from her garden every day in the summer.

## week

A **week** is an amount of time. There are seven days in one **week**. There are 52 **weeks** in one year.

> **Week** sounds the same as **weak**. Both words rhyme with **cheek**. What other words rhyme with **week, weak,** and **cheek**?

## weekend

A **weekend** is the time from Friday night through Sunday night. Most schools do not have classes on **weekends**. Would you like to come over and play this **weekend?**

## weekly

**Weekly** means that something happens every week. Devin and Sydney visit their grandparents **weekly**.

## weep

To **weep** means to cry. Riley **wept** when the sad movie ended. ■ **wept**

## weigh

To **weigh** means to measure how heavy something is. At the grocery store, my sister **weighed** carrots on a scale. They **weighed** three pounds.

◆ weigh

---

When we **weigh** something, we find out its **weight**. **Weight** is how heavy something is. Roger finds out his **weight** at the doctor's office.

---

## welcome

**1.** To be **welcome** means that someone is glad to see you. We tried to make our new neighbors feel **welcome** by inviting them to our house for dinner. **2.** You're **welcome** means that someone is happy to have done something for someone else. We say "You're **welcome**" to someone who says "Thank you."

## well

**1.** A **well** is a deep hole in the ground. Most **wells** are dug to get water, oil, or gas. **2.** Well means in a good way. Esther plays the violin **well.** Everyone likes to listen to her. **3.** Well also means healthy. Antonio stayed home because he was sick. When he is **well,** he will go back to school.

◆ well

## we'll

**We'll** is a short way to say **we will. We'll** see dolphins at the aquarium.

## went

**Went** is a form of **go.** Last Saturday Bob and Randy **went** bowling.

## wept

**Wept** is a form of **weep.** The baby **wept** when he hurt his toe.

## were

**Were** is a form of **be.** Jo and Eli will be home today. They **were** away on vacation last week.

## we're

**We're** is a short way to say **we are.** My sisters and I are very good at playing basketball. **We're** also good at painting.

## weren't

**Weren't** is a short way to say **were not.** Oliver and Howard **weren't** hungry after they ate their supper.

## west

**West** is a direction. The sun sets in the **west. West** is the opposite of **east.**

◆ west

## wet

**Wet** means covered with water or full of water. After I went swimming, I dried myself with a towel. Now the towel is **wet.** The leaves were **wet** after the rain. ■ **wetter, wettest**

◆ wet

The opposite of **wet** is **dry.** Our dog was **wet** after her bath. We rubbed her with a towel until she was **dry.**

## we've

**We've** is a short way to say **we have. We've** lived in our house for two years.

## whale

A **whale** is a large animal. It lives in the ocean, but it is not a fish. **Whales** are mammals.

There are many kinds of **whales.** The **blue whale** is the largest animal in the world.

## what

**1. What** is used to ask questions about people and things. **What** are you eating? **What** book are you reading? **2. What** also means the thing that. We wondered **what** was inside the box. We learned **what** happened in the story.

## whatever

**Whatever** means anything or everything. Sara eats **whatever** her father cooks for her.

## wheat

**Wheat** is a kind of plant. The seeds of **wheat** are made into flour. **Wheat** is used to make cereal.

◆ wheat

## wheel

**1.** A **wheel** is a round object. **Wheels** turn to help machines move or work. **2.** To **wheel** means to move something that has **wheels.** I **wheeled** my bicycle into the garage.

◆ wheel

A bicycle has two **wheels.** A car has four **wheels.** Some trucks have eight or more **wheels.**

## when

**1.** **When** is used to ask questions about time. **When** does the basketball game start? **2.** **When** means at the time that. All the snow melts **when** the weather gets warm. **When** I get home from school, I like to eat a snack.

## where

**1.** **Where** is used to ask questions about a place. **Where** did the cat go? **Where** were you born? **2.** **Where** also means at the place that. Sachi found the key on the table **where** her brother had left it.

## which

**1.** **Which** is used to ask questions about one person or thing in a group. **Which** of these coats is yours? **Which** girl is your friend? **2.** **Which** also means the one that. We saw two books and bought the longer one, **which** looked more interesting.

## while

**1.** **While** means during what time. Mason went to the store **while** it was open. **2.** A **while** is a small amount of time. Julian, Carter, and Addison played baseball for a **while,** and then they went home.

## whisper

To **whisper** means to speak in a soft voice. People **whisper** in a library so they won't bother other people who are trying to read or study.

## whistle

**1.** To **whistle** means to make a musical sound by blowing air through your teeth or lips. Many people learn to **whistle** songs. **2.** A **whistle** is a very small instrument that you blow into. **Whistles** make a noise like a bird.

◆ whistle

## white

White is a color. It is a very light color. This page is printed on **white** paper.

## who

**1. Who** is used to ask questions about a person. **Who** knocked on the door? **2. Who** also means the person that. The man **who** works in the movie theater is very friendly.

## whoever

**Whoever** means any person that. **Whoever** runs the fastest will win the race. My parents said to invite **whoever** I wanted to play games with us.

## whole

**Whole** means all together. Our **whole** class went to the museum to see fossils.

> The word **whole** sounds the same as the word **hole.** The **whole** class watched as the **hole** was dug for a new school.

## who's

**1. Who's** is a short way to say **who is. Who's** in the kitchen? **2. Who's** is also a short way to say **who has. Who's** been to the zoo?

## whose

**Whose** tells who something belongs to. The teacher found a glove that someone had lost. She wanted to know **whose** glove she had found.

## why

**Why** is a word people use when they ask about or explain what makes things happen. **Why** do birds fly south for the winter? Luanne doesn't know **why** so many students were absent from school today.

## wicked

**Wicked** means very bad and mean. The **wicked** king took land and money from the people.

## wide

**1. Wide** means having a lot of space between the two sides. The truck carried a very **wide** load. **2. Wide** tells how far something is from side to side. The island is three miles **wide**.

> The opposite of **wide** is **narrow.**

## width

**Width** is how wide something is. The **width** of Darla's paper is eight inches.

## wife

A **wife** is a married woman. The **wives** of my uncles are my aunts. ▪ **wives**

## wig

A **wig** is an object made from hair that may or may not be real. You wear **wigs** on your head. The clown wore a funny purple **wig**.

## wild

**Wild** means not usually cared for or kept by people. Lions and tigers are **wild** animals.

## will

**Will** tells about something in the future. Hermione **will** go to the pool with Eleanor tomorrow. ▪ **would**

## willing

**Willing** means that you agree to do something. My sister was **willing** to lend me her book.

## win

To **win** means to finish first or to do the best in a game or a race. I always **win** when I play checkers with my dad. ▪ **won**

> The opposite of **win** is **lose**. Yesterday we played Skylar's team in soccer. Her team **won**, and our team **lost**.

## wind

**Wind** is air that moves. Strong **winds** blew the tree down.

> If there is a lot of **wind**, we say that it is **windy**. During the storm, it was very **windy**.

## windmill

A **windmill** is a kind of machine. The power of the wind makes it work. Some **windmills** help make electricity.

◆ windmill

## window

A **window** is an open place in a wall. It lets light and air into a room. **Windows** usually have glass in them.

## wing

A **wing** is a long part that helps something to fly. All birds have **wings**. Bats and many insects also have them. Most airplanes have two **wings**.

◆ wing

(A) (B) (C) (D) (E) (F) (G) (H) (I) (J) (K) (L) (M)

## winter

**Winter** is a season. It comes after fall and before spring. **Winter** can be very cold in some places.

> The days of **winter** are called **wintertime.** Shauna likes to build a snowman during the **wintertime.**

## wipe

To **wipe** means to rub something so that it is clean or dry. Mitzi **wiped** the wet desk with a towel.

## wire

A **wire** is a piece of metal. It looks like a long string and is easy to bend. Electricity moves through **wires.**

◆ wire

## wise

**Wise** means very smart. **Wise** people have learned many things, and they often know the right thing to do.

## wish

**1.** A **wish** is something that you hope will happen. Rachel made a **wish** when she threw pennies into the well. **2.** To **wish** means to hope that something good will happen. Lincoln **wishes** that he could find a hidden treasure.

## witch

A **witch** is a woman who has magic powers in stories. We dressed like **witches** for the costume party.

## with

**1. With** means together. I went to the store **with** my sister. Jolie's hamburger came **with** onions on it. **2. With** tells what something has. A giraffe is an animal **with** a long neck. **3. With** can also tell what you use to do something. Hunter dug a hole **with** a shovel.

## without

**1. Without** means not having. People cannot live **without** air and food. **2. Without** means not with someone or something else. Casey walks to school alone. She goes **without** anyone else.

## wives

**Wives** means more than one **wife.**

## wizard

A **wizard** is a person who has magic powers in stories. The **wizards** in the movie had long, white hair and wore pointed hats.

## wobble

To **wobble** means to move in a way that is not steady. Cole **wobbled** the first time he tried to ride a bicycle.

## woke

**Woke** is a form of **wake.** Yesterday Sebastian **woke** up, got dressed, and ate breakfast quickly because he wanted to get to school early.

## woken

**Woken** is a form of **wake.** It is nine o'clock, but Jacques has not **woken** up yet.

## wolf

A **wolf** is a kind of animal. It looks like a large dog. **Wolves** hunt for food in groups.
■ **wolves**

◆ wolf

## woman

A **woman** is a grown female person. My mother and aunts are **women.** The **women** in our family all like to read. ■ **women**

## won

**Won** is a form of **win.** My sister's volleyball team is very good. They **won** almost all of their games this year.

> The word **won** sounds like the word **one.**

## wonder

To **wonder** means to think about something that you are curious about. Michaela **wonders** what she will be when she grows up.

## wonderful

**Wonderful** means very good. Giorgio thought the book he just finished reading was so **wonderful** that he lent it to his sister. My friends and I had a **wonderful** time playing at the park yesterday.

## won't

**Won't** is a short way to say **will not.** Iolana **won't** be seven years old until next spring. Our dog **won't** go outside during a storm.

## wood

**1. Wood** is what trees are made of. It is used to make houses, furniture, and paper. **2.** The **woods** is a place where a lot of trees grow. We went for a walk in the **woods.**

◆ wood

> If something is made from **wood,** we say that it is **wooden.** Natasha sat on a **wooden** chair.

## woodpecker

A **woodpecker** is a kind of bird. **Woodpeckers** have sharp, hard bills. The bills can make holes in trees to get insects for food.

◆ woodpecker

## wool

**Wool** is the hair that grows on sheep and some other animals. **Wool** is used to make yarn and cloth for clothes and blankets. Things made of **wool** keep you warm. Many sweaters are made of **wool.**

## word

A **word** is a sound or a group of sounds that means something. People speak **words** to share their thoughts with other people. Letters are symbols people use for **words.**

## wore

**Wore** is a form of **wear.** Everybody in the play **wore** a funny costume and a wig. Yesterday I **wore** a dress to school.

## work

**1. Work** is the energy you use to do or to make something. Digging a hole is hard **work. 2. Work** is also what someone must do. Some people earn money for their **work.** Colin's mother is a scientist. She loves her **work. 3.** To **work** means to do work. Claudia is writing a book. She **works** on it every day. **4.** To **work** also means to do what something is made to do. After the radio fell on the floor, it did not **work.**

> A **worker** is a person who **works.** Sherry and Heather are pilots. They work hard at their jobs. They are good **workers.**

## world

The **world** is the place where everyone lives. Our **world** is made up of land, water, and air.

## worm

A **worm** is a very small animal. It has a long, soft body and no legs. Many **worms** live in the ground.

## worn

**Worn** is a form of **wear.** Cody's jacket is new. He has not **worn** it before today.

◆ worm

When something has been **worn** a lot, it can become **worn-out.** It cannot be **worn** anymore. My **worn-out** slippers have holes in them.

## worry

To **worry** means to feel that something bad can happen. My parents **worry** sometimes if I am late coming home.
■ **worries, worried**

## worse

**Worse** means very bad but not as bad as the worst. Yesterday it rained. Today the weather was **worse.** It rained and snowed. **Worse** is the opposite of **better.**

## worst

**Worst** means worse than any other. Dwight did not like the soup his brother made at all. He thought it was the **worst** thing he had ever tasted.

**Worst** is the opposite of **best.** What is the **worst** book you have ever read? What is the **best** book?

## would

**Would** is a form of **will.** Damon said yesterday that he **would** go swimming with us today.

## wouldn't

**Wouldn't** is a short way to say **would not.** The cat **wouldn't** come down from the tree.

## wrap

To **wrap** means to cover with something such as paper or cloth. People usually **wrap** holiday presents and tie them with ribbons and bows. I **wrapped** myself in a towel.
■ **wrapped**

**Wrapping paper** is a special kind of paper that you use to **wrap** presents. It often has bright colors and is easy to tear.

(A) (B) (C) (D) (E) (F) (G) (H) (I) (J) (K) (L) (M)

## wreck

To **wreck** means to make something worse. The rain **wrecked** the castle we had made in the sand.

## wrinkle

A **wrinkle** is a crooked line on something. **Wrinkles** are places where the surface of something is folded. Our dog has many **wrinkles** on his face.

◆ wrinkle

If something has a lot of **wrinkles,** we say that it is **wrinkled.** If you throw your shirts on the floor, they will become **wrinkled.**

## wrist

A **wrist** is a part of the body. It is between your hand and your arm. You wave your hands by bending your **wrists.** Some people wear a watch on their **wrist.**

## write

**1.** To **write** means to make letters and words with a pencil, a pen, or a computer. I **wrote** my name in big letters. Lesley has **written** a letter to her friend. **2.** To **write** means to make a book, poem, play, or something else for people to read. Some people also **write** for magazines and newspapers.
■ **wrote, written**

A **writer** is a person who **writes.** Dave likes to tell stories. He wants to be a **writer.**

## wrong

**1. Wrong** means not correct. Margo gave the **wrong** answer to the question. The teacher told her the right answer.
**2. Wrong** also means the way something should not be. Jon knew it was **wrong** to lie.

## wrote

**Wrote** is a form of **write.** Morgan **wrote** the date at the top of the page.

# x-ray

**1.** An **x-ray** is a kind of energy. It can pass through objects. Doctors use **x-rays** to take photographs of the inside of the body. **2.** An **x-ray** is also the photograph that we can look at after **x-rays** are used. The doctor looked at the **x-ray** of the hand to see if any bones were broken.

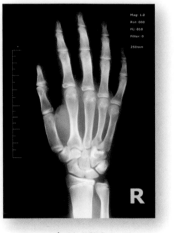

◆ **x-ray**

# xylophone

A **xylophone** is an instrument. It is made of a row of wood rectangles that are different sizes. **Xylophones** make music when they are hit with small hammers. Zoe is learning how to play the **xylophone.**

◆ **xylophone**

A B C D E F G H I J K L M

# Y

## yard

**1.** A **yard** is an amount of length. One **yard** is the same as three feet. A **yard** is almost as long as a meter. **2.** A **yard** is also an area of land around a house. Many **yards** are covered with grass.

> The **yard** behind a person's house is called a **backyard.** My friends and I like to play in my **backyard.**

## yarn

**Yarn** is a kind of string. It is made from wool, cotton, or other threads that are twisted together. **Yarn** is used to make sweaters and socks.

◆ **yarn**

## yawn

To **yawn** is to open your mouth wide and take a deep breath. People **yawn** when they are tired.

## year

A **year** is an amount of time. There are 12 months in one **year.** Sabrina has gone to my school for two **years.**

> Most **years** are 365 days long. In some **years,** there are 366 days. These years are called **leap years.**

## yell

To **yell** means to shout. The hockey game was very exciting. We **yelled** for our team to make a goal. When they made it, we **yelled,** "Woohoo!"

## yellow

**Yellow** is a color. Bananas and lemons are **yellow.**

## yes

**Yes** means that you agree. Audrey asked Noreen to come to her house after school. Noreen said, "**Yes,** I would like to come."

## yesterday

**Yesterday** is the day before today. It snowed **yesterday.** Today there is snow outside.

## yet

**Yet** means up to this time. The movie has not started **yet.** It will start in five minutes.

## yolk

A **yolk** is the yellow part of an egg. **Yolks** are food for an animal when it is inside an egg.

## you

**You** is a word that is used when one person speaks to another person. I like **you.** Do **you** like to dance? **You** are the best friends I have ever had.

## you'll

**You'll** is a short way to say **you will.** Let's play this new board game. I think **you'll** like it.

## young

To be **young** means to have been alive only a short time. Babies are very **young** people.

The opposite of **young** is **old.**

◆ young

## your

**Your** means belonging to you. That is **your** house. Can I borrow **your** book?

## you're

**You're** is a short way to say **you are. You're** tall for your age. **You're** a great group of actors.

## yours

**Yours** means belonging to you. That cup is **yours.** This one is mine.

## yourself

**Yourself** means you and nobody else. Did you earn that money **yourself**?

## you've

**You've** is a short way to say **you have. You've** got a nice smile.

## yo-yo

A **yo-yo** is a kind of toy. It is a round piece of wood or plastic with a string tied to it. The **yo-yo** goes up and down on the string. Some people can do tricks with **yo-yos.**

◆ yo-yo

# Z

## zany

To be **zany** means to be funny in an unusual way. Tenisha invents **zany** games that make me laugh.

## zebra

A **zebra** is an animal. It looks like a small horse. **Zebras** have black and white stripes. Samantha's favorite animals to see at the zoo are the **zebras.**

♦ zebra

## zero

**Zero** is a number. It's written 0. $1 + 0 = 1$. One hundred is written with a one and two **zeroes.** ■ zeroes

> **Zero** rhymes with **hero.**

## zest

**Zest** means extra flavor. Those spices give **zest** to soup.

## zigzag

**Zigzag** means first going one way and then another, over and over again. The truck followed a **zigzag** path down the hill.

## zip

**1.** To **zip** means to close with a zipper. Peyton **zips** her jacket when it is cool outside. **2.** To **zip** also means to move very fast. Muhammad **zipped** down the street on his bicycle.
■ zipped

## zipper

A **zipper** is used to hold parts of clothes together. **Zippers** are made of plastic or metal. They have two rows of little bumps that look like teeth. These rows fit together when the **zipper** is closed.

## zone

A **zone** is an area that is special because of where it is or how it is used. People must be careful when they drive in a school **zone.**

## zoo

A **zoo** is a place where animals are kept. Sometimes they stay in cages. You can see lions, tigers, and elephants at some **zoos.**

A person who works at a **zoo** is called a **zookeeper. Zookeepers** feed the animals. They also clean the places where the animals live.

## zoom

To **zoom** means to move suddenly and very fast. The rocket **zoomed** into the sky.

## zucchini

A **zucchini** is a kind of vegetable. **Zucchinis** are long and green.

◆ zucchini

Here are examples of different ways to spell vowel and consonant sounds.

# Short Vowel Sounds

### Short a

Short **a** (as in **at**) is often spelled **a**:

| | |
|---|---|
| act | cap |
| bad | dragon |
| bag | fast |
| began | glass |

Short **a** may be spelled **au**:

laugh

dragon

### Short e

Short **e** (as in **pet**) is often spelled **e**:

| | | |
|---|---|---|
| best | help | spend |
| desk | insect | step |
| egg | leg | tell |
| fed | mess | them |
| fresh | neck | wet |

Short **e** is sometimes spelled **ea**:

| | | |
|---|---|---|
| bread | instead | read (in the past) |
| dead | leather | spread |
| feather | meant | treasure |
| head | measure | weather |

help

Short **e** may also be spelled with these letters:

| | | | | |
|---|---|---|---|---|
| **a** | many | **u** | bury |
| **ai** | said | **ue** | guess |
| **ie** | friend | | |

### Short i

Short **i** (as in **pit**) is often spelled **i**:

| | | |
|---|---|---|
| big | ink | sick |
| bin | lid | sister |
| disk | lip | wish |
| fist | miss | with |
| fit | ring | zip |

feather

271

Short **i** is sometimes spelled **y**:

    gym

Short **i** may also be spelled with these letters:

| | | | |
|---|---|---|---|
| **e** | pretty | **u** | business |
| | | | busy |
| **o** | women | **ui** | build |
| | | | building |

rock

### Short o

Short **o** (as in **hot**) is often spelled **o**:

| | |
|---|---|
| body | monster |
| copy | pop |
| costume | rock |
| knot | solid |

Short **o** may be spelled **a**:

    watch

### Short u

skunk

Short **u** (as in **nut**) is often spelled **u**:

| | | |
|---|---|---|
| brush | hunt | must |
| bucket | luck | puppy |
| bus | lump | rung |
| butter | much | skunk |
| fun | mud | tub |

Short **u** may also be spelled **o**:

| | | |
|---|---|---|
| color | honey | some |
| done | month | son |
| from | mother | tongue |
| glove | nothing | |

In some words, short **u** is spelled **ou**:

| | |
|---|---|
| double | touch |
| rough | trouble |

glove

Short **u** may also be spelled with these letters:

| | | | |
|---|---|---|---|
| **a** | was | **oo** | blood, flood |
| **oe** | does | | |

272

# Long Vowel Sounds

### Long a

Long **a** (as in **ate**) is often spelled **a**. Many words that end in **a-consonant-e** have a long **a** sound.

| | | |
|---|---|---|
| able | radio | strange |
| made | rake | take |
| maple | safe | tape |
| page | same | wave |

maple

Long **a** may also be spelled with these letters:

| **ai** | aid | **ay** | hay | **ei** | eight |
|---|---|---|---|---|---|
| | daisy | | maybe | | neighbor |
| | grain | | played | | weigh |
| | paid | | | | weight |
| | pail | **ea** | break | | |
| | raise | | great | **ey** | they |
| | straight | | steak | | |
| | wait | | | | |

### Long e

Long **e** (as in **see**) is often spelled **e**. Many words that end in **e** or **e-consonant-e** have a long **e** sound.

straight

| | | |
|---|---|---|
| be | he | she |
| evil | me | these |

Long **e** may also be spelled **ee**:

| | |
|---|---|
| bee | freeze |
| cheese | seed |
| feel | tree |
| feet | week |

Long **e** may also be spelled **ea**:

| | |
|---|---|
| bead | leave |
| clean | please |
| east | seat |
| heap | speak |
| leaf | teacher |

leaf

273

Long **e** may also be spelled with these letters:

| | | | | | | | |
|---|---|---|---|---|---|---|---|
| **eo** | people | **i** | piano | **ie** | believe | **y** | family |
| | | | ski | | piece | | pretty |

### Long i

Long **i** (as in **ice**) is often spelled **i**. Many words that end in **i-consonant-e** have a long **i** sound.

smile

| | | | |
|---|---|---|---|
| describe | hide | like | size |
| dime | I | mine | smile |
| find | iron | nice | write |
| fire | ivy | pint | |

Long **i** may also be spelled **y** or **y** with another letter:

| | | | | | |
|---|---|---|---|---|---|
| **y** | by | **ey** | eye | **ye** | goodbye |
| | fly | | | | |
| | my | **uy** | buy | | |
| | rhyme | | | | |
| | xylophone | | | | |

Long **i** is sometimes spelled **i** plus one or more silent consonants:

| | | | |
|---|---|---|---|
| **igh** | flight | **is** | island |
| | sigh | | |

### Long o

Long **o** (as in **go**) is often spelled **o**. Many words that end in **o-consonant-e** have a long **o** sound.

| | | |
|---|---|---|
| both | joke | robe |
| fold | lone | rode |
| home | note | so |
| hope | owe | those |

rainbow

Long **o** may be spelled **oa**:

| | | |
|---|---|---|
| coat | loan | road |
| loaf | loaves | soap |

Long **o** may also be spelled **ow**:

| | | |
|---|---|---|
| below | know | throw |
| grow | rainbow | yellow |

Long **o** may be spelled **oe**:

> toe

## Long u

Long **u** (as in **use**) is often spelled **u**. Many words that end in **u-consonant-e** have a long **u** sound.

| computer | huge | uniform |
|---|---|---|
| cute | music | |

**huge**

Long **u** may also be spelled in these ways:

**ew** few     **eau** beautiful

## Other Vowel Sounds

The sound of **a** in **all** may be spelled with these letters:

| **a** | | **au** | | **aw** | | **ough** | |
|---|---|---|---|---|---|---|---|
| | ball | | caught | | awful | | fought |
| | fall | | saucer | | crawl | | ought |
| | small | | taught | | jaw | | thought |
| | talk | | | | paw | | |
| | tall | | | | saw | | |
| | walk | | | | straw | | |
| | | | | | yawn | | |

**ball**

The vowel sound in **how** may be spelled in these ways:

| **ow** | | **ou** | |
|---|---|---|---|
| | clown | | about |
| | cow | | house |
| | flower | | our |
| | now | | proud |
| | powder | | round |
| | towel | | |

The vowel sound in **good** may be spelled in these ways:

| **oo** | | **u** | | **ou** | |
|---|---|---|---|---|---|
| | book | | bull | | could |
| | hood | | full | | should |
| | look | | put | | would |
| | took | | | | |

The vowel sound in **moon** may be spelled in these ways:

| **oo** | cool | **o** | lose | **u** | June | **oe** | canoe |
|---|---|---|---|---|---|---|---|
| | food | | move | | ruby | | shoe |
| | loose | | to | | truth | | |
| | rooster | | who | | tulip | **ui** | fruit |
| | smooth | | whose | | | | suit |
| | soon | | | **ou** | group | | |
| | too | **ew** | blew | | soup | **ue** | blue |
| | tooth | | flew | | through | | glue |
| | troop | | grew | | you | | true |

The vowel sound in **joy** may be spelled in these ways:

| **oy** | cowboy | **oi** | boil |
|---|---|---|---|
| | enjoy | | noise |
| | toy | | oil |

fruit

## Consonant Sounds

Some consonant sounds have more than one spelling. Here are some to remember.

The sound of **f** as in **fun** may be spelled in these ways:

| **f** | after | **ff** | different | **gh** | enough | **ph** | phone |
|---|---|---|---|---|---|---|---|
| | fall | | off | | laugh | | |
| | if | | | | rough | | |
| | life | | | | | | |

The sound of **j** as in **jam** may be spelled in these ways:

| **j** | injure | **g** | energy | **dg** | edge |
|---|---|---|---|---|---|
| | jelly | | ginger | | judge |
| | jog | | imagine | | |
| | object | | page | | |

edge

The sound of **ch** as in **much** may be spelled in these ways:

| **ch** | bunch | **tch** | catch | **ti** | question |
|---|---|---|---|---|---|
| | chalk | | scratch | | |
| | child | | stretch | | |
| | choose | | watch | | |
| | rich | | | | |

**276**

The sound of **k** as in **kick** may be spelled in these ways:

| k | | c | | ck | |
|---|---|---|---|---|---|
| | kitten | | because | | back |
| | park | | can | | hockey |
| | sky | | car | | rocks |
| | speak | | magic | | |
| | woken | | picnic | ch | school |
| | wrinkle | | uncle | | |

**kitten**

The sound of **r** as in **red** may be spelled in these ways:

| r | | | | rh | |
|---|---|---|---|---|---|
| | border | | story | | rhinoceros |
| | far | | tree | | rhyme |
| | green | | work | | |
| | marble | | | wr | wrap |
| | ran | rr | borrow | | wrist |
| | spring | | hurry | | write |

**marble**

The sound of **s** as in **say** may be spelled in these ways:

| s | | c | | sc | |
|---|---|---|---|---|---|
| | base | | cent | | muscle |
| | disappear | | city | | science |
| | pants | | dance | | scissors |
| | sit | | exercise | | |
| | | | nice | st | castle |
| ss | miss | | pencil | | listen |
| | pass | | princess | | whistle |

The sound of **sh** as in **ship** may be spelled in these ways:

| sh | | ch | |
|---|---|---|---|
| | push | | machine |
| | shore | | |
| | wash | ci | magician |
| | | | special |
| s | sugar | | |
| | sure | ti | dictionary |
| | | | direction |
| | | | pollution |

**shore**

Words have special names that tell how they are used.

A **noun** is a word that names a person, a place, or a thing. In these examples, the nouns are underlined.

- The <u>dog</u> dug a <u>hole</u> in the <u>yard</u>.
- My <u>sister</u> read a <u>book</u> about <u>space</u>.
- <u>Basketball</u> is my favorite <u>sport</u>.

space

A **proper noun** is the name of a person, place, or thing. Proper nouns begin with a capital letter.

| | |
|---|---|
| Names of people | George Washington |
| Names of pets | Tabby |
| Names of cities or countries | New York |
| Names of days of the week | Sunday |
| Names of months | September |
| Names of holidays | Thanksgiving |
| Names of languages | English |

A **pronoun** is a word that can take the place of a noun. A pronoun names the same person, place, or thing as the noun it stands for. The words **I, you, he, she, it, we,** and **they** are pronouns. In each of these examples, the noun and the pronoun that takes its place are underlined.

- <u>Ava</u> read the book. <u>She</u> enjoyed the story.
- Bees make <u>honey</u>. <u>It</u> is very sweet.

A **verb** is a word that names an action. In these examples, the verbs are underlined.

- The cat <u>jumped</u> over the fence.
- Devin and his dog <u>pulled</u> on the rope.

pull

An **adjective** is a word that tells about a person, a place, or a thing. In these examples, the adjectives are underlined.

- The <u>little</u> child began to cry.
- The library was very <u>quiet</u>.
- The car was <u>clean</u> after we washed it.

# WORDS THAT SOUND ALIKE

Many words sound alike but do not have the same spelling or the same meaning. These words are called **homophones**. For example, **one** is a number and **won** is a form of the word **win**. The words **one** and **won** are spelled differently and have different meanings, but they sound alike when you say them out loud.

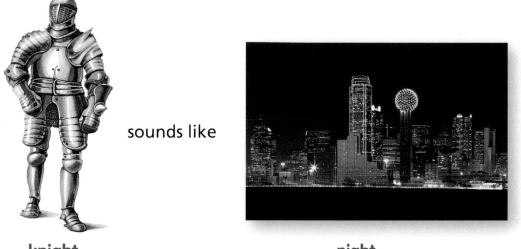

knight          sounds like          night

Here are some examples of words that sound alike in this dictionary. Many of these are pointed out in yellow note boxes.

| | | | | | |
|---|---|---|---|---|---|
| ate | eight | knew | new | sew | so |
| bare | bear | knight | night | son | sun |
| be | bee | knot | not | their | there |
| blew | blue | know | no | threw | through |
| buy | by | mail | male | to | too, two |
| cent | sent | meat | meet | wait | weight |
| dear | deer | one | won | way | weigh |
| eye | I | pair | pear | weak | week |
| flour | flower | peace | piece | wear | where |
| for | four | plain | plane | which | witch |
| heal | heel | right | write | wood | would |
| hear | here | road | rode | | |
| hole | whole | sea | see | | |

## COMPOUND WORDS

Many words are made up of two shorter words joined together. These are called **compound words.** Here are some examples from this dictionary.

| | | |
|---|---|---|
| afternoon | grownup | popcorn |
| backpack | homework | railroad |
| bathtub | horseshoe | rainbow |
| birthday | jellyfish | scarecrow |
| cowboy | keyhole | shoelace |
| doorbell | lighthouse | sidewalk |
| everywhere | newspaper | something |
| fireplace | nobody | toothbrush |
| flashlight | outside | tugboat |
| gingerbread | pancake | underground |
| grasshopper | playground | |

**jellyfish**

The **compound words** in the list below are made up of short words given in this dictionary. Can you tell what they mean?

corn + bread = cornbread
dish + towel = dishtowel
doll + house = dollhouse
farm + land = farmland
grape + vine = grapevine
hair + brush = hairbrush
moon + light = moonlight
paint + brush = paintbrush
pine + cone = pinecone
rain + drop = raindrop
sail + boat = sailboat

sun + rise = sunrise
tool + shed = toolshed
wheel + chair = wheelchair

**sunrise**

A **contraction** is also a way of joining two words together. Contractions are short ways of writing two words. An **apostrophe** (') takes the place of a letter or letters that have been taken out.

can't = cannot
don't = do not
I'm = I am

they're = they are
we're = we are
you've = you have

## Mammals

| | | |
|---|---|---|
| ape | giraffe | pig |
| bat | goat | puppy |
| bear | gorilla | rabbit |
| beaver | hamster | raccoon |
| calf | hippopotamus | rat |
| camel | horse | rhinoceros |
| cat | kangaroo | seal |
| cattle | kitten | sheep |
| cow | leopard | skunk |
| cub | lion | squirrel |
| deer | mice | tiger |
| dog | monkey | whale |
| dolphin | moose | wolf |
| donkey | mouse | zebra |
| elephant | ox | |
| fox | panda | |

dolphin

## Insects

| | | |
|---|---|---|
| ant | caterpillar | mosquito |
| bee | cricket | moth |
| beetle | fly | |
| butterfly | grasshopper | |

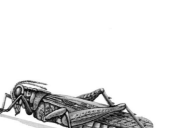

grasshopper

## Birds

| | | |
|---|---|---|
| chicken | hen | robin |
| crow | ostrich | rooster |
| duck | owl | swan |
| eagle | parrot | turkey |
| goose | peacock | woodpecker |
| hawk | penguin | |

## Other Animals

| | |
|---|---|
| alligator | lobster |
| crab | snail |
| crocodile | snake |
| dinosaur | toad |
| frog | turtle |

turtle

## Time

| | | |
|---|---|---|
| calendar | minute | watch |
| clock | month | week |
| hour | second | year |

clock

## Seasons

| | |
|---|---|
| winter | summer |
| spring | fall |

## Months

| | | |
|---|---|---|
| January | May | September |
| February | June | October |
| March | July | November |
| April | August | December |

## Days

| | |
|---|---|
| Sunday | Thursday |
| Monday | Friday |
| Tuesday | Saturday |
| Wednesday | |

## Number Words

| | | | | |
|---|---|---|---|---|
| zero | 0 | eight | 8 |
| one | 1 | nine | 9 |
| two | 2 | ten | 10 |
| three | 3 | | |
| four | 4 | | |
| five | 5 | hundred | 100 |
| six | 6 | thousand | 1,000 |
| seven | 7 | million | 1,000,000 |

two

## Sports

| | |
|---|---|
| baseball | skating |
| basketball | soccer |
| bowling | swimming |
| football | tennis |
| hockey | volleyball |

soccer

## Parts of the Body

| | | |
|---|---|---|
| arm | foot | nail |
| back | hair | neck |
| bone | hand | nose |
| brain | head | shoulder |
| cheek | heart | stomach |
| chest | heel | teeth |
| chin | jaw | toe |
| ear | knee | tongue |
| elbow | leg | tooth |
| eye | lung | wrist |
| face | mouth | |
| finger | muscle | |

tongue

## Family

| | | |
|---|---|---|
| aunt | grandfather | parent |
| brother | grandmother | sister |
| cousin | grandparent | son |
| daughter | husband | uncle |
| father | mother | wife |

## Furniture

| | | |
|---|---|---|
| bed | couch | sofa |
| bench | crib | table |
| chair | desk | |

chair

## Colors

| | |
|---|---|
| black | pink |
| blue | purple |
| brown | red |
| gray | white |
| green | yellow |
| orange | |

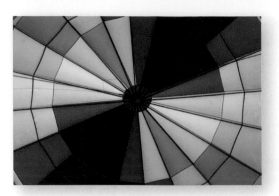

color

## Shapes

| | |
|---|---|
| circle | rectangle |
| cone | square |
| diamond | star |
| oval | triangle |

## Clothes

| | |
|---|---|
| apron | pajamas |
| belt | pants |
| bib | shirt |
| boot | shoelace |
| bowtie | shoes |
| cap | slipper |
| cape | sneaker |
| coat | sock |
| dress | suit |
| glove | sweater |
| hat | tie |
| helmet | trousers |
| hood | vest |

helmet

## Amounts and Distances

| | | |
|---|---|---|
| foot | kilometer | pint |
| gallon | meter | pound |
| gram | mile | quart |
| inch | ounce | yard |

## Foods

apple
banana
bean
beef
berry
bread
butter
cake
candy
carrot
cereal
cheese
cherry
chocolate
cookie
corn
cream
dessert
doughnut
egg
fish
fruit
gingerbread
grape

grapefruit
gravy
ham
hamburger
hot dog
ice cream
jam
jelly
ketchup
lemon
lettuce
lime
macaroni
marshmallow
meat
milk
mustard
onion
orange
pancake
pea
peach
peanut butter
pear

pepper
pie
pineapple
pizza
plum
popcorn
potato
pudding
pumpkin
rice
sandwich
sauce
soup
spice
steak
sugar
tomato
turkey
vegetable
waffle
watermelon
wheat

popcorn

## Land and Water

beach
cave
continent
desert
field
forest
harbor
hill
jungle
lake
marsh

meadow
mountain
ocean
plain
pond
river
sea
shore
stream
swamp
valley

valley

## Transportation

| | |
|---|---|
| airplane | jet |
| automobile | motorcycle |
| bicycle | rocket |
| boat | ship |
| bus | sled |
| canoe | submarine |
| car | train |
| carriage | truck |
| fire engine | tugboat |
| helicopter | wagon |

bicycle

## Jobs

| | |
|---|---|
| actor | guard |
| artist | judge |
| astronaut | librarian |
| author | magician |
| baker | mayor |
| barber | musician |
| blacksmith | nurse |
| carpenter | pilot |
| coach | police officer |
| cook | president |
| doctor | principal |
| dentist | sailor |
| engineer | scientist |
| farmer | singer |
| firefighter | teacher |
| fisherman | writer |
| grocer | zookeeper |

astronaut

## Instruments

| | | |
|---|---|---|
| drum | horn | tuba |
| flute | piano | violin |
| guitar | trombone | xylophone |
| harp | trumpet | |

trombone

# PAIRS OF OPPOSITES

| | | | |
|---|---|---|---|
| absent | present | loose | tight |
| asleep | awake | loud | soft |
| back | front | love | hate |
| backward | forward | male | female |
| beautiful | ugly | many | few |
| before | after | minus | plus |
| below | above | morning | evening |
| best | worst | narrow | wide |
| better | worse | neat | messy |
| big | small | new | old |
| borrow | lend | north | south |
| buy | sell | odd | even |
| cheap | expensive | on | off |
| clean | dirty | open | close |
| cold | hot | plain | fancy |
| comfortable | uncomfortable | possible | impossible |
| day | night | quiet | loud |
| deep | shallow | rich | poor |
| down | up | right | wrong |
| early | late | safe | dangerous |
| east | west | same | different |
| easy | hard | shout | whisper |
| empty | full | slow | fast |
| entrance | exit | smooth | rough |
| evil | good | start | finish |
| far | near | strong | weak |
| fat | thin | tall | short |
| frown | smile | thick | thin |
| good | bad | tight | loose |
| hard | soft | together | apart |
| here | there | top | bottom |
| in | out | true | false |
| inside | outside | under | over |
| large | small | up | down |
| left | right | warm | cool |
| less | more | wet | dry |
| light | heavy | wild | tame |
| little | big | win | lose |
| long | short | young | old |

1. Sometimes two short words can be joined to form a longer word. Match each word in column A with a word in column B to form a **compound word** that is in your dictionary.

| A | B |
|---|---|
| after | room |
| high | melon |
| score | board |
| bath | ball |
| base | case |
| water | rise |
| sun | noon |
| suit | bow |
| rain | chair |

2. Find the words that **rhyme.**

• Find a word on page 83 that rhymes with **sun.**

• Find a word on page 17 that rhymes with **tree.**

• Find a word on page 104 that rhymes with **mouse.**

• Can you find two words that rhyme with **two** and begin with the letter **d**? (Hint: The words are on pages 57 and 60.)

3. **Synonyms** are words that mean the same thing. Say the missing word or fill in the blank.

*A word on page 176 that means the same as* **gift** *is* _____.

*A word on page 96 that means the same as* **glad** *is* _____.

*A word on page 46 that means the same as* **sofa** *is* _____.

4. The words in the dictionary are in **ABC order.** Can you list these words in ABC order?

*scissors, knife, fork, spoon, dish, cup, pitcher*

*whale, camel, ape, hawk, turkey, woodpecker, cat*

*kite, chalk, marble, crayon, teddy bear, sled, bicycle*

Now see if you can find these words in your dictionary. Use the **guidewords** at the top of the pages to help you.

5. Match the word in column A with its **opposite** in column B. Look up these words in your dictionary.

| A | B |
|---|---|
| shout | crooked |
| early | spend |
| high | forget |
| asleep | entrance |
| straight | late |
| exit | find |
| save | low |
| lose | wet |
| remember | awake |
| dry | whisper |

The following source abbreviations are used throughout the credits: **AB** Albano Ballerini; **AG-RF** age fotostock royalty-free; **AL-RF** Alamy royalty-free; **COR-RF** Corbis royalty-free; **CC-RF** Cutcaster royalty-free; **EVC** Eva Vagreti Cockrille; **GI-RF** Getty Images royalty-free; **ISGI-RF** iStockphoto-Getty Images royalty-free; **HMH** © Houghton Mifflin Harcourt Digital Studio; **IS-RF** iStockphoto.com royalty-free; **GI-PD** Getty Images, Photodisc; **PF** Phoebe Ferguson; **ShS-RF** Shutterstock royalty-free; **SS-RF** Superstock, Inc. royalty-free

## Frontmatter credits

**bulldog and leaves** ShS-RF, Rita Kochmarjova **chameleon** AL-RF, Maria Gritsai **branch** Nature Picture Library, Larry Michael **dinosaur** EVC **paw** IS-RF, suemack **orange** Fotolia-RF, volff **chase** AL-RF, Jupiterimages, Comstock Premium **hug** IS-RF, Artistic Captures **panda** ShS-RF **blow** COR-RF, REB Images, Blend Images **thin** EVC **team** AL-RF, Jupiterimages, Brand X Pictures **collect** HMH **parrot** ShS-RF

## A-Z text credits

**above** ShS-RF, bikeriderlondon **acorn** AL-RF, Alistair Scott **against** HMH **airplane** ShS-RF, Mikhail Starodubov **alike** GI-RF, Susanne Walstrom **alligator** ISGI-RF **alone** COR-RF, Tim Pannell **anchor** EVC **ant** EVC **apron** GI-RF, PeopleImages, Digital Vision **armor** EVC **artist** ShS-RF, C. Jones **asleep** ShS-RF, Hung Chung Chih **astronaut** GI-PD **attic** GI-PD, Don Farrall **automobile** AL-RF, Roberts Ratuts **axe** EVC **baby** ShS-RF, Tatiana Gladskikh **backpack** ShS-RF, 2xSamara.com **ball** AL-RF, Jupiterimages, Polka Dot **balloon** HMH **barn** SS-RF, Ron Chapple **basket** AL-RF, D. Hurst **basketball** AL-RF, Jupiterimages, Brand X Pictures **bat (note)** AL-RF, MB1 **beak** EVC **bear** ShS-RF, Dave Allen Photography **bee** EVC **beetle** Getty Images, Barcroft Media **behind** COR-RF, Ron Chapple **bend** CC-RF, Anne-Louise Quarfoth **berry** AL-RF, Chris Pancewicz **beside** Disabilityimages.com-RF, Huntstock **between** Fotolia, Monkey Business Images **bicycle** AL-RF, Leonid Nyshko **bird (note)** ShS-RF, sakhorn **bite** AL-RF, Bananastock **blanket** EVC **blend (note)** GI-RF, kickstand **blow** COR-RF, REB Images, Blend Images **blue (note)** iStockphoto.com, stanley45 **boot** HMH **both** HMH **bowl** AB **braid** PF **branch** Nature Picture Library, Larry Michael **bridge** ShS-RF **bright** IS-RF, Iakov Kalinin **bubble** COR-RF, Monalyn Gracia **bucket** AG-RF, Liane Riss, Westend61 **bunch** AL-RF, Brand X Pictures **bus** AL-RF, Erick Nguyen **butterfly** ShS-RF, Holger Wulschlaeger **button** HMH **cactus** ShS-RF, CBH **camel** AL-RF, GFC Collection **camp** GI-PD, Chris Robbins **candy (note)** AG-RF, Ingebord Knol **canoe** AL-RF, imac **cape** PF **carpenter** COR-RF, Skip Nall **carrot** GI-PD **carry** AL-RF, Blend Images **castle** SS-RF, Exactostock **cat** GI-PD **caterpillar** ISGI-RF **caught** Getty Images, Stephanie Rausser **chair** GI-PD, C Squared Studios **chase** AL-RF, Jupiterimages, Comstock Premium **checkers** SS-RF, SOMOS **cherry** EVC **chicken** GI-PD, G.K. & Vikki Hart **circle** EVC **claw** EVC **clock** HMH **coach** ShS-RF, Monkey Business Images **coat** GI-RF, Mike Kemp **coin** HMH **collect (note)** HMH **color** AL-RF, Photolocate **cone** GI-PD **container** GI-RF, Lauri Patterson **cool (note)** GI-PD, C Squared Studios **corn** EVC **costume** GI-RF, Digital Vision **cotton** ShS-RF, Jerry Horbert **couch** GI-RF, Jose Luis Pelaez, Inc., Blend Images **cover** Getty Images, Dave King **crack** IS-RF, Susan Stewart **crane** GI-RF, Jim Kruger **crocodile** ShS-RF, defpicture **crooked** ISGI-RF, alexkar08 **crush** AL-RF, Collection 92, GlowImages **cub** AL-RF, Corbis Super RF **curly** GI-RF, Iliana Mestari **cut** GI-RF, George Doyle, Stockbyte **dam** Fotolia-RF, Bryan Busovicki **dandelion** EVC **deer** IS-RF, Bruce MacQueen **dentist** GI-RF, Echo **design** AL-RF, Igor Golovnov **diamond** EVC **different** ShS-RF, Jagodka **dinosaur** EVC **direction** EVC **dirt** HMH **dish** AB **dolphin** GI-PD, Tier und Naturfotografie, J & C Sohns **donkey** GI-PD **door** HMH **dragon** EVC **drawer** AL-RF, bobo **dress** GI-RF, Vikram Raghuvanshi **drink** HMH **drop** GI-RF, David Sacks **drum** COR-RF, Ocean **duck** AL-RF, John McKenna **ear** IS-RF, dolgachov **east** EVC **eat** AL-RF **edge** COR-RF, Jeff Greenough, Blend Images **egg** GI-RF, Brian T. Evans, Flickr **elephant** AL-RF, Corbis Super RF **engine** COR-RF, Monty Rakusen **entrance** GI-RF, ML Harris **equal** AB **everything** GI-RF, David Sacks **exciting** AL-RF, PureStock **exercise** AL-RF, Blend Images **expand** PF **explore** AL-RF, Blend Images **factory** ShS-RF, Vasily Smirnov **fan** IS-RF, gmnicholas **farm** ShS-RF, MaxyM **feather** EVC **feed** AL-RF, imagebroker.net **fence** AL-RF, Neal & Molly Jansen **field** GI-RF, Holly Cohn **fill** HMH **fireplace** AL-RF, JG Photography **fireworks** ISGI-RF **fish** COR-RF **flag** GI-PD **flashlight** IS-RF, Christopher Bernard **float** ShS-RF, Studio 1One **flour** ShS-RF, Wiktory **flow** ShS-RF, hakfin **fly** EVC **fog** GI-PD **foot** EVC **football** GI-RF, Comstock **form** COR-RF, Richard Gross **fossil** ShS-RF, Mario Jose Bastos Silva **fox** GI-RF, Les Piccolo, Flickr **frog** AL-RF, Byphoto **frost** CC-RF, Elena Elisseeva **frown** PF **fruit** GI-PD, C Squared Studios **full** AL-RF, Judith Collins **fur** ShS-RF, Zuzule **gallon** EVC **game (note)** HMH **garden** ShS-RF, goodluz **giant** ShS-RF, Joy Brown **gingerbread** EVC **giraffe** IS-RF, WLDavies **globe** HMH **glove** EVC **goal** AG-RF, Corbis **goat** ShS-RF,